Social Interactions and Status Markers in the Roman World

Edited by
George Cupcea
Rada Varga

Archaeopress Roman Archaeology 37

ARCHAEOPRESS PUBLISHING LTD
Summertown Pavilion
18-24 Middle Way
Oxford OX2 7LG

www.archaeopress.com

ISBN 978 1 78491 748 7
ISBN 978 1 78491 749 4 (e-Pdf)

© Archaeopress and the individual authors 2018

Cover: Stella of the *augustalis* Lucius Popilius Prunicus, from the Museo y Necrópolis Paleocristianos (MNAT), Tarragona. Inv. no. MNAT 25373.

All rights reserved. No part of this book may be reproduced, or transmitted, in any form or by any means, electronic, mechanical, photocopying or otherwise, without the prior written permission of the copyright owners.

This book is available direct from Archaeopress or from our website www.archaeopress.com

Contents

Notes on contributors v

Foreword xi

The *Barbii*, trade in Noricum and the influence of the local epigraphic habit on status display 1
Markus Zimmermann

    Traders of Noricum 1
    The *Barbii* 3
    Concluding remarks 6
    References 7

The professionals of the Latin West. 9
Rada Varga

    The problem 9
    State of research 10
    The encoding 13
    Conclusions and future prospects 16
    References 20

Latin occupational titles in Roman textile trade 23
Iulia Dumitrache

    Methodology 23
    Luxury garments traders: *barbaricarii, sericarii, purpurarii* 24
    Linen garments traders 30
    Wool garments traders: *panucularii, lanarii, centonarii, paenularii, sagarii, vestiarii* 32
    Conclusions 41
    Acknowledgements 42
    References 42

The professions of private slaves and freedmen in Moesia Inferior 47
Lucreţiu Mihăilescu-Bîrliba

    Introduction 47
    The epigraphic record 47
    The language of inscriptions and the dedicators 51
    Conclusions 54
    References 55

Prosopography of the leading families of Larinum in the Roman period 57

Elizabeth C. Robinson

- Introduction 57
- The Cluentii 59
- The Didii and the Paquii 61
- The Papii 65
- The Vibii 65
- The careers of the first five families 68
- Newly prominent families under the Roman Empire 69
- The Raii 69
- The Coelii 71
- The Gabbii 73
- The careers of the last three families 74
- Conclusions 74
- References 76

The kindred dimension of the Black Sea associations: between fictive and real meaning 79

Annamária-Izabella Pázsint

- Fictive familial language 79
- Mater 81
- Pater 81
- Adelphos 83
- Familial engagement in associations 84
- Conclusions 88
- References 89

Tarraco. Town and society in a 2nd-century AD Roman provincial capital 91

Diana Gorostidi, Ricardo Mar and Joaquín Ruiz de Arbulo

- Tarraco in the 2nd century AD 96
- Soldiers and civil society: the veterans of the VII Gemina legion settled in Tarraco 98
- Immigrants in Tarraco: the epigraphic evidence of *Africani* 100
- The urban society of Tarraco: some given names 101
- Town and territory: Tarraco society in its suburban villas 102
- References 108

Soldiers and their monuments for posterity: manifestations of martial identity in the funerary iconography of Roman Dacia 115
Monica Gui, Dávid Petruț

- Cuirassed representations 116
- Soldiers in battle gear 121
- Riders 123
- Soldiers in camp dress 128
- The funerary banquet scene (*Totenmahl*) 130
- Cloaked representations 134
- Conclusions 135
- Acknowledgements 135
- References 136

***Origo* as identity factor in Roman epitaphs** 139
Tibor Grüll

- Civis 139
- Domo 141
- Natione 143
- Conclusions 145
- References 147

Centurions: military or social elite? 151
George Cupcea

- Questions 151
- Why centurions? 151
- Are centurions soldiers? 153
- 'Political' centurions 155
- Centurions as judges 157
- Centurions in culture and religion 159
- Conclusions 161
- References 162

Notes on contributors

George Cupcea is a researcher at the National History Museum of Transylvania and the *Babeș-Bolyai* University of Cluj-Napoca, Romania. His interests lie in the field of Latin epigraphy, Roman military history, especially the hierarchy of the Roman army. His PhD was published with Archaeopress, in 2014, *Professional Ranks in the Roman Army of Dacia*, BAR International Series 2861, Oxford. He has also completed two post-doctoral projects with two universities in Romania and is currently a post-doctoral scholar at the University of Vienna, Institute for Ancient History and Epigraphy, holder of an *Ernst Mach grant* from *OeAD*. His second area of expertise is Roman provincial archaeology and non-invasive techniques, an interest that has mostly been applied to the study of the Roman frontier of the province of Dacia, in the frame of a national program which tries to enlist the Dacian frontier in the UNESCO World Heritage List, as part of the trans-national FRE site.

Iulia Dumitrache is a researcher at the Research Department of the Faculty of History, Alexandru Ioan Cuza University, Iași. She gained her doctoral degree in 2011. Her scientific interests are economic history, social history, Roman prosopography, and Latin epigraphy. Her doctoral research was focussed on the prosopography of traders in the Roman Empire; the analysis was not limited only to individual agents, but also encompassed the study of association mechanisms and of social and geographical mobility. Another field of interest is non-destructive methods in landscape archaeology and settlement archaeology. She has also studied the gromatic terminology in ancient literary sources (both Latin and Greek) and the exploitation of resources in Greek city hinterlands in Antiquity and the Middle Ages. Selected publications include: *Garum și salsamenta în lumea romană. Surse literare, epigrafice și papirologice*, Iași, 2014; *La colonisation dans le milieu militaire et le milieu civil de Troesmis*, Iași, 2012 (with L. Bîrliba); .*Acculturation – Romanization – Colonisation: The Role of the Army in the Roman Province of Moesia Inferior*, Mankind Quarterly, 54, 1, 2013, 75-92 (with L. Bîrliba); *The Halieutic Circuit in Scythia Minor. State of Art and Further Approaches*, in M. Alexianu, R.-G. Curcă, O. Weller, A. Dumas (eds.), *Mirrors of Salt. Proceedings of the First International Congress on the Anthropology of Salt, 20-24 August 2015, 'Al. I. Cuza' University, Iași, Romania*, Archaeopress, Oxford, 2016; *Les origine de la famille des Coccei en Scythie Mineure*, in Mihailescu-Bîrliba (ed.), *Migration, Kolonisierung, Akkulturation im Balkanraum und im Osten des Mittelmeerraumes*, Hartung Gorre Verlag, Konstanz, 2016, 175-179; *Ancient literary sources concerning fishing and fish processing in the Black Sea region*, Studia Antiqua et Archaeologica 21/1, 2015, 69-77.

Diana Gorostidi is full-time research fellow at the Catalan Institute of Classical Archaeology (ICAC) and Assistant Professor at the Rovira i Virgili University (Tarragona, Spain). She was awarded a full-time pre-doctoral research fellowship at the Spanish School of History and Archaeology at Rome of the Spanish Council for Scientific Research (CSIC) (Italy, 2000-2006). Upon completion of her PhD thesis, entitled 'The Roman inscriptions of ancient Tusculum (Latium, Italy)' at the University of Zaragoza (2008) (Pastor Foundation for Classical Studies award), she was appointed 'Juan de la

Cierva' Research Fellow at the ICAC (2010-12) and junior researcher (since 2012). She also has been visiting scholar at the Seminar of Ancient History of the University of Heidelberg (Germany, 2011), at the Corpus Inscriptionum Latinarum project of the Berlin-Brandenburg Academy of Sciences and Humanities (Germany, 2012) and at the Centre Ausonius – Bordeaux (France, 2014). In addition to her main interest in epigraphy and institutions from Rome and ancient Latium, she currently leads a R&D project on inscriptions from Tarraco and Hispania Tarraconensis (Officinae Lapidariae Tarraconenses) funded by the Ministry of Economy, Industry and Competitiveness – Government of Spain. In this time, she has taken part in several R&D projects and published a book (Ager Tarraconensis 3. The Roman Inscriptions (IRAT), Tarragona 2010. She was awarded the Latin Epigraphy Prize in 2012 by the AIEGL - Association Internationale d'Épigraphie Grecque et Latine, and has followed this with many scientific publications with an interest on historical and prosopographical questions, epigraphic supports and inscriptions on instrumentum. She is now coordinating the translation into Spanish of Géza Alföldy's works on Tarraco previously published in German.

Tibor Grüll, DSc, PhD habil., is associate professor at the University of Pécs. His main field of research is the social, religious and economic history of the Roman Empire under the early Principate, as well as Jewish history in the Greco-Roman period. He has written nine books (in Hungarian) and ca. 150 scholarly articles in English or Hungarian.

Monica Gui studied archaeology and classical studies at Babeș-Bolyai University in Cluj-Napoca, culminating in 2014 with the defence of her PhD thesis on the social and daily life aspects of the Roman army in Dacia. She has taken part in a number of archaeological excavations, most notably being involved in the research carried out by the Institute of Archaeology and Art History in Cluj-Napoca of the Romanian Academy at the ancient site of *Porolissum*. Her main area of research is the Roman army, particularly military equipment, but she is also interested in small finds, material culture and social phenomena in general. She has published several articles addressing pieces of equipment and other finds, as well as various aspects of the military life as disclosed by its material traces.

Ricardo Mar is professor at the Rovira i Virgili University from Tarragona. He is a specialist in the Roman era history and archaeology of Hispania Tarraconensis and especially Tarraco, and has a particular interest in the sphere of architectural engineering and cultural history. His most important publications are the books co-authored with J. Ruiz de Arbulo, listed below.

Lucrețiu Mihailescu-Bîrliba is professor of Roman history at Alexandru Ioan Cuza University of Iași. He specialises on Roman social history, Roman demography, Roman army and migration. Selected books include: *Individu et société en Dacie romaine. Étude de démographie historique*, Wiesbaden 2004; *Les affranchis dans les provinces romaines de l'Illyricum*, Wiesbaden 2006; *Ex toto orbe Romano. Immigration into Roman Dacia: with prosopographical remarks on the population of Dacia*, Leuven 2011. Edited books (selection): *Pax Romana. Kulturaustausch und Wirtschafts beziehungen in den Donauprovinzen des* *römischen Reichs*, Kaiserslautern 2012 (with Dilyana Boteva and Octavian Bounegru); *Migration, Kolonisierung, Akkulturation im Balkan raum und im Osten des Mittelmeer raumes (3. Jh. v. Chr.-6.Jh. n. Chr.)*, Konstanz 2017.

Annamária–Izabella Pázsint is a PhD Candidate at the Faculty of History and Philosophy, 'Babeș-Bolyai' University in Cluj-Napoca, where she is also a temporary research assistant. Within the same institution she is also member of two research units: Centre for Roman Studies, and Centre for Middle Eastern and Mediterranean Studies. Her PhD thesis is tackling the private associations from the Greek colonies of the Black Sea area, through which she is trying to offer an extensive view on the associative phenomenon in all its aspects, focusing especially on the ancient population, and on the network systems. Her main fields of research are the social dimension of life in the Black Sea colonies, ancient demographic studies, prosopographical and network studies. Among her more distant academic interests, heritage studies occupy an important position. In her scientific enquiries she is eager to apply research methodologies deriving from interdisciplinary fields of study (sociology, economics), in order to provide a comprehensive outlook on the topics she deals with.

Dávid Petruț studied at the Babeș-Bolyai University in the same town, completing his doctoral thesis in 2013 following a term as visiting PhD student at the University of Cambridge (Faculty of Classics). He previously worked as a researcher at the Mureș County Museum in Târgu Mureș and is currently a postdoctoral research fellow at the Babeș-Bolyai University in Cluj-Napoca. His main fields of research within Roman provincial archaeology include: social and economic life on the *limes*, production and consumption of Roman pottery, Roman sculptural art, as well as the history of archaeology and its connection with nation-building programmes in east-central Europe. Dávid Petruț has undertaken archaeological surveys in numerous sites of Roman Dacia, including *Porolissum*, *Napoca*, *Apulum* and Călugăreni.

Elizabeth C. Robinson is Affiliate Assistant Professor of Art History at the University of Dallas Rome Program in Marino, Italy. She received her PhD in Classical Archaeology from the University of North Carolina at Chapel Hill in 2013 with a dissertation entitled 'The Impact of Roman Expansion in Central-Southern Italy: The Case of Larinum.' While at UNC Chapel Hill she served as the Acting Director of the Ancient World Mapping Center from 2007 to 2009, during which time she co-edited a series of seven 'Wall Maps for the Ancient World' (Routledge, 2010). Her dissertation research was supported by a series of fellowships and grants, including a U.S. Fulbright Graduate Student Full Grant to Italy, the Olivia James Traveling Fellowship from the Archaeological Institute of America, and the Irene Rosenzweig / Samuel H. Kress Foundation Pre-Doctoral Rome Prize from the American Academy in Rome. She is the author of multiple articles and book chapters, as well as the editor of a volume for the *Journal of Roman Archaeology (Supplement 97): Papers on Italian Urbanism in the First Millennium B.C.* Among her many current projects is a monograph entitled 'Urban Transformation in Ancient Molise,' under contract with Oxford University Press. She is also the Regional Topography and Digital Data Coordinator for the Gabii Project excavations. Her research interests include the cultural and physical landscapes of Italy in the 1st millennium BC and the nature of

Roman interactions with the other inhabitants of the Italian peninsula in this period, as well as Italian urbanism. She is also interested in GIS and digital mapping, and in the integration of digital technologies in the fields of Classics and Classical Archaeology.

Joaquin Ruiz de Arbulo Bayona is senior researcher at the Catalan Institute for Archaeology and professor at the Rovira i Virgili University from Tarragona. He has great experience in the archaeology, epigraphy and social history of Hispania – and especially Hispania Tarraconensis. His university teaching experience is extensive, as he has been teaching at many important universities of Spain: Barcelona (1991-1992), Lleida (1992-1996) and Tarragona (since 1996). In 2006-2007, he taught a Blockseminar, Die römischen Städte Hispaniens, at the Archäologisches Institut, Hamburg University. He has also coordinated many national projects and been involved in numerous European projects. Among his coordinated projects are: 'Roma, las capitales provinciales y las ciudades de Hispania', Programa Nacional de Promoción General del Conocimiento. 2013-2015; 'Roma y las capitales provinciales de Hispania (Emerita, Tarraco, Carthago Nova). Subproyecto Tarraco', Programa Nacional de Promoción General del Conocimiento - Historia y Arte (BHA). 2010-2012. Also, he has participated in numerous European projects, such as 'TEMPUS IV. Project Network for Post-Graduate Masters in Cultural Heritage and Tourism Management in Balkan Countries. CHTMBAL'. 2012-2015; 'Water shapes: Meanings, uses and the architectural works of the most precious gift', Culture 2010, 2011-2012; 'Simulacra Romae: Roma y las capitales provinciales del Occidente romano', Culture 2000, 2001-2002; 'Origen, topografia y desarrollo urbanístico del area central de Roma', Culture 2000, 2000-2001. Among his publications, we will only mention the books: R. Mar, J. Ruiz de Arbulo, D. Vivo, J. A. Beltran, F. Gris. *Tarraco. Arquitectura y urbanismo de una capital provincial romana. Volumen II. La ciudad imperial*, Tarragona: Universitat Rovira i Virgili. 2015; R. Mar, J. Ruiz de Arbulo, D. Vivo, J. A. Beltran. *Tarraco. Arquitectura y urbanismo de una capital provincial romana. Volumen I. De la Tarragona ibérica a la construcción del templo de Augusto*. Tarragona: Universitat Rovira i Virgili. 2012; R. Mar, J. Ruiz de Arbulo. *Tarragona romana. Republica i Alt Imperi (anys 218 a.C. - 265 d.C.). Historia de Tarragona, vol. 1. Tàrraco Clàssica i Prehistòrica*. Tarragona: Pagès editors. 2011; J. Ruiz de Arbulo. *L´Amfiteatre de Tarraco i els espectacles de gladiadors al mon romà / El Anfiteatro de Tarraco y los espectáculos gladiatorios en el mundo romano / The amphitheatre in Tarraco and the gladiators' spectacles in the Roman world*. Tarragona: Fundació Privada Liber. 2006.

Rada Varga, PhD, is a researcher at the Babeş-Bolyai University and coordinator of the project *Romans1by1* (romans1by1.com). Her research interests lie within the areas of digital epigraphy, ancient population studies, Roman occupations and professions. She is and has been a team member in numerous national and international projects and has been the beneficiary of a DAAD scholarship at the Kommission für Alte Geschichte und Epigraphik München (2011), of a residence scholarship granted by the Fondation Hardt (2014) and of a Fritz Thyssen Stiftung award. Among her recent scholarly publications are the monograph *The Peregrini of Roman Dacia* (Cluj-Napoca, 2014) and the edited volume *Official power and local elites in the Roman Empire* (Routledge, 2016).

Markus Zimmermann studied Ancient History, Roman Provincial Archaeology and Classical Archaeology at the University of Freiburg. He finished his M.A. in 2011 and moved to the University of Bamberg to work on his PhD about the Romanization of Noricum which he finished in 2016. During his studies he spent time at Rome, St. Andrews, Munich and Salzburg. Since 2014 he has been a lecturer in Ancient History at the University of Bayreuth. His main research interests are the history of the Roman Empire, the history and archaeology of the Rhine and Danube provinces, and Latin epigraphy.

Foreword

The selection of articles presented in the current volume is based mainly on presentations from the *People of the Ancient World* international conference, held in Cluj-Napoca on October 13th-15th, 2016. The conference, organized within the framework of the project *Romans 1 by 1*, brought together around forty scholars, from universities and research institutes from Europe and the United States. The underlying purpose of all the research presented was to deepen knowledge about ancient populations, employing various methodologies, tools and research techniques.

The variety of the conference programme is reflected in the contents of this book. The approaches taken to study Roman provincial populations are diverse and the case-studies highlight the multi-faceted character of Roman society. We have prosopographic and social history researches on the inhabitants attested in various regions or settlements: Larinum, in E. C. Robinson's chapter and Tarraco in D. Gorostidi, R. Mar and J. Ruiz de Arbulo's study. An important group of researches is dedicated to profesional contexts: thus, M. Zimmerman deals with the merchants of Noricum, L. Mihăilescu-Bîrliba with the professions of slaves in Moesia Inferior, I. Dumitrache with the nomenclatures of the textile trade and R. Varga with the encoding of occupational titles. The associative aspects of profession and family life are dealt with by A.-I. Pázsint. Other aspects, always of interest when dealing with ancient people, are onomastics and naming practices – as the name is sometimes the only fact we still know about a person and extracting all possible information from it is of crucial scientific importance. In this line of work, we have T. Grüll's research on *origo* as an identity factor. Another socially-important group in Roman provincial society is that of the military, investigated by M. Gui and D. Petruț's research on the iconographic elements of soldiers' funerary monuments and G. Cupcea's chapter dealing with the social role of centurions.

All these elements highlight the great diversity of Roman social standings, of exhibited social markers and – maybe most importantly – the stress upon the variety of forms of expressing status and place within the community.

This volume was supported by several grants of the Romanian Ministry of Research and Innovation, through UEFISCDI, project nos. PN-III-P4-ID-PCE-2016-0252 and PN-III-P4-ID-PCE-2016-0255.

The *Barbii*, trade in Noricum and the influence of the local epigraphic habit on status display

Markus Zimmermann

Merchants often played an important role in the Roman provinces. Cicero for example tells us that he was on good terms with *negotiatores* and *mercatores* during his time as a governor.[1] He also mentions that these merchants often had freedmen as business partners.[2] Statements in the *Digests* regarding slaves and freedmen who did business in distant areas[3] tell us about the importance which freedmen could have in long distance trade operated by wealthy merchants. Beside such wholesale dealers there were also retailers who worked on their own and made only little profit. One of these retailers speaks about his life in the Metamorphoses of Apuleius:

> *I am Aristomenes from Aegium. And here's how I make my living: I deal in cheese and honey, all that sort of innkeeper's stuff, travelling here and there through Boeotia, Aetolia, and Thessaly. So when I learned that at Hypata, Thessaly's most important town, some fresh cheese with a fine flavour was being sold at a very good price, I rushed there, in a hurry to buy the lot. But as usual I went left foot first, and my hopes of a profit were dashed. A wholesale dealer called Lupus had snapped it up the day before.*[4]

Traders of Noricum

Retailers and wholesale dealers similar to those mentioned by Apuleius were operating in all Roman provinces. However, the literary evidence regarding the economic life of the province of Noricum is very scarce. Only a very limited number of literary sources provide us with information about trade and goods exported to Italy. We learn, for instance, about the good quality of the *ferrum*

---

[1] Cic. *Planc.* 64.
[2] Cic. *Verr.* 2, 5, 154.
[3] *Dig.* 40, 9, 10.
[4] Apul. *Met.* 1, 5, 3-5: *Sed ut prius noritis cuiatis sim; Aegiensis: audite et quo quaestu me teneam; melle vel casco et huiuscemodi cauponiorum mercibus per Thessaliam Aetoliam Boeotiam ultro citro discurrens. Comperto itaque Hypatae, quae civitas cunctae Thessaliae antepollet, caseum recens et sciti saporis admodum commodo pretio distrahi, festinus adcucurri id omne praestinaturus. Sed, ut fieri assolet, sinistro pede profectum me spes compendii frustrata est; omne enim pridie Lupus negotiator magnarius coemerat.*

Noricum,⁵ the alpine cheese⁶ or a pleasantly smelling and expensive herb called *saliunca*.⁷ The people involved in the trade with these goods, however, are not mentioned at all. Only for the neighbouring Pannonian town Carnuntum the expedition of a Roman knight is mentioned in the sources, who passed the area when he went to the Baltic Sea to get some amber for the emperor Nero.⁸

Because of the absence of literary sources providing us with details concerning the trading activities in Noricum we have to rely on the epigraphic and archaeological material. The archaeological finds of the *emporium* on the Magdalensberg are evidence for ongoing trade between the *regnum Noricum* and Rome from the middle of the first century BC onwards. Around 40 BC, the *forum* of the *emporium* was built. It was surrounded by *tabernae* which were used for commercial activities.⁹ In addition to wholesale dealers¹⁰ there were also retailers active on the Magdalensberg. Some graffiti attest that they obtained credits from the bankers to rent *pergulae* for temporary use to conduct their businesses.¹¹

South of the Alps towards Illyricum the army supply was an important economic factor since the end of the first century BC. This market was probably controlled by merchants from Aquileia.¹² Some of them were specialized on trade in the Alpine area. One of those specialists was the Aquileian freedmen and *merkator(!) transalpinus* Caius Licinius Philomusus.¹³ Others resided in Milan and were members of the local *collegium* of the *negotiatores cisalpini et transalpini*.¹⁴

In scholarship it is assumed that a considerable number of north Italian merchants, especially those from Aquileia, were constantly present in the province of Noricum.¹⁵ However, actually only very few citizens of this city are epigraphically attested in inscriptions found in the province,¹⁶ and an even smaller number can be assigned to commercial activities. One inscription found in the area of Virunum mentions the businessman Marcus Trebius Alfius who

---

⁵ Pertron. 70.
⁶ Plin. *N.H.* 11, 240.
⁷ Plin. *N.H.* 21, 43.
⁸ Plin. *N.H.* 37, 45.
⁹ Dolenz *et al.* 2008.
¹⁰ Alföldy 1974, 45.
¹¹ Graßl 2005.
¹² Horvat 2008: 118.
¹³ AE 1994, 671.
¹⁴ CIL V 5911.
¹⁵ Alföldy 1974: 45f.; Gallego Franco 1996: 232; Harding/Jacobsen 1988; Horvat 2009: 355; Piccottini 1987: 292f.; Scherrer 2002: 14.
¹⁶ CIL III 4869 and 5217.

was *conductor ferrariarum* in Noricum and *praefectus iure dicundo* at Aquileia.[17] The assumption of P. Scherrer who pleads in favour of a massive presence of Italians in Noricum has therefore called into question.[18]

O. Schlippschuh postulated a less important role of native traders for the economy of Noricum and the other Danube provinces.[19] However, in the neighbouring provinces of Germania Superior and Raetia epigraphic evidence demonstrates that Italian merchants were only prominent during the first century AD. Shortly after, native merchants as well as those coming from other provinces gained a share of the market.[20] Therefore the question arises whether the development in Noricum was similar to that in Germania Superior and Raetia. Certainly, there were Italian merchants in Noricum, but it is doubtful they were actually there in such a great number as often assumed.

The *Barbii*

Especially the *gens Barbia* is thought to have been an important trading family based in Aquileia. This idea is present in scholarship since the influential article of J. Sasel.[21] However, the roots of this idea go back to the early 20th century when A. von Domaszewski assumed, based on the inscription of the '*Youth of Magdalensberg*', that most of the *Barbii* attested in the Danube provinces were attached to trading activities and that their hometown was Aquileia.[22] S. Panciera was right, but widely ignored, when he questioned the idea of A. von Domaszweski in his book on the economy of Aquileia. He pointed out that apart from the inscription of the '*Youth of Magdalensberg*' there is little epigraphic evidence for the assumed trading activities of the *Barbii*. He argued instead, that in imperial times most of the *Barbii* were not occupied in the trading business at all.[23] Besides the already mentioned inscription of the '*Youth of Magdalensberg*', most probably dating from the time of Augustus,[24] mentioning a *procurator* of this family, there is no other merchant of the *gens Barbia* known by inscriptions from Noricum. In these matters the recently published prosopography of all merchants of the Western provinces by W. Broekaert is of great interest. In all other Danube provinces there are no members of the *gens Barbia* attested as

---

[17] CIL III 4788.
[18] Scherrer 2002: 13-32.
[19] Schlippschuh 1974: 156.
[20] Kuhoff 1984: 105.
[21] Sasel 1966: 134-136; vgl. Alföldy 1974: 45f.; Scherrer 2002: 14.
[22] von Domaszewski 1902: 159f.
[23] Panciera 1957: 95-99.
[24] Hainzmann 2000: 468 with further literature.

merchants.[25] For this reason, the importance of the *Barbii* in trade is indeed questionable.

A problem of the study of merchants active in Noricum is caused by the already mentioned small epigraphic evidence. Through the *tesserae nummulariae* found at the Magdalensberg there are several families known who were active in banking business, for example the *gens Pomponia* or the *gens Albia*.[26] However, being a *nummularius* was not the same as being a *negotiator*. The first was active in financial affairs, the latter in trade.[27] Despite these bankers known from the *tesserae* only a few merchants are attested by inscriptions in stone. The most famous is the already mentioned *procurator* Lucius Barbius Luci *libertus* Philotaerus,[28] the only member of the *gens Barbia* active in trade in the whole Danube area. In addition, there are only five more merchants attested by inscriptions in Noricum. Two of them are known by inscriptions of Celeia: Aurelius Adiutor[29] and Caius Iulius Attianus.[30] North of the Alps two further merchants are known from inscriptions: Marius Anicetus in Salzburg[31] and a wine trader from Trento called Publius Tenatius Essimnus.[32] The inscription of the latter was found in the Inn River near Passau and therefore he probably sold his wine in Raetia and Noricum. Finally, an activity in trade can also be assumed for the shipper Lucius Servilius Eutyches[33] who carried out his business on the Sava River.

This scarce epigraphic evidence for merchants in Noricum has to be discussed. Especially because of the higher number of merchants attested in inscriptions from the other Danube provinces. Some scholars assumed that some of those individuals, who had Italian *nomina gentilicia* were merchants.[34] This is an assumption without methodological value because not even every Roman with an Italian *nomen gentilicium* was an immigrant from Italy.

A closer look at the inscriptions of the Magdalensberg could help us to re-evaluate the presence of the *gens Barbia* and other Italian *gentes* at Emporium. Because of the relatively short time in which inscriptions where set up there, roughly from the reign of Augustus till the reign of Claudius, it is possible to

---

[25] See the index of names in: Broekaert 2013: 555.
[26] Gostencnik 2005a; Gostencnik 2008.
[27] Broekaert 2013: 19f.
[28] CIL III 4815.
[29] CIL III 5230.
[30] CIL III 5308.
[31] AE 2009, 988.
[32] AE 1984, 707.
[33] AE 1938, 151.
[34] See for example: Harding/Jacobsen 1988.

trace the spread of names among the local population. The above mentioned inscription of the '*Youth of Magdalensberg*' shows us that Italian merchants like the procurator Lucius Barbius Philotaerus cooperated with the native population. The business partners received Roman citizenship with the help of the Italians or through manumission. In the following time those new Roman citizens took on Italian *nomina gentilicia* just as their children and grandchildren, when they married a Roman citizen or had the right of *conubium*. This process caused a rapid spread of Italian *nomina gentilicia* and Latin *cognomina* among the native population.[35] One instructive example of the Latinization of names are Publius Barbius Rusticus and his son Publius Barbius Proculus.[36] Regarding onomastic criteria both of them could have an Italian origin but the father is also known from another inscription which allows us to identify him as a native[37] just like his son. This strengthens the assumption that several of the 'onomastic Italians' were in fact natives with Latinized names. This is quite plausible because the North Italian merchants did not need a large number of delegates on the Magdalensberg to conduct their business. It was certainly cheaper to assign the native population for the work which had to be done instead of settling a lot of slaves and freedmen across the Alps.

Of course there were some merchants from North-Italy operating in Noricum but they are not really attested by the inscriptions. Therefore, the question arises why this was the case. There was with certainty not less trade than in the neighbouring provinces were more merchants are attested. Yet it is striking, that we have less inscriptions from Raetia than from Noricum but more merchants attested in these inscriptions.[38] Some of the merchants active in Raetia were even part of the local elite. One *decurio* of Augsburg made his fortune by selling pigs[39]. Another merchant named Tiberius Claudius Euphrates was *sevir Augustalis*.[40] A third one was honoured with a burial place *ex decreto decurionum*.[41]

The explanation for this difference must be searched in the local epigraphic habit[42] which was influenced by the local social structure and the values shared in local society. I would assume that in the society of Noricum being a merchant was not a great achievement which the deceased wanted to communicate to

---

[35] See for example: CIL III 4886, 4990a, 11563, 11565, 11603.
[36] CIL III 11564.
[37] CIL III 11563.
[38] For the merchants in Raetia see: Gallego Franco 1996: 223-231; Kuhoff 1984: 89-102.
[39] CIL III 14370.
[40] CIL III 5824.
[41] CIL III 5816.
[42] For further literature on the nature of the epigraphic habit see: Alföldy 2004: 238, n. 79.

the public, whilst in Raetia it was. This could be explained by the continuity of the local elite in Noricum,[43] which was not the case in Raetia, where big parts of the province were not populated in the years before the Roman conquest.[44] Therefore merchants were able to gain political and social standing during the formation of the new social structure of Raetia and they were proud of their business which gave them the financial background needed for an entry into the upper class of Raetia. Unlike Raetia, in Noricum the native elite could maintain their power under the new circumstances. It was thus difficult for merchants to enter into this social group. And if a member of the local elite might have had a mercantile background he was not presenting this to the public because it was more common to present other achievements in the inscriptions like political or military positions.

Concluding remarks

All this point to the fact that Silvio Panciera was right when he questioned the importance of the *Barbii* as a big merchant family in Imperial times. There is no evidence that proves the theory, that the *Barbii* dominated the trade in Noricum or in any other Danube province. The inscription of the 'Youth of the Magdalensberg' shows that they still had some importance in the time of Augustus which they probably lost in the following time. Also other theories which postulate, that a large number of the people bearing an Italian *nomen gentilicium* were Italian merchants have to be dismissed. The inscriptions of Magdalensberg are demonstrating that several of them were natives and probably not related to commercial activities at all. However, the Latinization of the *cognomina* is a problem for onomastic research in this field of study. Only in some cases it could be solved, when the parents or grandparents could be identified as natives by their names. Surely merchants from northern Italy and other regions of the empire were active in Noricum but they are not attested a lot in the epigraphic evidence. The difference between Noricum und Raetia could be explained with the local epigraphic habit, which was heavily influenced by the local social structure and the values shared in society. Probably there were not less merchants active in Noricum than in Raetia, it was just not worth mentioning it in inscriptions in Noricum because other social markers were more important to classify the personal status in the provincial society.

---

[43] Alföldy 1974: 86f.
[44] Kellner 1995: 17; Löffl 2011: 178-181; Rieckhoff 2007: 414-434.

References

Alföldy, G. 1974. *Noricum*. London, Routledge.
Alföldy, G. 2004. Theodor Mommsen und die römische Epigraphik aus der Sicht hundert Jahre nach seinem Tod. *Epigraphica* 66: 217-245.
Broekaert, W. 2013. *Navicularii et Negotiantes. A prosopographical study of Roman merchants and shippers*. Rhaden, Leidorf.
Dolenz, H. et al. 2009. Zur vorannexionszeitlichen Siedlung auf dem Magdalensberg. *Fundberichte aus* Österreich 47: 235-266.
Ehmig, U. 2011/2012. Über alle Berge. Früheste mediterrane Warenlieferungen in den römischen Ostalpenraum. *Römisches Österreich* 34/35: 13-35.
Gallego Franco, H. 1996. Negotiatores en la estructura social de las provincias romanas del Alto y Medio Danubio. *Espacio, Tiempo y Forma, Serie II, Historia Antigua* 9: 221-247.
Gostencnik, K. 2005. *Die Beinfunde vom Magdalensberg*. Klagenfurt, Verlag des Landesmuseums Kärnten.
Gostencnik, K. 2008. Beinfunde als Schriftträger. Die Beinfunde aus der Stadt auf dem Magdalensberg und ihre Kleininschriften. In M. Hainzmann and R. Wedenig (eds.), *Instrumenta Inscripta Latina II*: 165-179. Klagenfurt, Verlag des Landesmuseums Kärnten.
Graßl, H. 2005. Das Gold der Noriker. *Münstersche Beiträge zur antiken Handelsgeschichte* 24, 1: 31-37.
Hainzmann, M. 2000. Aulus Publicus Antiochus. In G. Paci (ed.), *Epigraphai. Miscellanea epigrafica in onore di Lidio Gasperini*: 463-477. Rom, Ed. Tipigraf.
Harding, M. and Jacobsen, G. 1988. Die Bedeutung der zivilen Zuwanderung aus Norditalien für die Entwicklung der Städte in Noricum und Pannonien. *Classica et mediaevalia* 39: 117-206.
Horvat, J. 2008. Early Roman horrea at Nauportus. *Mélanges de l'École française de Rome. Antiquité* 120, 1: 111-121.
Horvat, J. 2009. Selected Aspects of Romanization in Western and Central Slovenia. In G. Cuscito (ed.), *Aspetti e problemi della romanizzazione. Venetia, Histria e arco alpino orientale*: 355-381. Trieste, Editreg.
Kellner, H.-J. 1995. Die Kelten im Alpenvorland. In W. Czysz et al. (eds.), *Die Römer in Bayern*: 13-17. Stuttgart, Theiss.
Kuhoff, W. 1984. Der Handel im römischen Süddeutschland. *Münstersche Beiträge zur antiken Handelsgeschichte* 3, 1: 77-107.
Löffl, J. 2011. *Die römische Expansion*. Berlin, Frank & Timme.
Maier-Maidl, V. 1992. *Stempel und Inschriften auf Amphoren vom Magdalensberg. Wirtschaftliche Aspekte*. Klagenfurt, Verlag des Landesmuseums Kärnten.
Panciera, S. 1957. *Vita economica di Aquileia in età romana*. Aquileia.
Piccottini, G. 1987. Scambi commerciali fra l'Italia e il Norico. In: *Vita sociale artistica e commerciale di Aquileia romana*: 291-304. Udine, Arti Grafiche Friulane.
Rieckhoff, S. 2007. Wo sind sie geblieben? – Zur archäologischen Evidenz der Kelten in Süddeutschland im 1. Jh. v. Chr. In H. Birkhan (ed.), *Kelten-Einfälle*

an der Donau: 409-440. Wien, Verlag der Österreichischen Akademie der Wissenschaften.

Sasel, J. 1966. Barbii. *Eirene* 5: 117-137.

Scherrer, P. 2002. Vom *regnum Noricum* zur römischen Provinz: Grundlagen und Mechanismen der Urbanisierung. In M. Sasel Kos and P. Scherrer (eds.), *The Autonomous Towns of Noricum and Pannonia. Noricum*: 11-70 Ljubljana, Narodni Muzej Slovenije.

Schlippschuh, O. 1974. *Die Händler im Römischen Kaiserreich in Gallien, Germanien und den Donauprovinzen Rätien, Noricum und Pannonien*. Amsterdam, Verlag Adolf M. Hakkert.

von Domaszewski, A. 1902. Die Beneficiarierposten und die römischen Strassennetze. *Westdeutsche Zeitschrift für Geschichte und Kunst* 21: 158-211.

The professionals of the Latin West

Encoding the occupational titles

Rada Varga

The problem

During the last decades, studies concerning the professions, labour and the social implications of work in the Roman world have greatly developed, but comprehensive research on provincial occupational epigraphy is still to be undertaken. The relative scarcity of individual (not *collegia* and other types of associations) inscriptions offering occupational/professional details is a hard fact and a drawback, but even so, cataloguing, centralizing and analyzing these pieces would and will be a step forward in understanding Roman society.

During the 3rd and 4th centuries AD, what we would define as the Roman middle class collapsed and subsequently re-constructed itself; these changes, impossible to render in all their details at a provincial level, have some of their primary causes in the social and professional structures of the 1st and 2nd centuries AD. There is a very high possibility that occupational epigraphy can offer additional hints on the labour market, as well as on people's attitude towards their professions. It is highly relevant to identify when and why one takes pride in a profession and considers it a mark of identification in front of men and gods. Eventually, the quantification analysis of the occupational epigraphs will give us important data on general and specific patterns of the 'epigraphic habit'.[1]

The current article is part of a larger research initiative,[2] focused on collecting and analyzing all occupational inscriptions from the Latin language provinces. The focus on the Latin provinces is justified by the differences and even discrepancies existing between the epigraphic habits, as well as the 'labour culture' of the Greek and Latin-language parts of the Empire; nonetheless, Moesia Inferior, the easternmost province included in our research plan, will serve as a case-study as well as a possible gateway to the future expansion of this scientific endeavour. Because we are interested not merely in those

---

[1] MacMullen 1982.
[2] The project *Carving a professional identity. The occupational epigraphy of the Roman Latin* West was developed and finaced through a Fritz Thyssesn Stiftung postodctoral fellowship.

occupations listed, but in the social significance of the monuments as well, we have only relied in this research on stone epigraphs.

State of research

The modern beginnings of work and labour studies of the Roman Empire were based on law sources – especially on Justinian's Digest (such as Mina Maxey[3]'s monograph) and Diocletian's edict on prices, but also on literary fragments, with the focus on Martial and Juvenal. A step forward was made by Harald von Petrikovits,[4] who combined the study of epigraphical, literary and juridical texts. But the research of occupational inscriptions, as we understand it today, truly evolved later. As was to be expected, the investigation of these inscriptions was born and carried out with extraordinary results for Italy and especially Rome. The success is due, of course, to the richness of sources and implicitly to their outstanding informational variety. Sandra Joshel's[5] book, analyzing all the occupational inscriptions from the city of Rome, was a breakthrough, as it offered a new perspective on the labour market, socio-professional structures and the relevance of profession in defining one's identity, at the level of the Empire's capital.

Certain professional categories enjoyed special attention, for several reasons, but mainly due to an increased number of sources and/or the attractive nature of the given profession. Such are the merchants (terrestrial and naval) and associated workers in trade – which aroused interest because of their great mobility, (relative) wealth, heterogeneous cultural background and implicitly by the mass of information their inscriptions can deliver. As a curiosity, we will only stress the fact that the first published monographs (that we are aware of) dedicated to Roman traders (Johann August Ernesti)[6] and ancient trade and navigation (Pierre-Daniel Huet)[7] date from the 18th century; of course, they are scientifically obsolete today, but remain important in outlining the evolution of research themes and interests. Coming back to modern historiography, while Italy and Rome are again a focus of renewed interest, the Latin provinces have enjoyed less attention and even less ample monographic study. Thus, Gabrielle Wesch-Klein's[8] article on private trade initiatives in North Africa or Octavian Bounegru's[9] books on the maritime merchants from the Black Sea come as

---

[3] Maxey 1938.
[4] Petrikovits 1981.
[5] Joshel 1992.
[6] Ernesti 1737.
[7] Huet 1763.
[8] Wesch-Klein 1989.
[9] Bounegru 2006; Bounegru 2013.

rarities. The last important contribution on traders is Wim Broekaert's[10] book from 2013, which provides a very valuable attempt at prosopographical reconstruction; though, in our opinion, building its catalogue of sources on rather subjective criteria, the book is a step forward in knowledge regarding the *navicularii* and the *negotiatores*, as well as in the advance of prosopographical studies for the Roman non-elites. Other recent collective contributions present various aspects of general trading phenomena: Droß-Krüpe's[11] volume centres around textile trade, Wilson and Flohr's[12] book deals with urban craftsmen and traders, etc.

Another set of professions that have attracted great interest are those related to manufacturing. Besides being epigraphically and literarily present, various crafts have become interesting due to their close connection to archaeology. Such are illustrated by Gerhard Zimmer's[13] ANRW study, with monographic features, on the Roman craftsmen, E. Marianne Stern's[14] social study on the artisans working in the glass industry, or the rather numerous researches focused on cloth and cloth-industry (Alexandra Croom[15] deals with fashion, as well as with the production of clothing, Miko Flohr[16] presents the world of the Pompeian *fullo*, etc.). Another point of interest seems to be metalworking, due to its fine products (from vessels to weapons, these artefacts go a step beyond the commonplace), the more complex production process, but also because of its relation to mining and the interest awoken by their legal status and administration. The bibliography is thus rather extensive, listing a huge number of articles and studies centred on specific matters or (types of) artifacts, general production monographs (David Sim and Isabel Ridge's[17] is the last we are aware of), local monographs (Harald Straube's[18] contribution on the *ferrum Noricum* is the most obvious example), and publications trying to place the artisan and his work in a wider social context (such as Anne Lehoërff's[19] edited volume).

---

[10] Broekaert 2013.
[11] Droß-Krüpe 2014.
[12] Wilson, Flohr 2016.
[13] Zimmer 1985.
[14] Stern 1999.
[15] Croom 2010.
[16] Flohr 2013.
[17] Sim, Ridge 1998.
[18] Straube 1996.
[19] Lehoërff 2004.

Currently, a series of significant projects and research groups deal with the economics of the Roman Empire; among them, *The Oxford Roman Economy Project*,[20] *Structural Determinants of Economic Performance in the Roman World*,[21] the *Centre for Economic History* from the University of Reading,[22] etc.

From this brief overview, one can clearly see that interest in the epigraphic sources has been secondary or adjacent. While this tendency is normal when research is focusing on production and artefact-related matters, it still reveals a scientific bias. Cataloguing all the attested craftsmen's inscriptions and integrating them in an epigraphical and social context will surely open new doors and will give an overview without which the role and place of work in Roman society will never be fully grasped.

Besides trade and craftsmanship, educational occupations have enjoyed special attention, being intertwined with the study of ancient educational systems and patterns, literacy, as well as with the study of childhood. Recently, Yun Lee Too[23] has delivered a number of interesting (and relevant in the context of our research) studies concerning the economics of pedagogical work.

We will not insist upon relating the historiographical development of researches in all areas of Roman professions, but a last group must be mentioned, due to their particular and peculiar character: the gladiators. Out of the 'invisible Romans'[24], they are definitely the highest-profile group for the modern reader, as scientific interest has gone hand in hand with a very vivid and acute general public curiosity in the matter. Unlike other groups, their inscriptions have been dealt with individually, as well as in clusters – but still the best provincial monographic approaches remain the rather old works of Louis Robert[25] (on the gladiators of the Greek provinces) and Georges Ville[26] (on the gladiators of the Occidental provinces).

As one can see, the research trends which mark(ed) the study of professions in the Roman Empire are manifold and very different in essence. But in this very colourful picture, a monographic approach to the occupational inscriptions of the Latin provinces, including all the aspects and data they reveal, is still lacking up to now.

---

[20] http://www.romaneconomy.ox.ac.uk. Last accessed 2017-05-10, 12.35 p.m.
[21] http://www.rsrc.ugent.be/sdep. Last accessed 2017-05-10, 12.35 p.m.
[22] http://www.reading.ac.uk/economic-history/. Last accessed 2017-05-10, 12.37 p.m.
[23] Too 2000.
[24] The very inspired syntagma belongs to Robert Knapp (Knapp 2011).
[25] Robert 1940.
[26] Ville 1981.

The encoding

After gathering and registering all the epigraphic material, the necessity to standardise and encode certain classes of information becomes paramount. For this, we have used and adapted HISCO[27]- *Historical International Standard Classification of Occupations*. The HISCO codes have later been classified in HISCLASS,[28] HISCAM[29] and SOCPO[30] – systems that connect profession with social status. Although efficient for the periods they were designed for, they are completely irrelevant for the Roman era (servile status is ignored, and they cannot be adjusted to the fact that the socio-economical high classes are basically excluded from any professional/occupational category, etc.); in the end, we have not resorted to any of them.[31]

On line and in print,[32] HISCO has been thoroughly documented, thus we shall not insist on relating all the details here. Basically, it offers a standard codification system for historically-registered occupations – albeit only from Early Modernity up to the present. The system is based on the HISCO-tree, which contains nine professional Major groups:

0/1 – Professional, technical and related workers;
2 - Administrative and managerial workers;
3 - Clerical and related workers;
4 - Sales workers;
5 - Service workers;
6 - Agricultural, animal husbandry and forestry workers, fishermen and hunters;
7-8-9 - Production and related workers, transport equipment operators and labourers.

Each Major group contains Minor groups (01- Physical scientists and related workers, 02 – Architects, engineers and related workers) and Unit groups (011 – Chemists, 012 - Physicists), Micro groups (01110 – Chemist general, 01120 – Organic chemist) and every occupational title from the Unit groups files is associated with a description and a link to equivalent occupational titles, in various languages. Of course, these are modern languages, directing the search

---

[27] http://historyofwork.iisg.nl/; Last accessed 2017-05-10, 12.25 p.m.
[28] van Leeuwen, Maas 2011.
[29] Lamber, Zijdeman, van Leeuwen 2013. Of later attestations he offers no explanation for the absence, linaru History, April-June 2013, 46, 2ve Research, i.
[30] van de Putte, Miles 2015.
[31] For example, in HISCLASS, a professional trader is included in Group 4 (out of 5), but we have attested *negotiatores* who were *decuriones*, thus being part of a local elite (assimilated with Group 2 in HISCLASS).
[32] van Leeuwen, Maas, Miles, 2002.

towards databases dealing with occupations and/or demographic databases for the eras indicated above.

Adapting the system for the Roman era occupational titles was rather challenging, as certain *mutatis mutandis* processes had to take place. We have recorded 689 individuals associated with their professions. Regarding occupational titles, we have identified 286 of them in the first, raw, phase (the number more or less corresponds to the one extracted from pre- and early-industrial era church registers, for an area more or less overlapping with a Roman province) and reached 225 after a minimum standardization. Why minimum? Because, even with the risk of getting some technical glitches in the database and having to do part of the work manually, we have preferred to keep true to the source and give more details on the occupation – rather than opting for a general standard form. So, we have *negotiator artis alicariae, negotiator artis cervesariae, negotiator artis clostrariae, negotiator artis cretariae, negotiator artis cretariae et flaturariae,* etc. We have opted for keeping them as separate occupational titles in the database and unifying them by an identical code. So, we can make statistical deductions based on the codes, if we don't need to get into many details, but we can also have in front of our eyes the information given by the stones themselves.

The best-represented Major group as occupational titles go is no. 4 (Sales Workers). Besides the large variety of types of sellers attested, this group also raised a serious problem and we were faced with the necessity of adapting the encoding system: in Latin and for the Roman world, it is often hard to make the clear-cut distinction (as HISCO does) between producer and seller. Thus, for example, the *ampullarius*, most probably didn't only produce flasks, but also sold them, just as the *sagarus*, at least sometimes, also produced the cloaks he sold, etc. These kinds of situations are quite frequent and a decision had to be made regarding the encoding, as HISCO does not have codes for any type of producer-seller, let alone for all the multiple sub-specializations attested in inscriptions. The options were to adapt the codes and create new ones or to assign a general and/or two codes. We have decided in favour of the second solution, Because to introduce new codes would make the system more opaque for outside users. Therefore, sometimes we assigned two codes: 4 3200 + 4 9090, the general codes for negotiator plus a specialized producer code. Coming back to one of the above examples: for *ampullarius*, we have 8 9190 (Other Glass Formers, Cutters, Grinders and Finishers) + 4 9090 (Other Sales Workers – as we do not know anything about his status as a seller). In what category do we integrate one of these double-coded occupations, for statistical purposes? Both, none or according to historical realties, one might say. In some cases, the choice is very obvious, but in others, it is a matter of personal decision and methodological (not historical content) correctness. Some cases, such as *nauta negotiator* are

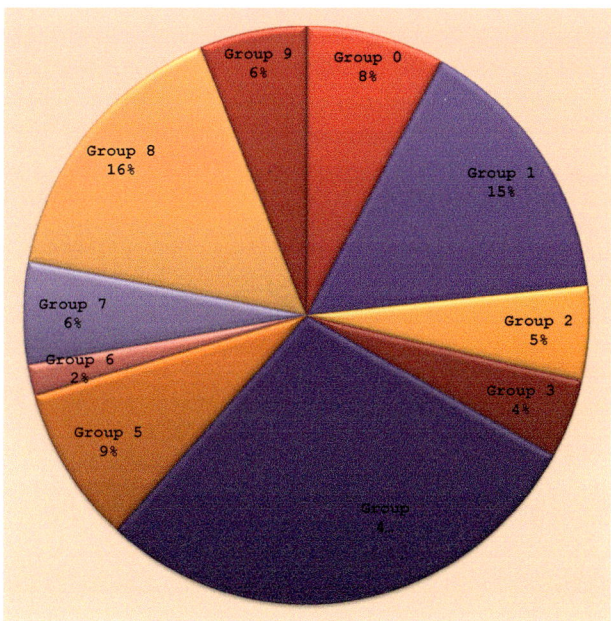

Figure 1. The group distribution of the professional titles

clear: 9 8135 + 4 3200 codes were assigned, for mariner and tradesman, and the occupational titles were introduced in group 9 and – respectively – group 4; this was an easy example, as we basically have two different titles, pertaining to two groups, but functionally it illustrates the same situation as when we allocate two codes to a single title. Generally we have included the double-coded professions in both groups, as this seems to be the correct and by-the-book option, when it comes to employing statistics. Another interesting case in group 4, from our point of view and from the point of view of social history analyses, was that of *venaliciarius* - slave dealer. HISCO doesn't provide anything remotely similar – even if traders of slaves existed in the periods the encoding system is mainly working with. It is hard to imagine this line of business as regular trade, but I had to assign it the general merchant code: 4 3200

Other problems faced when encoding in HISCO were connected to the inner structure of the system itself. Thus, the medical specializations do not have separate codes – which, in our opinion, would be very useful. For example, for *medicus ocularius*, one of the databases linked to HISCO, *TRA preliminary version 1803-1970*,[33] encodes ophthalmologist with 0 7520,[34] but the description

---

[33] http://www.inra.fr/. Last accessed 2017-05-10, 12.38 p.m.
[34] http://historyofwork.iisg.nl/detail_hiswi.php?know_id=47007&lang=. Last accessed 2017-05-10, 12.38 p.m.

of this code is: *Optometrist - Examines eyes and prescribes spectacles or treatment not involving the use of medicines, surgery or drugs, to conserve or improve vision.* We did not opt for this and did not consider it a solution, as writing *medicus* explicitly on one's monument implies pride in medical training and, in our opinion, excludes the auxiliary status. Equally, the system provides no separate codes for itinerant artists (we have *pictores pelegrini* attested); we have a code for journeymen, but then we lose track of the artistic profile of the profession. We neither have codes for amateur/private teachers,[35] as the encoding for teaching staff are completely dependent on the level they teach at (primary, secondary, university, etc.). In all these cases adjustments and integration into more general classes of codes were necessary.

Conclusions and future prospects

Regardless of the problems raised and the doubts faced during the encoding process, the codifications proved a useful step in analyzing the data, especially through social networks analyses (SNA),[36] connecting people based on common traits, obtaining and finally visualizing multiple types of connections.

In the general economy of research regarding occupational epigraphy, encoding is the first quasi-analytical step to be undertaken – right after the gathering and cataloguing of sources. Regarding social markers, what appears obvious from the table below (Table 1) is the fact that the most diverse and varied types of professionals took pride in their work status. Some of them have highly-specialized occupations (*architecctus, mensor, medicus*, etc.), others boast 'intellectual' professions (*pedagogus, grammaticus, adiutor tabularii*, etc.) and some definitely had a high economic status (*nauclerus, trierarchus*, etc.). These are the types of professions one would definitely expect to find on stone monuments. But we find a much larger variety of occupations, sometimes the information coming from evidently poor monuments. The complexity and multitude of the occupational titles is the hard proof for the fact that certain people identified with their profession regardless of which it was and that sometimes, even if modest, it became an important part of one's life and being.

---

[35] Present especially in the Greek world.
[36] For a general view on the method, see Barabási 2002.

Table 1. The encoded professional titles

Occupational title	HISCO code
architecctus	0 2120
fabrum navalium	0 2450
mensor	0 3010
agrimensor	0 3020
agens	0 3020
mensor aedificiorum	0 3150
nauclerus	0 4215
trierarchus	0 4215
pausarius	0 4230
architectus navalis	0 4330
medicus	0 6100
medicus ocularius	0 6100
pecuarius	0 6100
medicus; professor	0 6100 + 1 3120
medicus; professor	0 6100 + 1 3120
obstreticus	0 6120
veterinarius	0 6510
capsarius	0 7110
numerarius	1 1010
adiutor tabularii	1 1090
notarius	1 2310
notarius; obsonator	1 2310
educator	1 3000
grammaticus	1 3170
pedagogus	1 3390
praeceptor	1 3390
scholasticus	1 3390
retor	1 3990
lector	1 5990
sculptor	1 6120
picator	1 6130
pictor	1 6130
caelator anaglyptarius	1 6150

Occupational title	HISCO code
magister symforariorum	1 7135
musicarius	1 7145
mimographus	1 7320
scaenicus	1 7320
pilarius	1 7590
ursarius	1 7590
essedarius	1 8020
gladiator	1 8020
hoplomachus	1 8020
murmillo	1 8020
oplomachus	1 8020
pancratus	1 8020
provocator	1 8020
retiarius	1 8020
secutor	1 8020
venator	1 8020
doctor gladiatorum	1 8050
doctor retiarius	1 8050
navicularius	2 1240
navicularius marinus	2 1240
navicularius; auguarius	2 1240
ναύαρχος	2 1240
dissignator	2 2000
dispensator	2 2440
magister clavicularius	2 2440
ministra	2 2440
(ex) subaedianis	2 2490
actor	2 2520
dispensatoris vikarius	2 2520
vilicus	2 2520
apparitor	3 0000
coactor argentarius	3 1020
actarius	3 3120

Occupational title	HISCO code
scriba aerarii	3 3120
tabellarius	3 7000
scriba tabulari	3 9310
tabularius	3 9310
librarius	3 9990
scriba	3 9990
scriba coloniae	3 9990
frumentarius	4 1020
clavarius materiarius	4 1025
figlinarius	4 1025
emporos	4 3200
emporos (wine merchant)	4 3200
lixa	4 3200
mercator	4 3200
negotians	4 3200
negotians linatarius	4 3200
negotians vinarius	4 3200
negotiator (ferrarius)	4 3200
negotiator [vinarius ?]	4 3200
negotiator allecarius	4 3200
negotiator argenatrius vascularius	4 3200
negotiator artis alicariae	4 3200
negotiator artis cervesariae	4 3200
negotiator artis clostrariae	4 3200
negotiator artis cretariae	4 3200
negotiator artis cretariae et flaturariae	4 3200
negotiator artis cretariae, negotiator paenularum	4 3200
negotiator artis macellariae	4 3200
negotiator artis purpurariae	4 3200
negotiator artis ratiariae	4 3200
negotiator artis saponariae	4 3200
negotiator commerciator infectorius	4 3200
negotiator Durocortoro purpurario	4 3200
negotiator frumentarius	4 3200
negotiator gladiarius	4 3200
negotiator in ferro	4 3200
negotiator lanarius	4 3200
negotiator laudecenarius	4 3200
negotiator lignarius	4 3200
negotiator nummularius	4 3200
negotiator oleario	4 3200
negotiator olearius; diffusor	4 3200
negotiator pistoricius	4 3200
negotiator sagari	4 3200
negotiator salarius	4 3200
negotiator seplasiarius	4 3200
negotiator vestarius	4 3200
negotiator vestiario importator	4 3200
negotiator vinarius	4 3200
negotiator vinarius et artis cretariae	4 3200
negotiator vinarius et olearius; diffusor	4 3200
negotiatori artis prossariae	4 3200
olearius	4 3200
purpurarius	4 3200
sagarus	4 3200
scaenici negotiator	4 3200
seplasiarius	4 3200
thurarius	4 3200
unguentarius	4 3200
utricularius	4 3200
venaliciarius	4 3200
emporos (leather dresser merchant)	4 3200 + 4 5130

Occupational title	HISCO code
mensularius	4 4140
nummularius	4 4140
scrut(arius?)	4 4140
linarius	4 51 25
macellarius	4 5125
aquilegus	4 5220
propola salarius	4 5220
coponus	5 1020
cocus	5 3100
culinarius	5 3190
denudator	5 4030
famulus	5 4030
nutricius	5 4035
nutrix	5 4035
aedituus	5 5140
saltuarius	5 5190
scoparius	5 5290
ornatrix	5 7025
tonsor	5 7025
tonsor humanus	5 7025
defensor	5 8240
curator	5 8940
custos	5 8940
protector domesticus	5 8940
unctor sive pollinctor	5 9230 + 5 9220
ostiarius	5 9990
vicarius	5 9990
pecumarius	6 000
lardarius	6 2440
piscator	6 4100
vestigiator	6 4960
χαλκεύς	7 200
blacksmith (faber fabricalis)	7 2000
bronze smith	7 2000
cassidarius	7 2000

Occupational title	HISCO code
vascularius	7 2990
salinator	7 4470
vestiarius	7 5000
lanarius	7 5120
faber tignarius	7 5415
faber tignuarius	7 5415
fullo	7 5655
pistor	7 7610
tabernaclarius	7 9920
artis sutoriae	8 0110
calciarius	8 0110
sarcinatrix	8 0110
solearius	8 0110
sutor caligarius	8 0110
coriarius	8 0310
capistrarius	8 0320
faber lignarius	8 1000
cuparius	8 1930
columnarius	8 200
faber lapidarius	8 2000
lapicida	8 2000
lapidarius	8 2000
opifex lapidarius	8 2000
sculptor/lapicidus	8 2060
structor	8 2090
ferrarium	8 3110
sitularius	8 3110
faber limarius	8 3590
aerarius	8 7330
fabrum aerarius	8 7330
artificius argentarius	8 80 50
anularius	8 8010
argentarius	8 8050
aurifex	8 8050
faber argentarius	8 8050

Occupational title	HISCO code
τεχνειτης χρυσοχόος	8 8050
brattiarius	8 8070
vitriarius	8 9120
opificus artis vitriae	8 9190
ampullarius	8 9190 + 4 9090
sigillarius	8 9200
figulus	8 9210
lutor	8 9290
artis cretariae lixa	8-20.00
viminarius	9 4250
faber	9 4900
fabriciensis	9 4900

Occupational title	HISCO code
artis quadratariae	9 5140
marmorarius	9 5145
tignarius	9 5410
gypsarius	9 5510
diffusor olearius	9 7152
artis lintiariae	9 8100
lintiarius	9 8100
lintiarius; utricularius	9 8100 + 4 5125
nauta	9 8135
nauta; negotiator olearius	9 8135 + 4 3200
rector	9 8620
limarius	9 9910

References

Barabási, A.-L. 2002. *Linked: The Science of Networks*, Perseus Books Group.
Bounegru, O. 2006. *Trafiquants et navigateurs sur le Bas Danube et dans le Pont gauche à l'époque romaine*. Wiesbaden, Harrassowitz.
Boungeru, O. 2013. *Mercator: Studien zur antiken Wirtschaft im Pontosgebiet und in der Ägäis*. Kaiserslautern, Pantheon Verlag.
Broekaert, W. 2013. *Navicularii et negotiantes: a prosopographical study of Roman merchants and shippers*. St. Katharinen, Verlag Marie Leidorf.
Croom, A., 2010. *Roman Clothing and Fashion*. Stroud, Amberley.
Ernesti, J. A. 1737. *De negotiatoribus Romanis diputatiuncula*. Leipzig.
Droß-Krüpe, K. (ed.). 2014. *Textile trade and distribution in Antiquity*. Wiesbaden, Harrassowitz Verlag.
Flohr. M. 2013. *The world of the fullo. Work, economy and society in Roman Italy*. Oxford-New York, Oxford University Press.
Huet, P.-D. 1763. *Histoire du commerce et de la navigation des anciens*. Lyon, Desaint & Saillant.
Joshel, S. R. 1992. *Work, identity and legal status at Rome. A study of occupational inscriptions*. Norman-London, University of Oklahoma Press.
Knapp, R. 2011. *Invisible Romans*. Cambridge Ma., Harvard University Press.
Lamber, P. S., Zijdeman, R. L. and van Leeuwen, M. H.D. 2013. The Construction of HISCAM: a Stratification Scale Based on Social Interactions for Historical Comparative Research. *Historical Methods* 46, 2: 77-89
van Leeuwen, M. H. D., Maas, I. 2011. *HISCLASS. A Historical International Social Class Scheme*. Leuven, Leuven University Press.
van Leeuwen, M. H. D., Maas, I. and Miles, A. 2002. *HISCO: Historical International Standard Classification of Occupations*. Leuven, Leuven University Press.

Lehoërff, A. (ed.). 2004. *L' artisanat métallurgique dans les sociétés anciennes en Méditerranée occidentale: techniques, lieux et formes de production*. Rome, École Française de Rome.
MacMullen, R. 1982. The epigraphic habit in the Roman Empire. *American Journal of Philology* 103: 233-246.
Maxey, M. 1938. *Occupations of the lower classes*. Chicago, University of Chicago Press.
Petrikovits, H. V. 1991. Die Spezialisirung des römischen Handwerks. In H. Jankuhn, W. Janssen, R. Schmidt-Wiegand and H. Tiefenbach, *Das Handwerk in vor- und frühgeschichlichter Zeit*. Göttingen, Vandenhoeck & Ruprecht: 63-132.
van de Putte, B., Miles, A. 2015. A Social Classification Scheme for Historical Occupational data. *Historical Methods* 38, 2: 61-94.
Robert, L. 1940. *Les gladiateurs dans l'Orient grec*, Amsterdam, Adolf M. Hakkert.
Sim, D., Ridge, I. 1998. *Beyond the Bloom. Bloom refining and iron artifact production in the Roman world*. Oxford, Archaeopress.
Stern, E. M. 1999. Roman Glassblowing in a Cultural Context. *American Journal of Archaeology* 103: 441-484.
Straube, H. 1996. *Ferrum Noricum und die Stadt auf dem Magdalensberg*. Wien, Springer Verlag.
Too, Y. L. 2000. *The pedagogical contract: the economies of teaching and learning in the ancient world*. Ann Arbor, The University of Michigan Press.
Ville, G. 1981. *La gladiature en Occident des origines à la mort de Domitien*. Roma, Ecole Française de Rome.
Wesch-Klein, G. 1989. Private Handelsförderung im römischen Nordafrika. *Münsterschen Beiträge zur Antiken Handelsgeschichte* 7.1: 29-38.
Wilson, A., Flohr, M. (eds.). 2016. *Urban craftsmen and traders in the Roman world*. Oxford, Oxford University Press.
Zimmer, G. 1985. Römische Handwerker. *ANRW* 12.2: 205-228.

Latin occupational titles in Roman textile trade

Iulia Dumitrache

Methodology

Some methodological observations are to be acknowledged from the beginning. Using Greek and Latin inscriptions and documentary papyri as a source for analyzing specialization in crafts and trades creates a certain problem regarding the status of occupational or professional terms in these types of sources. The sample contains all recognizable individuals involved, in one way or another, in the textile trade. Considering that occupational titles are often vague and interpretable, it cannot be stated whether one person also performs handicraft, not only commercial activities. The opinion of Broekaert according to whom only the presence of the term *negotiator* within the occupational title is the doubtless mark of a commercial specialization[1] is worthful but limitary. First of all, in many cases, it is impossible to decide whether a specific term designates a craft or a trade. It should be recorded that some of the individuals, attested in Rome, are mentioning the location where they practice their business: Vicus Tuscus, Cermalus Minusculus, Horreum Volusianum, Horreum Agrippianum, all of these known as commercial spots.[2] They own shops where they sell their self-crafted products or other garments they acquired earlier. The iconographical sources often present images of deliverables garments that might signify disposal scenes.[3] It should be added the ambiguous semantics of Greek and Roman terminology.[4]

Individuals bearing names derived from occupational titles have been excluded from the analyzing.

The graphic representation of the Latin inscriptions containing occupational titles in textile trade, ordered in the legend alphabetically (hereinafter, they will be treated according to the raw material of the merchandises) reveals the following values: the most numerous are *centonarii*, actually the attestations of *collegia* (196), followed by *vestiarii* (101), *purpurarii* (46), *sagarii* (37), *lanarii* (23) *lintiarii* or *lintearii* (11), *sericarii*, *paenularii* and *barbaricarii* (4 each), and one *panucularius*.

---

[1] Broekaert 2013: 9.
[2] Coarelli 2012: 129; Richardson 1992: 429.
[3] Demarolle 2001: 32; Drinkwater 2001: 298; Larsson Lovén 2001: 45; Young 2000: 219.
[4] Ruffing 2016: 118; Wild 2000, 209.

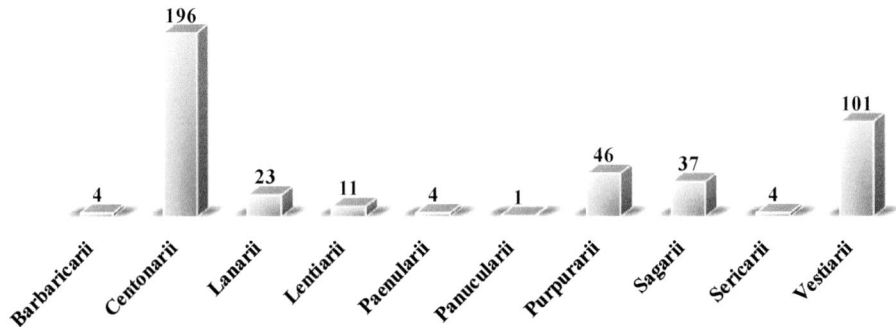

Figure 1. Occupational titles in Latin inscriptions

The analysis targets initially the most precious raw materials: gold, silk, and purple, followed by the most common: wool and linen.

Luxury garments traders: *barbaricarii, sericarii, purpurarii*

Figurative gold embroidery (*barbarica, aurea ornamenta*) was named after the 'barbarians', who, in contrast to the civilized Romans and Greeks, used to adorn their bodies and garments with all sorts of ornaments, even in the case of men. This is followed by the name of the **barbaricarii**, as defined in *Totius Latinitatis Lexicon: textores artificesque barbaricae vestis*,[5] or in *Notitia dignitatum* as follows: *exprimentes ex auro et coloratis filis hominum formas et diversorum animalium et specierum imitatam [?imitantes] subtilitate veritatem*.[6] Details about the production of such luxury garments are offered by Pliny: 'More than any other substance gold is immune from rust or verdigris or anything else emanating from it that wastes its goodness or reduces its weight. Moreover, in steady resistance to the overpowering effect of the juices of salt and vinegar, it surpasses all things, and over and above that it can be spun into thread and woven into a fabric like wool, even without an addition of wool. Verrius informs us that Tarquinius Priscus celebrated a triumph wearing a golden tunic. We have in our own times seen the Emperor Claudius's wife Agrippina, at a show at which he was exhibiting a naval battle, seated at his side wearing a military cloak made entirely of cloth of gold. For a long period gold has been woven into the fabric called cloth of Attalus, an invention of Kings of Asia'.[7] From the earlier imperial period, and still under Constantine, they appear as private craftsmen, and their merchandise was at great prize firstly within the imperial family, since garments, embroidered with gold, pearls, and precious stones, became the insignia of the imperial dignity.[8]

---

[5] *Lexicon* I: 371.
[6] Not. Dign. X, 58.
[7] Plinius, 33.62-63.
[8] Suetonius, *Nero*, 6. 50; SHA, Pertinax, 8. 2-4; SHA, Marcus Aurelius, 17. 4; SHA Elagabalus 23. 3-4.

There are only four *barbaricarii* attested in inscriptions (CIL V 785; XIII 1945; VI 33766, 9641): one is attested in Italy, two are mentioned in Rome, and one in Lyon (Figure 2). Aurelius Cassianus (CIL V 785) is a Syrian trader settled, probably as consequence of his business, in Italy. His success and an impressive wealth help him enter into the local elite from Forum Iulii Iriensium, where he became a *decurio*.[9] Another Syrian, Constantinus Aequalis (CIL XIII 1945) leaves his small hometown Germanicia for the Gallia. He settles down for life in Lugudunum, where he becomes a *sevir augustalis*. He seems to be involved also in craft activities as his funeral inscription suggests. He is called *homo optimus artis barbaricariae*, so he enters the category of merchants who deal their own products.[10] The two *barbaricarii* from Rome: Hermes and Diasmenus, have an inferior legal status. The first is a freedman (CIL VI 9641) and attendant – *ministrator*, and the latter is an imperial slave (CIL VI 33766). His funeral monument was erected by Tychicus, called 'collibertus', a term that makes the relationship between the two ambiguous. There are known cases when *collibertus* designates one's own freedmen (CIL VI 9010), but since Diasmenus is a slave, he has not the right to own slaves or to manumit them. All four *barbaricarii* date from the early imperial period.

The silk dealers manage their business where there are enough customers for their thoroughly expensive products. From the four **sericarii** epigraphically attested, three lead their trade in Rome: one man and two women (Figure 3). It is interesting to notice the occupational terms employed in silk-cloth commerce: there are two *sericaria* (CIL VI 9891, 9892), one *negotians sericarius* (CIL VI 9678), and one *negotiator sericarius* (CIL XIV 2793, 2812). There is a gender issue that implies that women were particularly involved, as epigraphically sources indicate, in activities linked to textile industry, and in the trade with luxury products.[11]

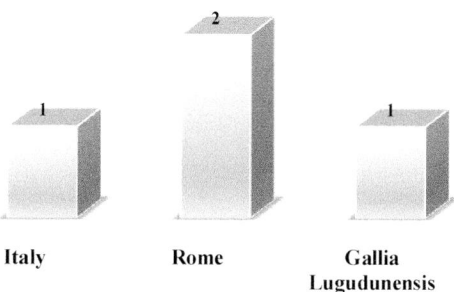

Figure 2. Geographical distribution of barbaricarii

---

[9] Vicari 2001: 38; Zaccaria 2009: 298.
[10] Wierschowski 2001: 325.
[11] Groen-Vallinga 2013; Holleran 2013; Larsson Lovén 2016.

Data and Thymele are involved in the silk garments trade, but very likely in the silk garments production, too. Both of them have a servile condition: the first is the freedwoman of an unknown person (CIL VI 9891), wealthy enough to facilitate her the access to such a revenue-bringing business, while the second (CIL VI 9892) is the slave of a certain Marcella.

The two attested men are clearly involved in trade: Marcus Aurelius Flavius (CIL VI 9678) is *negotians sericarius* in Rome, most probably in Vicus Tuscus, and Aulus Plutius Epaphroditus is an important member of the local elite in Gabii, a small town near Rome. He is known from two inscriptions (CIL XIV 2793, 2812). The first is dated in AD 169 and indicates Epaphroditus as an everget. He finances the building and the decoration of the temple of Venus Vera Felix Gabina. On this occasion, he offers as a gift five *denarii* to each decurion, three to each sevir Augustalis and one to each *tabernarius intra murum negotiantes*.[12] He also spends 10,000 sesterces for the birthday of Plutia Vera, his daughter.[13] His benevolence worth several thousands of sesterces, proving not only how fruitful his trade was, but also his importance within the local business and social milieu. The same idea is expressed by his quality of *accessus velatus* – magistrate in charge of Roman official cult, recruited from among the *ingenui* holders of prestigious careers and even from among the rich freedmen, due to the social permeability which, by virtue of individual wealth, promotes the social mobility.[14] Bessir Amiri suggests that Epaphroditus' legal status was low, rather of a freedman, and his donations were meant to facilitate social promotion for a man in an otherwise potentially marginal occupation. The second inscription confirms the wealth status of Epaphroditus. His freedmen honor him as patron, not forgetting to mention his qualities of *accenssus velatus* and *negotiator sericarius*.[15]

Aulus Plutius might have had connections with the silk dealers from Rome, where apparently also functioned a professional association of *sericarii* (CIL VI 9890).

Symbol of both wealth and power, purple represented one of the most expensive raw materials used in Roman textile industry, both through the rarity of the murex shell (taking into account that about 10,000 shells were necessary to produce 1 lb. of purple), and the complexity of the production process. Given 'the number of separate work roles and skills used in manufacturing a single product', as vertical specialization has been defined,[16] it becomes clear how and

---

[12] Ruffing 2016: 122.
[13] Ruffing 2007: 45; Tran 2007: 127-8.
[14] Di Stefano Manzella 1994: 262.
[15] Amiri 2012.
[16] Ruffing 2016: 117.

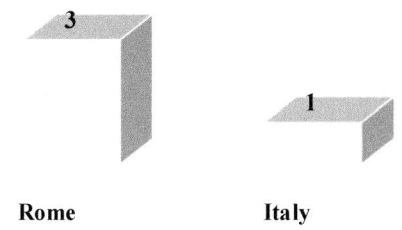

Figure. 3. Geographical distribution of sericarii

why veritable production and processing networks arose along the Roman world. Not much information about production costs remained (although apparently dyeing textiles was a low-status work,[17] but it is agreed that the finite products were exclusive merchandises. According to the Price Edict of Diocletian, there are five categories of purple-dyed garments: 'simple or once-dyed purple', 'best genuine Milesian purple', 'second quality Milesian purple', 'archil purple' of four different qualities, 'light purple', and 'bright Tyrian purple'.[18]

The occupational term '**purpurarius**' designated a 'producer of purple dye stuff', or 'someone selling purple products', or more likely, 'a person who combined producing and selling purple products'.[19] The majority of dealers (out of 46) in purple-dyed cloth comes, as expected, given the assumption that their merchandise is expensive, from Rome (17) and Italy (14), followed by Raetia (5), Syria and Baetica (2), and Moesia Inferior, Macedonia, Achaia, Gallia Narbonensis, Gallia Lugdunensis, and Aquitania (1). Although the great majority of them define themselves through the occupational term *purpurarius*, there are some different cases. Tiberius Claudius Euphras (CIL III 5824) is called *negotiator artis purpurariae* (so he is involved in the production process as well). Maybe he is the owner of a shop in Augusta Vindelicum, where he was able to sell the garments he created. Another trader, whose name was partially preserved –]eius – entitled himself *negotians purpurarius* (CIL VI 3388). Finally, a freedmen called Publius Murrius Zetus, native from Placentia – from northern Italy – was *mercator purpurarius* in Montecassino (AE 1972, 74), so he dealt a single type of products. His *collibertus* Eros took Zetus' remains back to his hometown.[20] In Aquino, near Montecassino, Publii Murii are attested; probably among them is also the patron of Zetus and Eros (CIL XI 1270). Several questions still remain: which is the link between them? Were the Murii involved in trade? Did they have interests in purple-dyed garments? Where Zetus and Eros business partner, or only their servile fellowship and friendship determined Eros' behavior?

The Murii would not be the only members of a Roman family involved in purple trade. One Lucius Bennius, *purpurarius* from the 1st century AD (AE 1994, 283),

---

[17] Larsson Lovén 2001: 45.
[18] Croom 1988: 25.
[19] Larsson Lovén 2001: 45.
[20] Broekaert 2013: 169.

very probably of a servile condition,[21] might be linked to Lucius Bennius Mida, attested in another inscription from Rome (CIL VI 32454) together with Lucius Modius Philomusus, also a purple-dealer. Some freedmen of the Vicirii: a man whose name was not preserved, freedman of the Numeri; Viciria, and Viciria Creste – freedwomen of Aulus; Viciria Ta?, and Victoria Nice – freedwomen of Numerus, are *purpurarii* in Rome at c. 1st century AD. Gian Luca Gregori sets a connection between the Vicirii from Rome and the senatorial branch of this family, originary from Rusellae, involved in marble trade.[22] When an occupational group like this of the Vicirii of mixed sex occurs in an inscription with a job title in the masculine form, it is obvious that it refers to male work, but it does not exclude that women were involved in the business as well. According to L. Larsson Lovén, 'If, in analysing the inscriptions with such job titles, women are more regularly considered, this still does not constitute direct evidence of female work, but it does offer a better understanding of women's occupational possibilities and of their roles in urban economies and the labour market'.[23] The last example of a family focused on purple-trade is the Veturia family. Decimus Veturius Atticus (AE 1923, 59) is a freedman of the Veturii who deals in purple in Vicus Iugarius. The inscription also mentions Veturia Tryphea but does not specify whether the woman worked in the purple trade; it is possible that both the man and the woman worked in the shop. Another *purpurarius*, attested in Castrimoensius (CIL XIV 2433), but who has his business in Rome, in Vicus Tuscus, married Veturia Attica, a freedwoman of another branch of the Veturii.

Another Decimus Veturius, bearing the cognomen Diogenes (CIL VI 9846) is mentioned together with Decimus Nicephor, Veturia Flora, and Decimus Veturius Philargurus as *purpurarii a Marianeis*. Little is known about the *monumenta Mariana*. They were erected by Marius after the victory against the cimbri and the teutons, but their location is not known. In summary, members of the Veturii are purple-traders concentrated in what we might call 'clusters': in Vicus Tuscus, Vicus Iugaris, or near the *monumenta Mariana*. However, it is not documented, but very likely, that the patrons of these freedmen had interests in these shops, but their freemen and the freedmen of their freedmen took care of the family business.

The wealth gathered allowed the purple-traders to enter the local elite and to gain different dignities. Taking into account that their great majority had a low legal status, the highest rank they were able to reach was *augustalitas*. Tiberius Claudius Euphras (CIL III 5824) settled in Raetia, in Augusta Vindelicorum,

---

[21] Gregori 1994: 739.
[22] Gregori 1994: 740.
[23] Larsson Lovén 2016: 205.

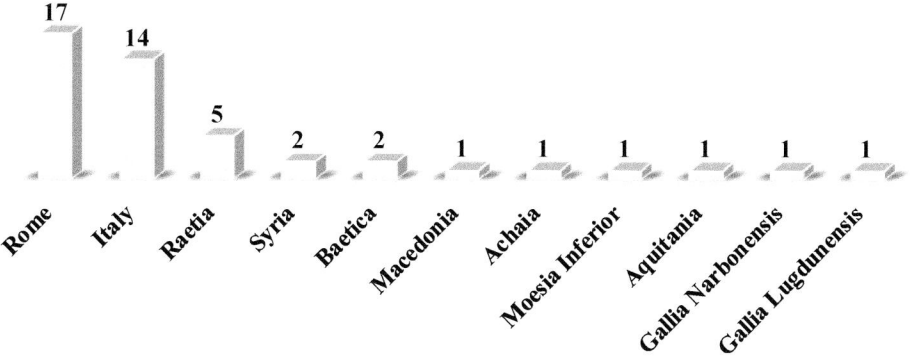

Figure 4. Geographical distribution of purpurarii

where he married a woman from a local family.[24] His origin is not known, but apparently, he integrates himself into the local Romanized landscape: his children bear Roman *cognomina*, and he is involved in the official cult. He is probably an imperial freedman or a descendant of an imperial freedman, and he reaches the dignity of *sevir augustalis* in Augusta Vindelicorum. Cnaeus Haius Doriphorus (CIL X 540) is *augustalis* in Puteoli in the 2nd century AD. He added to this title *dupliciarius*, so he receives a double part from the allotments, where the link between his success within the business milieu and the civic titles stems from.[25] The citizen Marcus Satellius Marcellus (CIL XI 6604) was *sexvir* in Mevaniola, and Caius Marcilius Eros (CIL IX 5276) is *quinquevir* – a commissioner responsible for the allotment of public funds – in Truentum.

In order to make their trade prosperous, the merchants had to move following the raw or a profitable market. Thus, Publius Murrius Zetus has his hometown in Placentia, but he leads commercial activities in Montecassino (AE 1972, 74). Victorius Regulus (AE 1982, 709) comes from the tribe of the Nemetes, located by the Rhine, and moves to Reims, probably due to his business.[26] He specializes in the purple trade between Durocotorum and Lugudunum, where he meets his end. It is possible that his destiny is connected to his brother's career. Vicrius Tetricus was a soldier in *legio XXII Primigenia Pia Fidelis*, stationed near Lyon from AD 197. As a veteran, Tetricus choose to settle in Lyon, probably a good reason for his brother to develop his business in the same place. Maybe Tetricus had good connections to his former legion brothers, a fact that opened a new and profitable market for Regulus.

---

[24] Broekaert 2013: 51.
[25] Tran 2007: 127.
[26] Broekaert 2013: 119.

Linen garments traders

Linen was very prized as raw material due to its irrefutable qualities: the tensile strength and durability; the fineness of fibers; the smooth handle, and, not least, its whiteness.[27] Tarsus, Laodicea, and Alexandria were well known for the production of high-quality **linen** garments.[28] Indeed, Dio of Prusa was mentioning a large number of linen workers at Tarsus and the political unrest resulting from their exclusion from full participation in civic life.[29] But many more cities and villages were involved in the production of more common items of clothing that could be purchased by a much broader buying public, much like the ceramic ware that is found all over the empire. The weaving of flax, like that of wool, was known and practiced in Gaul well before the Roman domination, and a canvas of Gaulic tribes enjoyed a certain reputation in the time of Pliny: *Cadurci, Caleti, Ruleni, Bituriges, ullimique hominum exislimati Morini, immo vero Galliæ universæ vela texunt.*[30] The Cadurcians also manufactured linen garments – very esteemed for the manufacture of mattresses and upholstered beds, the invention of which belongs to Gaul.

The are only 11 **lintearii/lintiarii** (Figure 5) attested on inscriptions (taking into account the variants *lintearii/lintiarii*): five in Rome, two in Italy, two in Gallia Lugudunensis, one in Aquitania, and one in Gallia Narbonensis.

Rolomagus (nowadays Rouen) was the capital of the Veliocasses. By coming to establish their commercial residence (*consistere*) in a community, the traders never neglected to secure all the rights they could claim or acquire. This remark finds the following: the inscription constituting the profession of Illiomarus Aper (CIL XIII 1998), its origin, its substitution in the Lyonnaise colony, and its aggregation to the *utricularii*, which would seem to indicate that the *lintiarii* did not have a special college at Lugdunum. The smaller cities, even the countryside, could also attract elements of an allogene population. They also determined interprovincial movements, along with the development of large economic zones, often on the frontiers of the empire, whose role was that of a market based on exchanges with the barbaric world and the purchasing power of the military units. Craftsmen, merchants, and others still gathered there in colleges.[31] Titus Iulius Secundus (CIL VI 9670) is involved in another trade than linen cloth, but because of the poor preservation state of the inscription it remains unknown. Broekaert assumes a commercial activity that implies textiles too (*centonarius* or *lanarius*).[32]

---

[27] Wild 1970: 14.
[28] Jones 1960.
[29] Dio Chrys. *Or.* 34.21–3.
[30] Pliny 19,2.
[31] Lassère 2006: 62-65.
[32] . Broekaert 2013: 74.

Titus Pontius Maior (CIL V 5932) is a linen trader from Milan that provides the military staff from the *limes* with linen garments. Quintus Aebutius Chrestus (CIL XI 6228), the freedman of a certain Quintus Abutius, became *sevir* in Fanum and affords to manumit his own slaves (as the case of Epaphra). Maybe the success of his business is due to a special type of linen products: sails that could have been sold in the harbor of Fanum.[33] Two freedmen, Entimus et Zmaragdus, care for the construction and the funerary inscription of their patron, Titus Matuccius Pallans.[34] The two were working together, but it is not known if they had learned the trade from their former master.

An association of the *negotiatores vestiariae et lintiariae* is known from Augusta Vindelicorum (CIL III 5800).

The *paenula* was a very simple type of a long sleeveless Roman cloak consisting of a piece of material with a central hole allowing the wearer to slip the cloak over the head. It was worn by both men and women, generally used as protection against bad weather. It has been considered as a low- or middle-quality garment, but, taking into account that the *Price Edict* mentions *paenulae* made of Laodicean wool, a high-rated raw material, this idea requires reflection. The four **paenularii** mentioned in the inscriptions traded cloaks in Rome (CIL VI 4000), in Puzzuoli (CIL X 1945), Peltuinum Vestinum (CIL IX 3444) and Sumelocenna (CIL XIII 6366).

The character Caius Aponio (CIL IX 3444) is probably originally from Amiterninus since this *nomen gentile* is widespread in this area, as in CIL IX 4374 (C. Aponius Celer) and CIL IX 4322 (C. Aponius Sabinus). From Peltuinum comes another inscription mentioning two women, landowners in the city (CIL IX 3446). Testimonials of this *nomen* are also found in Marruvium (CIL IX 3727); Pinna (CIL IX 3363); Forum Novum (CIL IX 4777), and Cupra Marittima (CIL IX 5293).

Marcus Meccius Fortunatus (CIL XIII 6366) devotes, in AD 225, an inscription *in honorem domus divinae* in Sumelocenna, as a consequence of his responsibilities associated with the sevirat. It does not seem an extraordinary financial effort, given his double commercial specialization. He deals *panuculae*, but he also produces and sells white pottery, as a *negotiator artis cretariae*. There are other three *negotiatores artis cretariae* in Germania Superior (CIL XIII 6524, 7228, 7588), but Fortunatus is the only one who practices diversified *negotium*, and the only one who mentions his quality of *sevir augustalis*.

---

[33] Agnati 1999: 416.
[34] Gordon 1983: no. 70.

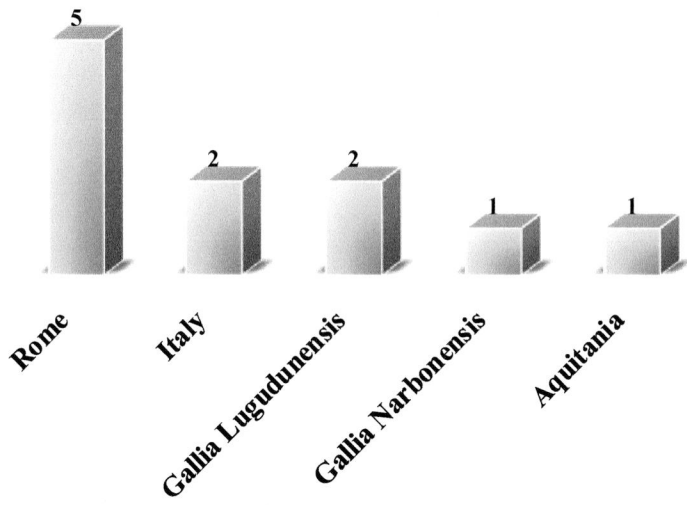

Figure 5. Geographical distribution of lintiarii

Wool garments traders: *panucularii, lanarii, centonarii, paenularii, sagarii, vestiarii*

Wool was the most common raw material used in the textile industry. Wool shearing and washing, spinning, dyeing, weaving, felting (the action of which the wool fabric becomes dense as the felt) and fulling (textile finishing operation consisting of compacting the fleece by binding together the fibers; it is carried out by pressing them through rotating cylinders or by hammering in moist and warm acid or basic environment) involves not only skills, but also various work activities. Wool processing, especially with the intent to obtain and prepare threads, consumes more time. In fact, spinning is considered key for the textile industry. This activity would involve a much larger labor, home provided. The wool threads trade may have been an integral element in the textile economy.

The word *panuculus* would be the diminutive of *panus*, that is to say, the coil around which the thread is wound. The **mercator panucularius** was then probably a yarn and threads merchant.[35] There is only one *mercator panucularius*, epigraphically attested in Narbo (CIL XII 5973), who deals only wool yarns.

There are only 23 epigraphically mentioned **lanarii**: 10 in Rome, 8 in Italy, 2 in Gallia Narbonensis and one in Hispania Citerior, Dalmatia, and Numidia (Figure 6) Beside *lanarius*, there are few occupational titles, derived from *lanarius*, that

---

[35] Bonsangue 2002: 211.

suggest wool-trade: *negotians lanarius* (CIL IX 862), *negotiator lanarius* (CIL VI 9669; AE 1925, 60), and *lanarius coactiliarius* (CIL VI 9494), title that suggest that the character was involved also in some craft activities. Publius Blerra (CIL XI 6367) is member, together with a *stuctor*, a *vestiarius* and another character, in the association of the *magistri vici* from Pisaurum. This association, however, as it is shown in the epigraph, have taken charge of the expanses for the construction of a porch, on which was placed the above-mentioned inscription, after having received a favorable opinion on the part of the assembly of decurions. Therefore, the *magistri vici* disposed of a common fund (*arca*), from which the same members drew to achieve in this case a work of public utility in behalf of the entire community of Pisarium. This new display will certainly contribute to the embellishment of the colony in a monumental way, but also to foster a feeling of gratitude from the part of the inhabitants.[36]

The funerary inscription of Mecia Dynata (CIL VI 9493) was set up according to her will and her donations. The epigraph reveals a family certainly involved in wool-processing and in wool-trade. The mother of the deceased is a wool-comber – *tonstrix*, while her brother, Lucius Mecius Rusticus, is a *lanarius* and owns a shop near the temple of Fors Fortuna.[37] Other places where wool-shops were located in Rome are vicus Caesaris (CIL VI 9492), that cannot be mapped[38] and Suburra (CIL VI 9491).

Quintus Alfidius Hyla (CIL XI 862) is a *sevir* in Forum Sempronii, in central Italy, and he is dealing in wool probably in Mutina. His connection to the *collegium hareniorum* from Rome led to different interpretation: cloth dealer for the gladiators,[39] game sponsor[40] or sand dealer.

Centonarii are identified as 'artisans and tradesmen in low-to-medium quality woolen. The members of the *collegia centonariorum* were recruited on the basis of their trade'.[41] Most of the mentions of the *centonarii* are linked to a *collegium*, connected at its turn to other professional or cultic *collegia*, related to other craft, trade or transport activities (Figure 7).

As for the internal organization of these *collegia*, there have been identified more honorifical or executive functions within them (Figure 8). There are to be noticed some clear cases where important members of the local or provincial elite were

---

[36] Valchera 2012: 14.
[37] Hawkins 2016: 193-194.
[38] Ball Platner 1929: 571.
[39] Nicolas 1998: 25.
[40] Liu 2013: 131.
[41] Liu 2009: 295.

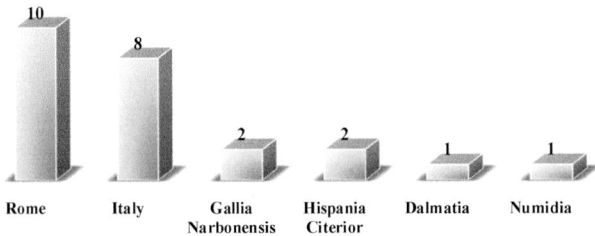

Figure 6. Geographical distribution of lanarii

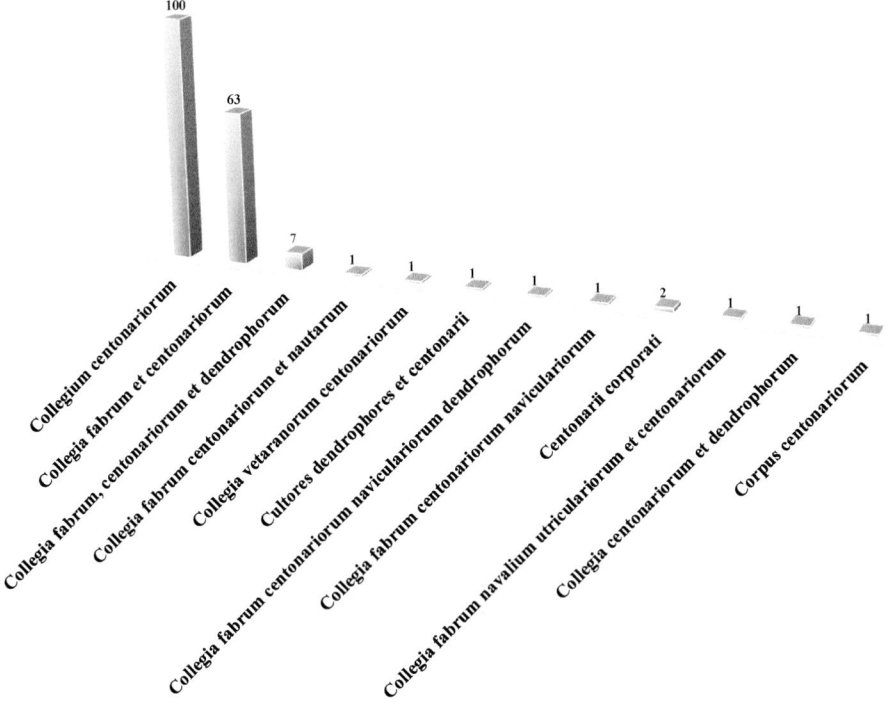

Figure 7. Epigraphical mentions of collegia centonariorum

mentioned as members of the associations: Attalus, from Gallia Lugdunensis (AE 1982 702), who is *sevir augustalis* in Lyon, member of the association of *nautae Rhodanae* and *corporatus* in *collegium centonariorum Luguduni consistentes*, or Publius Aelius Strenuo from Apulum (CIL III 1209) – *equus publicus, sacerdos arae Augusti*, augur, *duumvir* of Sarmizegetusa, *augustalis* in Apulum, decurion in Drobeta, but at the same time patron of the *collegium fabrum, centonariorum et nautarum* and *conductor pascui et salinarum et commerciorum*.

Aside from *centonarii*, the best attested occupational titles in textile in the Roman imperial period are *sagarii* and *vestiarii*.

The **sagarii** were makers and dealers of *saga*. As an outer cloak, the *sagum/sagus* was part of the basic costume for civilians and soldiers alike. According to *Dig.* 34.2.23.2, *saga* belonged to *vestimenta virilia* and *familiarica*, suitable for adult men and slaves, but not for children or women (*puerilia aut muliebria aut communia*). It was of Gallic origin. According to Strabo, the Gallic *sagi* were rough. In Martial, *saga* was used almost as a synonym for low-quality clothing. However, *saga* must have ranged in quality, since all kinds of people wore them. Indeed, in Diocletian's list, the price of *saga* ranged from 500 to 8,000 denarii. A *sagum* is easily identifiable in visual presentations: it is oblong and fastened by a bula on one shoulder. *Saga* were closely associated with the military, to the extent that as early as the time of Cicero, *ad saga ire* or *saga sumere/ponere* had the symbolic meaning of 'prepare for war'. There are 37 *sagarii* mentioned by the inscriptions: 15 from Rome, 12 from Italy (the most numerous appear in Mediolanum – four), six from Gallia Narbonensis (among them, four come from Vindobona), two from Gallia Lugdunensis, and one for Baetica and Germania Superior (Figure 9).

Beside the occupational title of *sagarius*, there are some other appelations added to this, according to the level of trade or the type of the merchandise: *Mercator*

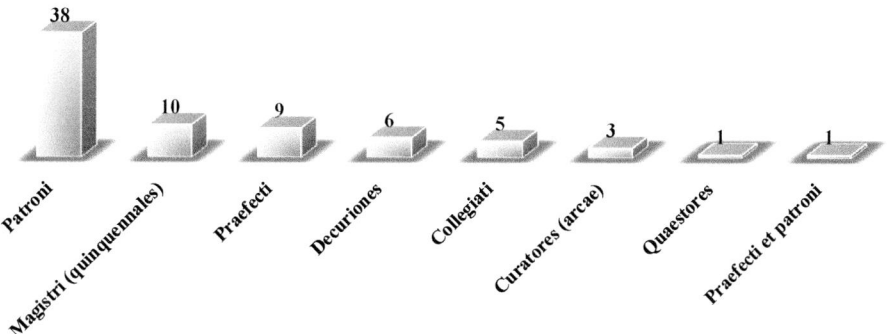

Figure 8. Honorifical titles within the collegia centonariorum

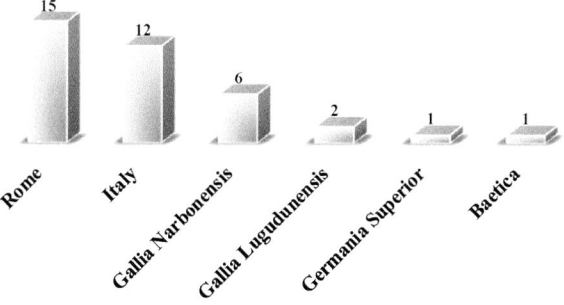

Figure 9. Geographical distribution of the sagarii

sagarius (CIL VI 9675), *negotiator sagarius* (CIL V 5925 and 5929; CIL VI 9675 and CIL XIII 2010), and *negotiator sagarius et pellicarius* (CIL V 5928).

From the 15 *sagarii* attested in Rome, seven bear the name Cornelius: four Quinti Cornelii (CIL VI 9866, 9867, 9868, 9869) and one Aulus Cornelius (CIL VI 33906). Menippus and Priscus mention also the location of their shop. Joshel 1992: 144 suggests that they acted as branch offices of a family business or they were 'the freedmen of patrons who were themselves connected by family ties or the relations generated by slavery and manumisson'. The same situation applies to the two Lucii Salvii (CIL VI 9870, 37378, 7971), and the two Lucii Arleni (CIL VI 9675, 12331, 12332).

Lucius Arlenus Demetrius and Lucius Arlenus Artemidorus are freedmen of a Lucius Arlenus residing in Rome. Demetrius is originary from Paphlagonia, and Artemidorus from Cilicia. Maybe the Arlenii sold on the Roman market came from their homelands, well-known for the textile industry. It is difficult to say if the two characters hold a shop in Rome or they were managing the textile import from the East. There is no other information that proves that were some *institores* for the family business.[42]

Marcus Cluvius Tertullus (CIL V 5925) sells in Milan the *saga* produced in Apulia, a region famous for sheep-raising and wool-processing. Milan seems to be an important market for the Gallic cloaks, as both the funerary reliefs and inscriptions show.[43] Thus, the presence of foreign traders here appears inherent. Marcus Matutinius Maximus (CIL V 5929), a citizen of the Mediomatrici (from the territory of Metz), settled and died in Milan, being involved in the commerce with *saga* between Gallia Belgica and Italy.[44] Quintus Lucilius Charinus (CIL IX 5752) *sagarius* from Milan, choses to build, during his lifetime, for him and his friend, a funeral monument in Ricina. The reasons for which he takes this decision stays unknown. It is possible that he has had commercial interests in Ricina, but since his main business was in Milan, where he was also a sevir, it is to assume that Mediolanum was his hometown.

Caius Latinus Reginus (CIL XIII 2008), originary from Durocortorum (Reims), resides and trades in Lugudunum. It is very likely that his move to Gallia Lugudunensis came as a business opportunity. His homeland was prized for textile, especially *saga* production.[45] Fryan suggests[46] that the *negotiatores sagarii*

---

[42] Pilhofer 2005: 171; Flohr 2014: 7.
[43] Young 2000: 219.
[44] Van Nijf and Meijner 1992: 106; Wierschowski 2001: 64.
[45] Wierschovski 2001: 345.
[46] Fryan 1984: 153.

brought the raw materials or the finished fabrics from the north-eastern Gallia Belgica, and the rest of the *sagarii* sold these items or made up the cloacks from this material.

Littavius (CIL XIII 2016) from the Carnutenses resided in Lugudunum in the second half of the 2nd century AD.[47] Caius Rusonius Secundus and Caius Rusonius Myron (CIL XIII 1898) decide to leave Vindobona for Lugudunum.[48] The two friends and freedmen, probably business partners, build impressive careers in Lugudunum. The Roman Publius Vettius Gemellus (CIL XII 1928) moved in the 2nd century AD in Vindobona and involved in the trade of the Gallic *saga*, very probably in Rome.[49] Since he died at the age of 21 in Gallia Narbonensis, and his father is the dedicant of his funerary inscription, it is possible that the latter has been involved at his turn in the commercial life of ancient Vienna. Myron develops his economic status by entering some professional associations linked to the textile trade (*centonarii* and *sagarii*). The both characters receive the *augustalitas*, the highest position they could have hold in the local hierarchy according to their legal status. The same situation is emphasized by another *sagarius*, whom name is unknown (CIL XII 2619), attested in Genava. This time, he moves from Lugudunum to Genava, in Gallia Narbonensis, where he became a *sevir*.

The economic prestige gained by the *sagarii* helps them in acquiring rather honorific dignities, connected to the imperial cult: they could have been *augustales* (CIL X 1872 – in Puteoli and Neapolis; AE 1996, 450 – in Luceria) or *seviri* (CIL IX 5752). In Baetica, at Corduba, the freedman Felix was a *magister Larum Augustorum*, the same as his patron (CIL II/7, 323).

Three professional associations of the *sagarii* are attested: in Pompeii (CIL IV 753), where an inscription that documents the *sagarii* refers to Caius Rufus, a candidate for the positions of *aedilis* and *duumvir* around AD 65-73; in Lugudunum (CIL XIII 1898), where Caius Rusonius Myron was a *sagarius corporatus*, and, finally, in Rome (CIL VI 956), where *sagarii theatri Marcelli*, together with the *cultores domus Augustae*, finance a votive inscription to the emperor Trajan, around AD 103-104. The Cornelii located *a theatro Marcelli* (CIL VI 9868) may have joined that *collegium*. Although there were also other locations preferred in Rome for the *saga* shops, *horrea Galbiana* (CIL VI 33906) or *aedes Castoris* (CIL VI 9872), there is no other evidence for a geographical association of the cloack-dealers.

---

[47] Verboven 2007: 308.
[48] Verboven 2007: 308.
[49] Wierschowski 2001:156.

Vestiarii – the cloth dealers – are the most numerous category of textile traders. There have been identified 101 individuals, as follows: more than half in Rome (56), and the rest distributed in Italy (26); Gallia Belgica (4); Gallia Narbonensis and Raetia (3); Africa Proconsularis (2); Gallia Lugudunensis, Germania Inferior, Aquitania, Baetica, Numidia (1), and one whom location is not known (Figure 10). The geographical distributions of the epigraphic records of the *vestiarii* and *sagarii* do not substantially overlap: epigraphic records of both titles have been found only in Rome, Pompeii, Capua, Corduba, and Bononia.

Luxury or high quality garments were sold by a distinctive category of traders, named *vestiarii tenuiarii*. They were heavily concentrated in Rome (CIL VI 1926, 6852, 7782, 9977, 33923, 33924, 37826; CIL V 6777; *InscrAqu* 1, 222), and they were mentioned mainly in vicus Tuscus, the most expensive commercial area of the Imperial Rome. An epitaph from Aquileia mentions a T. Claudius Syntrophus, who was described as a *vestiarius centonarius* (CIL V 50). If the inscription is not false,[50] then this inscription would be a further proof of the involvement of the *centonarii* in the textile industry. There are also attested a *negotiator vestiarius* (CIL III 816) in Augusta Vindelicorum, a *negotiator vestiarius importator* (CIL XIII 8568), and a *negotiator vestitor urbicus* (CIL VI 33889).

In Rome, the cloth shops were concentrated in few areas. The *vestiarii* use the location of their trade as an effective commercial, and as an assurance of their high quality service. They proudly affirm that their businesses rise *de vico Tusco* (CIL VI 9976, 33923, 37826); *de Cermalo Minusculo* (CIL VI 33920; *EURom* 52); *a Quirinis* (CIL V 9975); *a compito Aliario* (CIL VI 4476, 9971); *ab aedes Caereris* (CIL VI 9968); *ab Iuco Libitinae* (CIL VI 9974); *de Dianico* (CIL VI 33922); *de horreis Agrippianis* (CIL VI 9972 and XIV 3958), and *de horreis Volusianis* (CIL VI 9973). Within these clusters grow prosperous family businesses. Four freedmen (one woman and three men) of a certain Publius Avillius are selling cloth in Cermalus Minusculus – a part from the Palatine Hill, near the obelisk of Augustus from the Circus Maximus.[51] It is not specified if they have worked in the same shop (or workshop) as business partners or as employees of their former master, a freedman himself, to whom they dedicate the monument after his death.[52]

Cameria Iarine and the Lucii Camerii – Thraso, Alexander and Onesimus (CIL VI 37826) are involved in a luxury garments business, located in vicus Tuscus - 'the main route between the Forum Romanum and lower Forum Boarium, and hence to the Circus Maximus'.[53] The woman is the author of the dedication to

---
[50] Liu 2009: 79.
[51] Joshel 1992: 131; Coarelli 2014: 325.
[52] Orlandi 1994:765; Lázaro Guillamón 2003.
[53] Richardson 1992: 429

his former master (Thraso, a freedman himself), to the patron of her patron (Alexander) and to her *collibertus* and husband Onesimus). It might be an example of a family business. The occupation passed from patron to freedman to freedman's freedman.⁵⁴ Titus Statilius Hilarus was buried, in the first half of the 1st century AD in the *columbaria* of the Statilii, a senatorial family that flourished at the beginning of the 1st century AD.⁵⁵ Hilarus worked until the end of his life for his former patron, the consul Taurus Corvinus. There are no other characters from the *Monumentum Statiliorum* involved in the textile trade.⁵⁶ A group of three freedmen named Publii Sulpicii/Sulpicia might be connected to Publius Sulpicius Quirinus, who was in charge with the census in Judaea and Syria at beginnings of the Christian era.⁵⁷ Maybe after their manumission they associated in a trade or continued work together, as before, in the same shop kept by the same owner.

Alike in all other cases of textile dealers, the *vestiarii* have a low legal status. As a consequence, they could climb in the local hierarchy only to the position of *augustalis* (CIL VI 3680 and XII 4520) or *sevir augustalis* (CIL XII 3202). Lucius Lupercus Excessus is documented in the first half of the 2nd century AD in Fara Novarese (AE 2000, 632). His *nomen gentile* is extremely rare and can be met only once in an inscription from Salona. Following a Celtic tradition, the name is likely to be derived from the *cognomen* Lupercus. That he riched an honorary position of *sevir augustalis* in *civitas Helvetica*, probably his homeland, can support this hypothesis. Excessus's professional life can be considered a success, since he left a large sum of money to be distributed to his fellow merchants. The exact amount is unknown, because of the conservation status of the stone. The specific reference to the name of the city reveals an association that otherwise would have remained completely unknown in Novara. Also, it is still more interesting that he declares his affiliation to the *corpus splendidissimus Cisalpinorm et Transalpinorum*, a large association of traders covering an area of the central Gaul to northern Italy. Thus, the inscription suggests that the Cisalpine and Transalpine association have more 'divisions', each of them specialized in a particular type of goods. This theory is supported by the inscription of Q. Otacilius Pollinus (CIL XIII 11480), who was the patron of the subdivision of slave traders (*venalicii corporis Cisalpinorum et Transalpinorum*). Obviously, the decision of Excessus to give money only to his fellows is perfectly justifiable. He aspired to be considered a benefactor by the people who directly interacted with him. A donation to the corpus of the Alpine merchants would have been certainly less effective: many merchants hardly would have known Excessus,

---
⁵⁴ Joshel 1992: 138-139.
⁵⁵ Mouritsen 2013: 44-45.
⁵⁶ Hackworth 2011:3.
⁵⁷ Orlandi 1994: 765.

and more importantly, the distribution of money among his colleagues would have brought them each a nice gift, while dividing the same amount to all members of a large *corpus* would have hardly qualified him to aspire to the title of benefactor.

A certain Sextus Baebius (CIL V 774), cloth-seller from Aquileia, mentions his quality of former member of the Roman fleet (*veteranus ex classe*). Although it was not mentioned, he may have been acting within the *classis Venetum*, based at Aquileia and operating in the northern Adriatic Sea. Since the military milieu formed into a constant and consistent market, Herma seems to have profited from the vicinity of his colleegues. Sextus Baebius is not a unique example of a cloth-dealer who chooses the military garnments for his *negotium*. Iulius Victor, deceased in Augsburg, in Raetia, around AD 150-225, had a brother, serving within *legio III Italica*, based in this province. Did the ties his brother had in the army facilitate Victor's access to the unit's supply with different clothes? He may have been originary from the northern Italy, taking into account the recruitment area for this legion. Another inscription (AE 2006, 1827) is taken care by an auxiliary troup of *legio I Adiutrix* in honor of Aemilianus – cloth-seller and agent in Gallia. A certain Lucius Priminius Ingenuus (CIL XIII 8568) was selling finished cloth in Stockhum. His merchandise came most likely from the centers of Gaul, such as Trier and Reims.[58] Ingenuus might have traded on the military units located on the *limes*, the same way as Sextus Baebius or Iulius Victor. He could have been related to L. Priminius Provincialis, who dedicated an inscription to Mercury near Neuss. A woman belonging to the Priminii married a bread merchant from Cologne (CIL XIII 8545). Finally, Maxsiminus (sic!), who had the workstation in Marsal, in Gallia Belgica appears to have exported clothes to the *limes* (CIL XIII 4564).

A *civis Trever* (CIL XIII 542) is mentioned in Elusa (in Aquitania), where he sells clothes made in Gallia Belgica.[59] For Quintus Catusio Severianus it has been raised a tomb by his wife and son, sometime between AD 150-250, in Pola (InscrIt 10/1,163). Severianus was a Gallic merchant, as clearly specified in the inscription: *cives Gallus negotians vestiarius* origin confirmed by the Celtic root of his name. Probably Severianus and his family settled in northern Italy in order to organize the import and then the distribution of goods. It may be that other family members have lived still in Gallia to oversee production, but sources lack.

---

[58] Wierchowski 2001: 409; Broeckaert 2013: 93.
[59] Lavagne 1990: 345; Wierschowski 1995: 192; Wierschowski 2001: 267.

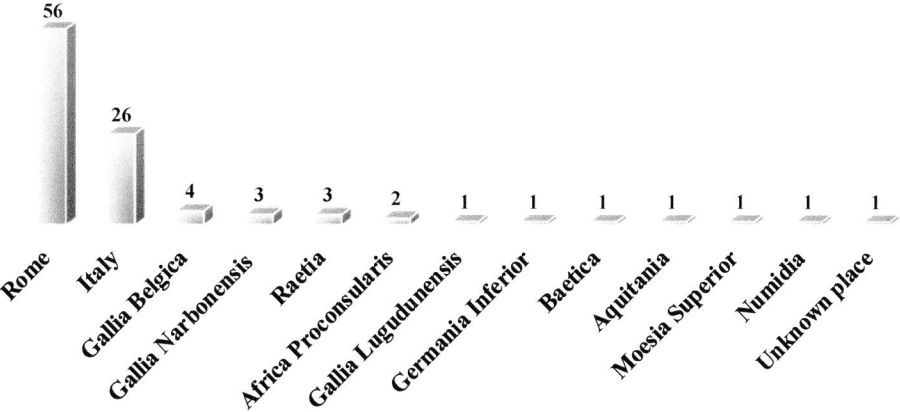

Figure 10. Geographical distribution of the vestiarii

Finally, Quintus Aurelius Herma (CIL XII 3202) includes in his occupational title a geographical clue – *Italicus*. He lived and died in Gallia Narbonensis, at Nemausus, but he had interests in the trade between this province and Italy.

As for the *collegia vestiariorum* the epigraphical evidence is rather poor. There is a *collegium* attested in Mauretania Tingitana (CIL VIII 21848) and another association *negotiatores vestariae et lintiariae* in Augusta Vindelicorum, in Raetia (CIL III 5800). There are also some clues for possible associations in Numidia – a *basilica vestiaria* (CIL VIII 20156) in Cuicul and a *forum vestiarum* in Timgad (AE 1988, 1583), and in Raetia – a *monumentum vestiariorum* in Aquileia (*Inscr.Aqu* 1, 687 and 1, 284; AE 1931, 96).

Conclusions

Roman textile production and trade were strictly specialized. Rarely there are traders who deal more different products. One *sagarius* and *centonarius* from Vienna, and one *negotiator artis cretariae* and also *negotiator paenularis* from Rottenburg, are exceptions. As the digits showed, textile dealers are better represented in Rome, Italy and the Gauls. The textile traders were organized in typical professional associations The geographical distributions of the epigraphic records of the *sagarii, vestiarii,* and *centonarii* are complementary to each other. The geographical coincidence and close association between these clothiers occur only in larger urban centers, such as Rome, Lugudunum, and Aquileia. It seems likely that the occupational spheres of these clothes-dealers overlapped to a great extent; they all catered mostly to the need for low- and medium-quality textiles. The term *centonarius* quite possibly served as a collective name for all the clothiers in many places. Dealers and tailors of luxurious/high quality textiles had their own distinctive name, that is, *vestiarii tenuiarii*. They were heavily concentrated in Rome, and were found in the Vicus Tuscus, the expensive shopping area of Imperial Rome. Some dealers are epigraphically attested in other places than their homeplaces: Romans in Vienna, Italians in Gaul or Gauls in Italy. Important markets and production centres could be identified. Patavium and Faventia were important centres in the textile industry, while the latter was also the starting point of a trans- Appennine road, the Via Faventina. Brixia was an important centre of the wool trade, where the raw material was also manufactured into goods. Milan, too, was an important textile market, as well as being a trading city with links through the Alps to Gaul and southwards to Apulia. Similar conditions prevailed at Verona, which was a wool-market in addition to the starting point for trade routes into the central Alps. *Sagarii*, probably due to the specificity of their merchandise are mentioned on the main route in Gaul. Textiles from southern Gaul and northern Italy not only migrated to Rome and central Italy, but also to the military border, where there was a high concentration of consumers. Hispania, on the other hand, seems to have played the role of a supplier of wool. According to Strabo, in his time, Baetica exported wool, mostly black, instead of cloth or clothing. Regarding Gallia Belgica, Strabo said that this region has provided abundant coarse clothing (*saga*) in Rome, and in most parts of Italy. Several gravestones spread in this province seem to indicate textile and retailing visible in 2nd and 3rd centuries AD.

Acknowledgements

This work was supported by the Project PN-III-P4-ID-PCE-2016-0271, financed through the Romanian Ministry of Research.

References

Agnati, U. 1999. *Per la storia romana della provincia di Pesaro e Urbino*. Roma, L'Erma di Bretschneider.
Amiri, B. 2012. Negotiator sericarius: sur la route de la promotion sociale. *L' Antiquité classique* 81: 125-143.
Ball Platner, S. 1929. *A Topographical Dictionary of Ancient Rome*. London, Oxford University Press.
Bonsangue, M. 2002. Aspects économiques et sociaux du monde du travail à Narbonne, d'après la documentation épigraphique (Ier siècle av. J.-C. - Ier siècle ap. J.-C.). *Cahiers du Centre Gustave Glotz* 13: 201-232.
Broekaert, W. 2013. *Navicularii et Negotiantes A prosopographical study of Roman merchants and shippers*. Rahden/Westf., Marie Leidorf.
Coarelli, F. 2012. *Palatium: il Palatino dalle origini all'impero*. Roma, Quasar.
Coarelli, F. 2014. *Rome and Environs: an Archaeological Guide*. Oakland, University of California Press.

Croom, A.T. 1988. *Roman Clothing and Fashion*. Charleston, Tempus Publishing Inc.

De Boissieu, A. 1846. Inscriptions antiques de Lyon: introduites d'après les monuments ou recueillies dans les auteurs. Lyon, L. Perrin.

Demarolle, J.-M. 2001. Un corpus en question, l'iconographie lapidaire des métiers en Gaule Belgique. In M. Polfer (ed.), *L'artisanat romain: évolutions, continuités et ruptures (Italie et provinces occidentales). Actes du 2e Colloque d'Erpeldange (26-28 octobre 2001), organisé par le Séminaire d'Études Anciennes du Centre Universitaire de Luxembourg et Instrumentum.*: 31-42. Montagnac, Monique Mergoil.

Deniaux, É. 1995. L'artisanat du textile en Gaule: remarques sur quelques inscriptions, *Cahiers du Centre Gustave Glotz* 6(1): 195-206.

Di Stefano Manzella, I. 1994. Accensi velati consulibus apparentes ad sacra: Proposta per la soluzione di un problema dibattuto. *Zeitschrift für Papyrologie und Epigraphik* 101: 261–279

Drinkwater, J. F. 2001. The Gallo-Roman woolen industry and the great debate. The Igel column revisited. In D. J. Mattingly and J. Salmon (eds.), *Economies beyond agriculture in the classical world*: 297-308. London and New York, Routledge.

Flohr 2014. Towards an Economic History of Textile Manufacturing and Trade in the Roman World. In K. Dross-Krüpe (ed.) *Textile trade and distribution in antiquity*: 1-16. Wiesbaden, Harassowitz.

Fryan, J.M. 1984. *Sheep-Rearing and the Wool Trade in Italy during the Roman Period*. Liverpool, Francis Cairns.

Gordon, A.E. 1983. *Illustrated Introduction to Latin Epigraphy*. Oakland, University of California Press.

Gregori, G.L. 1994. Purpurarii. In *Epigrafia della produzione e della distribuzione. Actes de la VIIe Rencontre franco-italienne sur l'épigraphie du monde romain (Rome, 5-6 juin 1992)*: 739-743. Rome, École Française de Rome (*Publications de l'École française de Rome*, 193).

Groen-Vallinga, M. 2013. Female Participation in the Roman Urban Labour Market. In E Hemelrijk and G. Wolf, (eds), *Women in the Roman City of the Latin West*: 295– 312. Leiden and Boston, Brill (Mnemosyne Supplement, 360).

Hackworth Petersen, L. 2011 *The freedman in Roman Art and Art History*. Cambridge, Cambridge University Press.

Hawkins, C. 2016. *Roman Artisans and the Urban Economy*. Cambridge, Cambridge University Press.

Holleran, C. 2013. Women and Retail in Roman Italy. In E Hemelrijk and G. Wolf, (eds), *Women in the Roman City of the Latin West*: 313– 330. Leiden and Boston, Brill (Mnemosyne Supplement, 360).

Joshel S.R. 1992. *Work, Identity and Legal Status at Rome. A Study of the Occupational Inscriptions*. Norman and London, University of Oklahoma Press.

Larsson Lovén, L. 2001. Images of textile manufacture in funerary iconography. In M. Polfer (ed.), *L'artisanat romain: évolutions, continuités et ruptures (Italie et provinces occidentales). Actes du 2e Colloque d'Erpeldange (26-28 octobre 2001), organisé par le Séminaire d'Études Anciennes du Centre Universitaire de Luxembourg et Instrumentum.*: 43-53. Montagnac, Monique Mergoil.

Larsson Lovén, L. 2016. Women, Trade, and Production in Urban Centres of Roman Italy. In A. Wilson and M. Flohr (eds.), *Urban Craftsmen and Traders in the Roman World*: 200-221. Oxford, Oxford University Press.

Lassère J.-M. 2006. La mobilité de la population. Migrations individuelles et collectives dans les provinces occidentales du monde romain. *L'Africa romana* 16(1): 57-92.

Lázaro Guillamón, M.d.C. 2003. Mujer, comercio y empresa en algunas fuentes jurídicas, literarias y epigráficas. *Revue internationale des droits de l'antiquité* 50: 155-194.

Liu, J. 2009. Collegia Centonariorum: *The Guilds of Textile Dealers in the Roman West*. Leiden and Boston, Brill.

Liu, J. 2013. Trade, Traders and Guilds (?) in Textiles: the Case of Southern Gaul and Northern Italy (1st–3rd Centuries AD). In M. Gleba and J. Pasztokai-Szeöke (eds.), *Making Textiles in pre-Roman and Roman Times: People, Places, Identities*: 126-141. Oxford, Oxbow.

Mouritsen, H. 2013. Slavery and manumission in the Roman elite: a study of the columbaria of the Volusii Saturnini and the Statilii Tauri. In M. George (ed.), *Roman Slavery and Roman Material Culture*: 43-68. Toronto, Toronto University Press.

Nicolas, M. 1998. Les Alfidii dans le monde romain (fin IIe siècle avant J.-C. - début IIIe siècle après J.-C.): étude d'un nom. *Annales de Bretagne et des pays de l'Ouest* 105(1): 7-33

Orlandi, S. 1994. Vestiarii (2). In *Epigrafia della produzione e della distribuzione. Actes de la VIe Rencontre franco-italienne sur l'épigraphie du monde romain (Rome, 5-6 juin 1992)*: 763-766. Rome, Collection de l'École française de Rome.

Pilhofer, S. 2005. *Romanisierung in Kilikien? Das Zeugnis der Inschriften*. München, Herbert Utz.

Richardson, L. Jr. 1992. *A New Topographical Dictionary of Ancient Rome*. Baltimore, The Johns Hopkins University Press.

Ruffing, K. 2007. Textilien als Wirtschaftsgut in der römischen Keiserzeit. In S. Gunther, K. Ruffing, and O. Stoll (eds.), *Pragmata: Beitrage Zur Wirtschaftsgeschichte Der Antike Im Gedenken an Harald Winkel*: 41-53. Wiesbaden, Harrasowitz (Phillipica).

Ruffing, K. 2016. Driving Forces for Specialization: Market, Location Factors, Productivity Improvements. In A. Wilson and M. Flohr (eds.), *Urban Craftsmen and Traders in the Roman World*: 115-130. Oxford, Oxford University Press.

Tran, N. 2007. La mention épigraphique des métiers artisanaux et commerciaux en Italie centro-méridionale. In J. Andreau and V. Chankowski (eds.) *Vocabulaire et expressions de l'économie dans le monde antique*: 119-141. Bordeaux, Ausonius.

Valchera, V. 2012. *Pisaurum*. Le associazioni professionali di età romana. *Studi pesaresi Rivista della Società pesarese di studi storici* 1: 7-20.

Van Nijf, F and Meijner, O. 1992: *Trade, Transport and Society in the Ancient World: a sourcebok*. London, Routledge.

Verboven, K. 2007. Good for business. The Roman army and the emergence of a 'business class' in the north-western provinces of the Roman empire. In L. de Blois and E. Lo Cascio (eds.), *The Impact of the Roman Army (200 BC-AD 476): Economic, Social, Political, Religious, and Cultural Aspects : Proceedings of the Sixth Workshop of the International Network Impact of Empire (Roman Empire, 200 B.C.-A.D. 476), Capri, March 29-April 2, 2005*: 295-314. Leiden and Boston, Brill.

Vicari, F. 2001. *Produzione e commercio dei tessuti nell'Occidente romano*. Oxford, Archaeopress (British Archaeological Reports – International. Series, 916)

Young, A. 2000. Representations of cloth vendors and the cloth trade on funerary reliefs in Roman Gaul and Italy. In D. Cardon and M. Feugère (eds.), *Archéologie des textiles. Des origines au Ve siècle. Actes du colloque de Lattes, octobre 1999*: 215-233. Montagnac, Monique Mergoil.

Wierschowski, L. 1995. *Die regionale Mobilität in Gallien nach den Inschriften des 1. bis 3. Jahrhunderts n. Chr: quantitative Studien zur Sozial- und Wirtschaftsgeschichte der westlichen Provinzen des Römischen Reiches*. Stuttgart, Franz Steiner.

Wierschowski, L. 2001. *Fremde in Gallien- 'Gallier' in der Fremde: die epigraphisch bezeugte Mobilität in, von und nach Gallien vom 1. bis 3. jh. n. Chr.* Stuttgart, Franz Steiner.

Wild, J.P. 1970. *Textile Manufacture in the Northern Roman Provinces*. Cambridge, Cambridge University Press.

Wild, J.P. 2000. Textile Production and Trade in Roman Literature and Written Sources. In D. Cardon and M. Feugère (eds.), *Archéologie des textiles. Des origines au Ve siècle. Actes du colloque de Lattes, octobre 1999*: 209-214. Montagnac, Monique Mergoil.

Zaccaria, C. 2009. *Novità* sulla produzione lanaria ad Aquileia, *Epigraphica* 27:277-29.

The professions of private slaves and freedmen in Moesia Inferior

The epigraphic evidence

Lucrețiu Mihăilescu-Bîrliba[1]

Introduction

The epigraphic evidence of private slaves is generally scarce, a fact which can be explained by their limited possibilities of erecting inscriptions. Their mention is mainly related to their masters; otherwise, they are trusted people and they are charged with various duties related to household economy. The epigraphic information on freedmen is richer, because their affluence is sometimes remarkable; in most cases however, they are mentioned along with their patrons or by their patrons.

Moesia Inferior is no exception to the rule. Nonetheless, we have tried to determine whether the texts attest professions for the slaves and the freedmen and whether in these provinces there were also professions specific for these social categories.

The epigraphic record

The evidence of inscriptions is not particularly rich concerning the professions of slaves and freedmen in Moesia Inferior; nonetheless, we have identified 12 characters with a profession, within 15 inscriptions (4 texts feature the same person,[2] while in one text the profession is indirectly identifiable). These features have been pointed out based either on direct evidence (the attestation of the *villa*, of the estate or of the boundary stones that delimited a private rural property) or on indirect mentions (the attestation of administrative managers of a *villa* – *vilici* or *actores* – or of discovery places in relation with the characters mentioned by the texts). I must also highlight that the number of owners was definitely larger, as shown by the numerous veterans attested at Tomis.[3]

---

[1] 'Alexandru Ioan Cuza' University Iași; blucretiu@yahoo.com. This paper was elaborated within the PN-III-P4-ID-PCE-2016-0271. I express my gratitude to the Romanian National Research Council (CNCS) for its financial support.
[2] ISM I 359-360; ISM I 374/377.
[3] Bărbulescu and Buzoianu 2013: 175.

However, I preferred to discuss only those examples that prove – directly or indirectly – beyond doubt the existence of *villae*. Hence, we can complete the catalogue of *villae* in Moesia Inferior (carefully elaborated by A. Bâltâc).[4]

On one hand, the Greek cities on the West-Pontic coast are rather well represented concerning the attestations of *villae*. On the territory of Istros, a votive inscription – erected for the health of L. Valerius Victorinus and his wife and sons by the *actor* L. Valerius Nilus, their freedman – provides indirect proof of the existence of a *villa* at Ulmetum.[5] I have included Ulmetum in the territory of Istros, even though there are still debates whether *vicus Ulmetum* actually belongs to the territory of Capidava. I will not detail the discussion; however, I tend to agree that village belonged to the territory of Istros, for several reasons (organization of the territory of Istros similar to *vicus Quintionis*, the possible existence of another *vicus* at Capidava, etc).[6]

Concerning the territory of Tomis, the texts attesting the professions of private slaves were written in Greek. Castresios – πραγματευτής of the *primipilaris* Iulius Fronto – erects a funerary monument for himself and his wife Euphrosyna, who lived 25 years.[7] His position – the Greek equivalent of the Latin *actor* – leads me to the assumption that he was a slave (with a wife of similar status), not a freedman, as posited by A. Bâltâc, M. Bărbulescu and L. Buzoianu.[8] The fact that he writes the text in Greek is due to his Greek-speaking origin: he may come from one of the Greek cities on the West-Pontic coast. Nonetheless, the owner is certainly Latin speaking; his status of former *primipilus* stands to show a wealth that allowed him to own property.

I would also highlight the series of four vows for Mithra, fulfilled by Flavius Horimos, steward (οἰκονόμος) and freedman of a certain Flavius Macedo, in a cave situated not far from Târguşor (Constanţa County).[9] I am tempted to date the inscription in the first half of the third century, not between the third and the fourth centuries, as D. M. Pippidi believes.[10] Beyond the vows *per se*, the position of Horimos makes me think of a rural estate belonging to Flavius Macedo.

The Roman cities situated along the Danube and within the province have other attestations concerning the professions of slaves and of private freedmen.

---

[4] Bâltâc 2011: 231-268.
[5] ISM V 72; Bâltâc 2011: 241.
[6] See more recently Mihăilescu-Bîrliba 2015a: 151, including the entire discussion.
[7] ISM II 289; Bâltâc 2011: 264-265; Bărbulescu and Buzoianu 2013:185.
[8] Bâltâc 2011, table I. 13; Bărbulescu and Buzoianu 2013: 185.
[9] ISM I 374-377; Bărbulescu and Buzoianu 2013: 188.
[10] ISM I 374-377, *sub numero*; see also Pippidi 1969: 284-310.

Tropaeum Traiani is the origin of another altar dedicated to Heros the invincible by Iaehetav, the *vilicus* of senator L. Aelius Marcianus.[11] Thus, the *villa* belongs to a member of the Roman Senate: does he come from this province or did he have administrative tasks in Moesia Inferior? For the moment, it is impossible to answer to this question. His steward is a slave and, considering his name, has a Semitic origin.

At Abrittus, a Greek inscription attests Christos, the πραγματευτής of M. Antonius Theodoros.[12] The owner and his steward-slave were both Greek-speaking; however, the master had the right of citizenship. Archaeological researches have highlighted a pre-Roman establishment where Greeks and natives cohabitated;[13] however, the presence of Roman troops[14] have contributed decisively to the development of a *civitas* inhabited by the Latin-speaking population.

On the territory of Nicopolis ad Istrum (modern-day village of Kramolin), a text mentions Herculanus, *actor* of Flavius Gemellus.[15] Herculanus was certainly the slave of Gemellus; unfortunately, there is no other information available concerning the master. We know he is a Roman citizen and that he is quite wealthy, with an estate in the countryside. Also at Nicopolis ad Istrum, T. Iulius Soterichus, freedman of T. Iulius Saturninus, has the function of deputy customs taxes cashier of Illyricum (*dispensatoris publicii portorii vikarius*).[16] I will speak below about T. Iulius Saturninus and his slaves.

The territory of Oescus provides another text, which attests Narcissus, slave and *actor* of M. Titius Maximus, *duumviral* and *quinquennalis* of the colony, *flamen perpetuus* and *prafectus saltus*.[17] The owner is part of the municipal elite and he definitely had a considerable fortune. His family had acquired the right of citizenship during the reign of Trajan, the founder of the colony; Titius Maximus is part of the Papiria tribe, of Trajan's tribe. The same person erects an altar for Mithra.[18] There are several Titii attested in the inscriptions of Moesia Inferior: C. Titius Similis, probably procurator during the Severi, mentioned at Novae,[19] a certain Titius at Tomis, who died at 45,[20] Titius Crispus, *corniculum* of governor

---

[11] ISM IV 34, Bâltâc 2011: 267.
[12] IGB V 527; Bâltâc 2011: 235.
[13] Ivanov 1980: 10.
[14] Matei-Popescu 2010: 220.
[15] ILB 403; Bâltâc 2011: 260.
[16] CIL III 14427; ILB 361.
[17] ILB 16; Bâltâc 2011: 262.
[18] CIL III 6127 (=7426); ILB 29.
[19] IGLN 63.
[20] ISM II 349.

Marcius Turbo, also at Tomis (around 155),[21] Titius Marcianus at Sacidava.[22] It is difficult to establish a parenting relationship between all of these characters.

At Dimum, another text was discovered attesting a slave, who subsequently became a freedman of a *conductor* of customs. It concerns Quintillus, *servus* and *libertus* of T. Iulius Saturninus, who has the position of *vilicus* related to customs.[23] His function is different from the one of a *vilicus* on a rural estate. The first is an agent charged with tax collection and the technical management of an office.[24] T. Iulius Saturninus is known from several texts as a *conductor* of Illyricum responsible for the Moesias, the Dacias and Thrace. He conducted his activities during the reign of Antoninus. The sources of other provinces attest the slaves of Saturninus who had positions in customs administration, such as Maturus, Mercator (stewards) or Amandus, controller.[25] In Moesia Inferior, except for T. Iulius Soterichus, there is another freedman of Saturninus, Tertullus, whose position is no longer visible in the text (which is actually fragmentary).[26]

In the territory of the *civitas Dianensium*, a text mentions the *vilicus* Primus, whose wife Aurelia Victorina erects an altar for Apollo and for Diana.[27] Primus seems to have been a slave; his relation with a female citizen is not surprising, because several such cases have been pointed out,[28] mostly considering this was a quite wealthy steward. It is possible for Aurelia Victorina to have been a freedwoman or a former *peregrina*; considering his name, I would tend to date the text towards the end of the second century or the first quarter of the third.

Another text comes from Montana. An inscription mentions Sergilianus, a *vilicus* who dedicated an altar for Diana Lucifera.[29] We do not know who the owner of the *villa* is. Nonetheless, the vows for Diana are frequent in the rural environment of Moesia Inferior[30] and mostly at Montana and in the surroundings.[31]

I saved for the end an inscription from Troesmis, erected by the Roman *eques* Terentius Iunior, *tribunus militum* of *legio V Macedonica*, for his deceased slave

---

[21] ISM II 56.
[22] ISM IV 178.
[23] CIL III 12363.
[24] Carlsen 1995: 43-55; Mihăilescu-Bîrliba 2006: 39.
[25] CIL III 4720.
[26] ILB 73 (Novae).
[27] ILB 233; Bâltâc 2011: 242.
[28] CIL VI 1930; 2365, 2374, 5062, 9110; AE 1912, 191; 1975, 64; 1988, 153, etc.
[29] AE 1987 874; Bâltâc 2011: 258-259.
[30] CIL III 12372, 12386, 13722; ILB 193, 197, 207; ISM V, 246-247, etc.
[31] CIL III 7445, 7447, 12370-12371; AE 1985, 747; 1987, 868, 875, 882, etc.

Euticus. The iconographic part of the stone depicts a patera-shaped mirror framed by two strigils. I will not comment again concerning the text, as I have done it before.[32] I just have to notice that Terentius Iunior belongs to the Terentii Iuniores branch of *gens Terentia*, a branch that has given consuls. The fact that the master has put up an epitaph for his slave shows that they had a close relationship, all the more as Euticus is a *verna*. One could even consider that the slave may have been the biological son of the tribune, but there are certain elements that compel me to advance another hypothesis. First, the slave's age is not mentioned in the text, which means that there is no way of knowing whether Terentius Iunior was the father of Euticus. Moreover, the strigils featured on the lower side of the tomb suggest that the slave had duties related mostly to the personal hygiene of his master. The question that arises – considering that Euticus, even as *verna*, accompanied his master to Moesia Inferior and that his *dominus* put up an epitaph in his memory – is whether this relationship between master and slave went beyond a simple emotional relationship.[33]

The language of inscriptions and the dedicators

According to the information provided by the epigraphic sources, 15 texts are available in this respect; six texts are written in Greek, the others in Latin; five inscriptions come from the territory of Tomis. Out of the five inscriptions, four texts make up the series of vows of Flavius Horimos for Mithra.[34] However, who are the dedicators in the Greek inscriptions? I have already presented Flavius Horimos, freedman and steward of Flavius Macedo. He was definitely Greek speaking, and this is why he dedicated his vows in Greek. Another dedicator is Castresios, πργματευτής (*actor*) of the *primipilaris* Iulius Fronto.[35] Finally, the sixth Greek text comes from the territory of Abrittus, where Latin speakers cohabitated with Greek speakers and natives; however, I have to underline that it concerns a vow of Christos, πραγματευτής of a Roman citizen, M. Antonius Theodorus.[36] Both master and slave were Greek speakers, but the slave was the one who put up the inscription. In other words, the persons who write the inscriptions are the slaves and the freedmen of owners and they write it using their languages of origin.

---

[32] Mihailescu-Bîrliba 2015b, 109-112.
[33] The sexual (including homosexual) relationships between the masters and their slaves have represented the subject of numerous studies (e.g., Cantarella 2002: 103–105; Parker 2007: 281; Williams 2010: 36–38).
[34] ISM I 374-378.
[35] ISM II 289.
[36] IGB V 5271.

The other texts are written in Latin. Who are the characters who erect the monuments? Valerius Victorinus is a Roman citizen; his wife has a Greek surname (Nicandra); however, his ancestors have acquired citizenship during the reign of Trajan; as for his sons, two have Latin surnames (Victorinus and Turbo) and another one has a Greek surname, Soter.[37] Greek surnames can be related to the divinity to which the inscription is dedicated and whose name was not preserved. The estate of Victorinus is seemingly well organized; one of his *actores*, the freedman Valerius Nilus was the dedicator of the text. Whereas his surname may suggest an Egyptian origin, he had served Victorinus for a long time and he definitely spoke Latin.

At Tropaeum Traiani, the master is a Roman senator, P. Aelius Marcianus, who must have been a great owner.[38] His *actor* slave writes the inscription in Latin, though his name suggests a Semitic origin.

In the territory of Nicopolis ad Istrum, a city where Greek was used intensely, I mention the owner Flavius Gemellus whose *actor* slave Herculanus also seems Latin speaking.[39] There is no mention on the origin of Flavius Gemellus, however it is certain that he was a citizen with estates in this region.

Another *actor*, Narcissus, is present on the territory of Oescus: he is the slave of M. Titius Maximus, a magistrate of the colony, *flamen perpetuus* and *praefectus saltus*.[40] Consequently, this person – considering the duties he fulfilled – must have possessed an important wealth and he definitely had rural estates. Whereas the slave has a Greek name, he writes the text in Latin, (the language of his master and the most common language in the city and within the territory of Oescus). Latin is also the language used for writing the texts of *civitas Dianensium* (a vow dedicated by the wife of a *vilicus*)[41] and on the Montana territory.[42] Concerning the last region, one of the dedicators is a veteran who married a native *peregrina* who acquired her citizenship post AD 212, and the other is a slave, steward of an estate. I have already posited that the veteran may have also been a native who completed his service and then returned home (the *vicus* has a Thracian name).

Finally, the epitaph of Euticus is erected by his master, a Roman *eques*, definitely Latin speaking. Whereas the slave has a Greek name (the most common name among *servi*), he was also Latin speaking, considering his status of *verna*.

---

[37] ISM V 72.
[38] ISM IV 34.
[39] ILB 403.
[40] ILB 16; Bâltâc 2011: 262.
[41] ILB 233; Bâltâc 2011: 242.
[42] AE 1969-1970, 568; Bâltâc 2011: 258; AE 1987, 874; Bâltâc 2011: 258-259.

Table I. The masters and the patrons, their families and the staff of servile origin

Name	Legal and/or social status	City or territory	Source(s)
Valerius Victorinus	citizen, patron	Ulmetum (Istros)	ISM V, 72
Ulpia Nicandra	female citizen, wife of Valerius Victorinus	Ulmetum (Istros)	ISM V, 72
Valerius Nilus	freedman of Val. Victorinus, actor	Ulmetum (Istros)	ISM V, 72
Iulius Fronto	primipilaris, master	Tomi	ISM II, 289
Castresios	slave of the person stated above, πραγματευτής (actor)	Tomi	ISM II, 289
Flavius Macedo	citizen, patron	Tomi	ISM II, 374-377
Flavius Horimos	freedman of the person stated above, οœκονόμοß (vilicus)	Tomi	ISM II, 374-377
Terentius Iunior	equestrian military tribune, master	Troesmis	Mihailescu-Bîrliba 2015, 121-124
Euticus	verna of the person stated above, charged probably with personal hygiene	Troesmis	Mihailescu-Bîrliba 2015, 121-124
P. Aelius Marcianus	senator, master	Tropaeum Traiani	ISM IV, 34
Iaehetav	slave of the person stated above, vilicus	Tropaeum Traiani	ISM IV, 34
M. Antonius Theodoros	citizen, master	Abrittus	IGB, 527
Christos	slave of the person stated above, πραγματευτής	Abrittus	IGB, 527
Flavius Gemellus	citizen, master	Nicopolis ad Istrum	ILB 403
Herculanus	slave of the person stated above, actor	Nicopolis ad Istrum	ILB 403
T. Iulius Saturninus	conductor P. P. I., master	Nicopolis ad Istrum, Dimum	ILB 361, CIL III 12363
T. Iulius Soterichus	slave of the person stated above, dispensatoris publicii portorii vikarius	Nicopolis ad Istrum	ILB 361
M. Titius Maximus	local prominent citizen, master	Oescus	ILB 16
Narcissus	slave of the person stated above, actor	Oescus	ILB 16
Quintillus	slave, then freedman of T. Iulius Saturninus (see supra), vilicus	Dimum	CIL 12363
Primus	slave, vilicus	civitas Dianensium	ILB 233
Aurelia Victorina	female citizen, wife of Primus	civitas Dianensium	ILB 233
Sergilianus	slave, vilicus	Montana	Montana II, 32

The texts mention 7 masters, 2 patrons, 10 slaves and 2 freedmen (maybe 3, considering that Aurelia Victorina may have been a freedwoman herself). Four masters are part of society elite: a senator (P. Aelius Marcianus), two knights (Terentius Iunior and T. Iulius Saturninus) and a local prominent citizen (M. Titius Maximus). The other masters and patrons are Roman citizens or, in the case of Iulius Fronto, *primipilaris*. Thus, the status of masters and patrons explains the presence of their slaves and freedmen in the texts of inscriptions. On the other hand, the status – even of slaves and freedmen – that proves great wealth can explain this presence in the texts. Valerius Nilus, Castresios, Christos, Herculanus and Narcissus are *actores*, while Flavius Horimos, Iaehetav, Primus and Sergilianus are *vilici*, all for rural estates. Quintillus and T. Iulius Soterichus work in customs administration, as *vilicus* and *vikarius* of *portorium* cashier. It is remarkable that, except for customs clerks, all professions of slaves and freedmen in Moesia Inferior are related to agricultural exploitation. This confirms the important role of servile personnel in rural provincial economy: Moesia Inferior is no exception. Certainly, slaves and the freedmen must have had other professions; however, the only ones mentioned in the inscriptions were those in charge of rural customs administration. This also stands to prove that there were important estates, which required numerous personnel. Moreover, other texts attest the existence of *villae* in the province. The organization of *villae* in Moesia Inferior confirms, at least from a certain standpoint, the typically Roman organization of villages, even in the territories of Greek-speaking cities.

Conclusions

Whereas they may not be numerous, the texts of Moesia Inferior attesting the professions of slaves and of freedmen are almost exclusively related to the agricultural field. This explains the wealth of these slaves and freedmen, which enabled them to put up inscriptions. Furthermore, their masters and patrons were great rural landowners. There are also two customs clerks, slaves and freedmen of the farmer T. Iulius Saturninus. The case of Euticus – *verna* of the knight Terentius Iunior – is special: the iconography of the inscription and the fact that the master himself erects the epitaph for his *servus* indicates not only the profession of the slave related to personal hygiene, but also a close relationship with his *dominus*.

References

Bâltâc, A. 2011. *Lumea rurală în provinciile Moesia Inferior și Thracia (sec. I-III p. Chr.)*. Bucharest, Renaissance.

Bărbulescu, M. and Buzoianu, L. 2013. Teritoriul Tomisului în epoca romană timpurie în lumina documentelor epigrafice. I. In F. Panait Bîrzescu, I. Bîrzescu, F. Matei-Popescu, A. Robu (eds)., *Poleis în Marea neagră. Relații interpontice și producții locale*: 174-202. Bucharest, Humanitas.

Cantarella, E. 2002. *Bisexuality in the Ancient World*[2], translation C. Ó Cuilleanáin. Yale, Yale University Press.

Carlsen, J. 1995. *Vilici and Roman estate management until 284 AD*. Rome, L'Erma di Bretschneider.

Ivanov, T. 1980. *Abritus – a Roman castle and early byzantine town in Moesia Inferior* (in Bulgarian with English summary). Sofia, BAN.

Matei-Popescu, F. 2010. *The Roman army in Moesia Inferior*. Bucharest, Conphys.

Mihailescu-Bîrliba, L. 2006. *Les affranchis dans les privinces romaines de l'Illyricum*. Wiesbaden, Harrassowitz.

Mihailescu-Bîrliba, L. 2015a. Colonisation in the Vicus Ulmetum during Early Roman Empire. In L. Mihailescu-Bîrliba (ed.), *Colonisation and Romanization in Moesia inferior. Premises of a contrastive approach*: 143-155. Kaiserslautern-Mehlingen, Parthenon.

Mihailescu-Bîrliba 2015b. An eques Romanus and his slave in a new funerary inscription from Troesmis. In R. Kogălniceanu, M. Gligor, R.-G. Curcă, S. Stratton (eds.), *Homines Funera Astra 2. Life Beyond Death in Ancient Times (Romanian Case Studies)*: 109-112. Oxford, Archaeopress.

Parker, H. 2007. Free Women and Male Slaves, or Mandingo Meets the Roman Empire. In A. Serghidou (ed.), *Fear of Slaves, Fear of Enslavement in the Ancient Mediterranean. Peur de l'esclave - Peur de l'esclavage en Méditerranée ancienne (Discours, représentations, pratiques). Actes du XXIXe Colloque du Groupe International de Recherche sur l'Esclavage dans l'Antiquité (GIREA). Rethymnon 4-7 November 2004*: 281-298. Besançon, Presses universitaires de Franche-Comté.

Pippidi, D. M. 1969. *Studii de istorie a religiilor antice. Texte și interpretări*. Bucharest, Editura Științifică.

Williams, C. A. 2010. *Roman Homosexuality*[2]. Oxford, Oxford University Press.

Prosopography of the leading families of Larinum in the Roman period

Elizabeth C. Robinson

Introduction

The ancient town of Larinum was located on the eastern edge of Samnium between the Samnites to the west, the Frentani to the north, and the Apulians to the south (Figure 1). Habitation at the site began in the Prehistoric period, and by the 3rd century BC Larinum had become an important Italic center. The first Roman involvement in this region occurred in the 3rd century BC, yet there was no permanent Roman presence installed here at that time. Things changed dramatically, however, during the Social War and shortly afterward, when all of Italy came under Roman domination and was granted Roman citizenship. Larinum became a Roman *municipium*, and it continued to remain a place of strategic significance until the 3rd century AD. The later history of building activity near this site led to a significant portion of the ancient inscriptions of Larinum being built into the structures of the historic center in the Medieval period. Their preservation, although they have been removed from their original archaeological contexts, gives Larinum one of the richest epigraphic records in this part of Italy.

In addition to a recently published corpus of almost 300 inscriptions, there is a wealth of historical information about the town. References to Larinum can be found in at least ten different ancient authors including Cicero, Livy, Pliny the Elder and Appian. The longest and most detailed account comes from Cicero's *pro Cluentio* oration, delivered in 66 BC in Rome in defense of Aulus Cluentius Habitus, a citizen of Larinum. Despite all this evidence, however, the history of Larinum that has previously been published is one based largely on an uncritical reading of the literary sources and on the use of only select pieces of archaeological evidence to corroborate those sources. The traditional narrative given for Roman expansion in this region has been one of collapse and conquest. Earlier studies saw the disappearance of local families after the Social War, followed by their replacement by Roman citizens and colonists who moved into the area from the 1st century BC onward. Recent archaeological work in this area of Italy, including this study, is helping to overturn these previous narratives.

Figure 1. Map showing the location of the town of Larinum. Copyright 2016 Ancient World Mapping Center (http://awmc.unc.edu/wordpress/), modified by author. Used by permission.

The current work to which this study belongs is the first to take into consideration the whole epigraphic corpus of Larinum. Through the study of the survival and prominence of local names in the epigraphic record, evidence emerges that indicates the various ways that the citizens of the town successfully navigated the transition from independence to Roman citizenship. In particular, the Cluentii, the Didii, the Papii, and the Vibii, families that all have pre-Roman roots in this area, each provided politicians in the Augustan period who were active in Rome. The Paquii family likewise rose to prominence under Augustus and was active both in Larinum and in Rome. A second group of families from Larinum represented by the Raii, the Coelii and the Gabbii, seems to have risen to political prominence only on a local level, and then mostly in the second half of the 1st century AD and slightly later. The majority of these eight family names continue to appear in the epigraphic record of Larinum until at least the middle of the 2nd century AD, and many appear at the end of the 2nd century AD, if not later. This suggests the significant stability of these local aristocratic families in the Imperial period, and implies that the population of Larinum remained largely stationary from before the Social War until well into the Imperial period. It also suggests that although the families of the aristocracy changed over time, the political, and presumably economic power at the site continued to remain in the hands of locals, rather than shifting to outside groups arriving from Rome or elsewhere.

This paper investigates the epigraphic evidence related to these eight different families from the town of Larinum in the period from the 1st century BC to the 3rd century AD.[1] It is part of a larger study that investigates the local-level history of Larinum from the ground up, tracing the lived experiences of people who survived the Roman conquest of Italy.[2] The focus of the current paper is the effects that the integration of Larinum into the Roman state had on the leading citizens of the town in the period from approximately 89 BC to AD 250, as displayed in the epigraphic record. Contrary to previously published findings, this paper will argue for the survival of these local families in Larinum and its surrounding area, and the successful integration of Larinum into the Roman state, led in part by the local elites of the town who were interested in participating in politics and state-sponsored cults at both the local and statewide level. Some highlights of the prosopographical analyses of these families will be used to illustrate these points. Particular attention will be paid to inscriptions that show the political successes of these eight families.

The Cluentii

Perhaps the most famous family from Larinum is the Cluentius family. Aulus Cluentius Habitus made a name for himself in Larinum and Rome through his connections to Cicero, and his descendants went on to hold offices in Larinum and maintain a presence there for centuries. The Cluentius family appears in at least three inscriptions from Larinum and one from Britain.

One inscription that points to the political success of the Cluentius family most likely belonged to a funerary monument, but is currently lost.[3] The inscription reads: *C(aio) Cluentio C(aii) f(ilio) Clu(stumina tribu) Attico | aed(ili) ((quattuor)) vir(o) i(ure) d(icundo) q(uaestori) ((iterum)) | Cluentia Asiatice Mater filio pio fecit et | C(aio) Cluentio C(aii) L(iberto) Evangelo Aug(ustali) viro suo | de suo*. The stone was dedicated by Cluentia Asiatice to both her son and her husband. It dates no later than the 1st century AD, and shows that in this period the freedmen of the gens furnished an important office-holder in the town of Larinum. Although the son of a freedman, Gaius Cluentius Atticus was an aedile, a *quattuorvir iure dicundo*, and a *quaestor* multiple times. All of these offices point to a successful local political career, and also indicate the presence of the gentilician at the site in the 1st century AD, being borne by the son of a freedman. The inscription also highlights the swift upward mobility of Gaius Cluentius Atticus. Although

---

[1] In many ways this paper builds on the analyses presented in Robinson 2013.
[2] Broader conclusions pertaining to this study are being revised for submission for a manuscript currently under contract with Oxford University Press, entitled *Urban Transformation in Ancient Molise: The integration of Larinum into the Roman state*.
[3] AE 1997, 335; Stelluti 1997, number 80.

his father was not eligible for a magistracy, Atticus became an important local office holder. It is likely that the Cluentius family name helped in this process. His mother must have been wealthy, since she paid for the monument de suo.

But perhaps the most interesting inscription pertaining to this family was found in situ inside a mithraeum in Britain at the site of Carrawburgh; it dates to between AD 198 and 211 (Figure 2).[4] It is an altar dedicated to Mithras by Aulus Cluentius Habitus, a prefect of the First Batavian cohort, who names his hometown as the Colonia Septimia Aurelia Larinum. Aulus Cluentius Habitus seems to have been a member of the same family as that of Cicero's defendant.[5] This is clear and remarkable gentilician continuity in the town – lasting over three centuries – and is comparable to that of the Didii, the Papii, and the Vibii, discussed below. The Cluentius in the Carrawburgh inscription is a prefect, the first rank in an equestrian military career.[6] This indicates his social standing as an *eques*, exactly like his ancestor who was defended by Cicero.[7] The family was therefore still relatively wealthy and had maintained its social status over time. The inscriptions associated

Figure 2. Photograph of the inscription on the mithraic altar from Carrawburgh. The inscription reads: D(eo) In(victo) M(ithrae) s(acrum) | Aul(us) Cluen\<t\>ius | Habitus pra(e)f(ectus) | coh(or)t(is) | Batavorum | domu\<s\> V⁻o⁻lti | n\<i\>a colon(ia) | Sept(imia) Aur(elia) L(arino) | v(otum) s(olvit) l(ibens) m(erito). Photograph provided by the Great North Museum: Hancock and the Society of Antiquaries of Newcastle upon Tyne. Used by permission

---

[4] AE 1951, 125b; Collingwood and Wright 1965 vol. 1, number 1545; Stelluti 1997, number 7A. For its location see Birley 1951: 45.
[5] Buonocore 1997: 49-50; Silvestrini 1996: 270.
[6] Keppie 1984: 177, 184.
[7] Birley 1951: 51; Cic. *Clu*. 156.

with the town of Larinum thus show that the *gens Cluentia* continued to fill important posts in the town and elsewhere within the Roman Empire, while maintaining its lineage and its social status in Larinum, too.[8]

The Didii and the Paquii

Another family that shows gentilician continuity within and around the area of Larinum is that of the Didii, who appear in inscriptions spanning three centuries. The earliest inscription pertaining to this family dates to the second half of the 1st century BC, while the latest inscription dates to the second half of the 2nd century AD. Inscriptions naming this gens appear at both Larinum and Histonium, providing evidence of the links between these two cities and their aristocratic families, including ties of marriage.[9]

One inscription comes from a first-century BC round funerary monument, comparable in size and shape to the mausoleum of Caecilia Metella in Rome and the mausoleum of Gaius Ennius Marsus at Saepinum (Figure 3).[10] It tells us that two daughters made the tomb for their mother, Didia Decuma, the daughter of Barbus. The use of this elegant and popular style of round funerary monument was a deliberate choice on the part of the daughters to portray their family's status. It could be construed as an act of self-representation to position themselves more prominently vis-à-vis Rome and the other major cities of the

Figure 3. Photograph of the inscription from the late first-century BC round funerary monument, currently walled in the bell tower of Larino. The inscription reads: Didiae Barbi f(iliae) | Decumae | Oppianica et Bil | liena matri fec(erunt). Photograph by author.

---

[8] Buonocore 1997.
[9] Camodeca 1982: 109; Ricci 2006: 40; Silvestrini 1996: 271; Torelli 1982: 183.
[10] For the mausoleum of Caecilia Metella see Claridge 2010: 430-431, and Gerding 2002. For the mausoleum of C. Ennius Marsus see De Benedittis *et al.* 1984: 131-134.

Mediterranean whose elites were erecting similar monuments. Their choice of this tomb type for their mother shows that the women of Larinum were concerned with their image and status in the town in this period, much like other elite women throughout Italy.

The story of the Didii at Larinum continued with Aulus Didius, a *quaestor* named on the famous Senatus Consultum of Larinum at the official formulation and writing of the text.[11] His presence there was a major political step forward for the local aristocracy of Larinum in the early 1st century AD.

Support for the Didii's links with Histonium can be found in two inscriptions on the inside of a monumental double sarcophagus found at Vasto (Figure 4).[12] This large sarcophagus was for Publius Paquius Scaeva and his wife Flavia, and the inscriptions represent the family by means of its lineage, allowing for different possible reconstructions of the family tree depending on how the inscriptions are read (Figure 5).[13] The inscriptions trace the origins of the couple all the way back

ab una parte :

P · PAQUIUS · SCAEVAE · ET · FLAVIAE · FILIUS · CONSI · ET · DIDIAE · NEPOS ·/ BARBI · ET · DIRUTIAE · PRO · NEPOS | SCAEVA ·/ QUAESTOR · DECEM · VIR · STLITI · BUS · IUDICANDIS · EX · S · C · POST · QUAESTURAM · QUATTUOR · VIR | CAPITALIS · EX · S · C ·/ POST · QUAESTURAM · ET · DECEM · VIRATUM · STLITIUM · IUDICANDARUM · TRIBUNUS · PLEBIS | AEDILIS · CURULIS · / IUDEX · QUAESTIONIS ·/ PRAETOR · AERARII ·/ PRO · CONSULE · PROVINCIAM · CYPRUM · OPTINUIT | VIAR · CUR · EXTRA V · R · EX · S · C · IN QUINQ · PRO · COS · ITERUM · EXTRA · SORTEM · AUCTORITATE · AUG · CAESARIS · | ET · S · C · MISSO · AD · COMPONENDUM · STATUM · IN · RELIQUUM · PROVINCIAE · CYPRI · FETIALIS · | CONSOBRINUS · IDEMQUE · VIR · FLAVIAE · CONSI · FILIAE ·/ SCAPULAE · NEPTIS ·/ BARBI · PRONEPTIS ·SIMUL · CUM · EA · CONDITUS

ab altera parte :

FLAVIA · CONSI · ET · SINNIAE · FILIA ·/ SCAPULAE · ET · SINNIAE · NEPTIS ·/ BARBI · ET · DIRUTIAE · | PRONEPTIS ·/ CONSOBRINA · EADEMQUE · UXOR · P · PAQUII · SCAEVAE · FILII · SCAEVAE · CONSI | NEPOTIS · BARBI · PRONEPOTIS ·/ SIMUL · COME · EO · CONDITA

Figure 4. The two inscriptions on the inside of the double sarcophagus from Histonium, as recorded in CIL IX 2485-2486. Rewritten by author.

---

[11] AE 1978, 145; AE 1983, 210; AE 1984, 249; AE 1990, 189; AE 1991, 515; AE 1992, 300-301; AE 1995, 354; AE 2006, 27; De Felice 1994: 32; Stelluti 1997, number 100a. Levick 1983: 98, 100, Ricci 2006: 39 and Torelli 1982: 183 all give this individual as Aulus Didius Gallus. Malavolta 1978: 367 says that this individual could be the son or grandson of Aulus Didius Postumus.
[12] CIL IX 2485, 2486; CIL XI *29, 2; Torelli 1973: 350-351.
[13] CIL IX 2845, 2846; PIR² P.126; Torelli 1973: 350-351.

to their shared great-grandparents and provide evidence of a woman who could be Didia, daughter of Barbus, from the Larinum inscription.[14] By the last generation mentioned in the sarcophagus, the family may have been trying to consolidate property or to preserve their status in the area by marrying within the family.

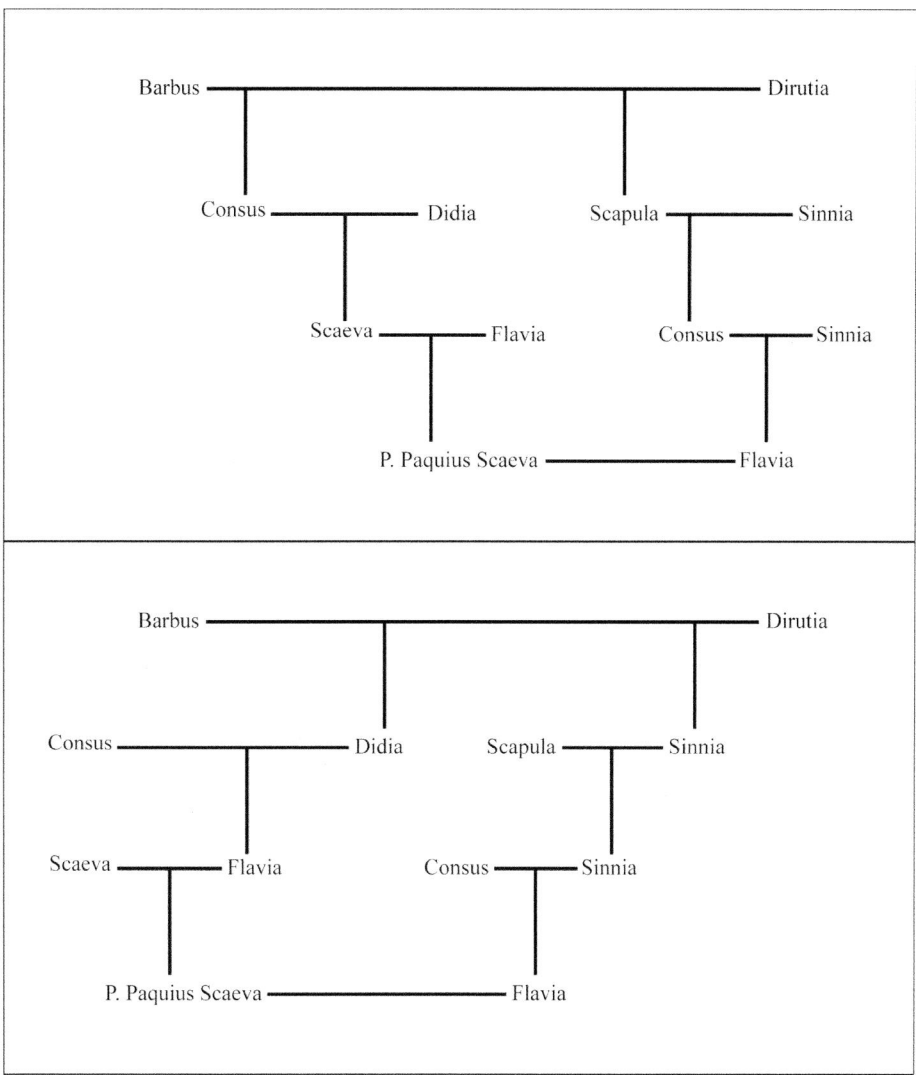

Figure 5. Two possible reconstructions of the family tree as given on the inside of the double sarcophagus from Histonium. The upper version follows only male heirs, the lower follows only female heirs. Drawn by author.

---

[14] Syme 1939: 361 note 1. If, however, the inscription traces only the male ancestors, then the Didia in the inscription was married to Consus, son of Barbus, and thus is not likely to be the woman mentioned in the Larinum inscription.

The informal nomenclature in the Didia Decuma inscription and the sarcophagus inscriptions, especially their use of *cognomina*, makes them seem meant for a local audience familiar with the family. It also suggests that the family was of significant status in the immediate zone. The sarcophagus inscriptions show the intermarriage of multiple families, suggesting that this occurred frequently at the top level of society, and implying that the ruling class was fairly small.

The Paquius family linked to the Didius family through the sarcophagus was certainly on the rise in the late Republic and early Empire. Publius Paquius Scaeva was a homo novus whose political career unfolded largely during the second half of the 1st century BC.[15] The inscription tells us that he held several magistracies, but his career is somewhat difficult to interpret since it comes so early in the Principate. He held several offices in the city of Rome and even extended his career to Cyprus, but his progression is somewhat slow, beginning with three junior positions and culminating with his assignment to a fairly insignificant province.

It is clear, however, that people liked him and desired to keep him in Rome. His position as *praetor aerarii* gave him the administration of the treasury of the Senate, and he is only the third person known to have held this post after Octavian removed the urban quaestors from the administration of the treasury in 28 BC.[16] He must have served not long after 23 BC.[17] Because this was such a new position, it is likely that Augustus would have chosen trusted men for it. It is thus probable that Scaeva's connections with and loyalty to Augustus were responsible for his advancement and achievements.[18] Without his family's aristocratic standing in Histonium and the surrounding territory, though, he would never have been able to garner the attention of the aristocrats in Rome, since he clearly used his wealth and influence to achieve his offices there.[19]

Additional evidence of the wealth and prestige of the gens Paquia in Histonium can be seen in three tile stamps[20] belonging to the same Publius Paquius Scaeva son of Publius from the sarcophagus, and in an inscription dating to around AD 70 involving a boundary dispute between Tillius Sassius and the *municipium* of Histonium, where Marcus Paquius Aulanius acted as actor

---

[15] Corbier 1974: 28.
[16] Corbier 1974: 9, 26.
[17] Corbier 1974: 26, 29. Tacitus (*Ann.* 13. 29) notes that the *praetor aerarii* was chosen by lots from the existing praetors, but this seems to have lasted only temporarily.
[18] Corbier 1974: 30. Such sentiments are echoed by Wiseman 1971: 180-181, 180, note 3.
[19] Corbier 1974: 28.
[20] CIL IX 6078, 128; Torelli 1996: 294.

municipii Histoniensium.[21] Publius Paquius Scaeva was also honored by a funerary inscription erected in Rome by three freedmen,[22] and by another inscription in Rome for his freedmen and his family.[23]

The fairly large group of inscriptions pertaining to the Didii and their kin, of which this is only a subset, testifies to an aristocratic family line that lasted in the area of Larinum and Histonium for at least four generations, if not longer. They intermarried with other families whose interests coincided with theirs and who were seeking political advancement both locally and in Rome. A prosopographical analysis of the inscriptions from Rome, Larinum and Histonium shows that these families managed not only to send forth successful politicians to the capital, but also to maintain a strong aristocratic presence within the local area of Larinum and Histonium. They seem to disappear from the epigraphic record around AD 200, but only after having left their mark on politics at both the local and state levels.

The Papii

Another gens with significant longevity in the area of Larinum is the gens Papia. The family name appears in the pro Cluentio, and it is represented at Larinum in two inscriptions that show its continuity here into at least the 2nd century AD (Figure 6).[24] At least one member of the family who was likely from the area near Larinum had political success in Rome under Augustus: this was the consul who gave his name to the lex Papia Poppaea in 9 BC.[25]

The Vibii

Another family from Larinum that saw considerable political success is the Vibius family. The *pro Cluentio* mentions two murdered men from this family, and also proves that the Vibii intermarried with the Cluentii. Marriage alliances between two powerful families in the town would have boosted the social status of both, and the results appear as early as the first decade of the 1st century AD.

In these years during the reign of Augustus two brothers from the Vibius family held high offices in Rome. The more accomplished was Gaius Vibius Postumus whose name occurs in three inscriptions from Larinum suggesting

---

[21] AE 2000, 68; AE 2006, 54; CIL IX 2827; ILS 5982; Stelluti 1997, number 161. For the dating, see Stelluti 1997: 240.
[22] CIL VI 1483.
[23] CIL VI 1484.
[24] Cic. *Clu.* 27 and elsewhere.
[25] Di Niro 2007: 248; La Regina 1991: 152; Ricci 2006: 66.

Figure 6. Photograph of an inscription pertaining to the Papius family dating to the second half of the 2nd century AD. The inscription reads: D(is) M(anibus) s(acrum) | Papiae Secun | dae Papia Spes | filiae | pientissimae | b(ene) m(erenti) p(osuit). Photograph by author.

that throughout his career he continued to have strong ties to his hometown. He held the offices of praetor, proconsul, suffect consul, governor of Dalmatia, and proconsul of Asia.

The first inscription was dedicated by the citizens and other inhabitants of the *municipium* of Larinum (Figure 7).[26] The second was erected in Larinum but dedicated by the *colonia Romulensis* (Figure 8).[27] This suggests that other towns began to seek Gaius Vibius Postumus' patronage as his political career grew and his influence spread. The final inscription dedicated to him is an unpublished inscription that was found in ongoing excavations at Larinum. It belonged to a large monument erected to Postumus by the urban plebs, honoring him as patron.[28] It likely stood in a public part of the town and would have been a

---

[26] CIL IX 730; Stelluti 1997a, number 6.
[27] At least five different cities seem to have held this title, making it difficult to tell the exact source of the dedication (AE 1966, 74).
[28] The information on this inscription was very kindly provided to me by Professor Enzo Lippolis and Professor Gianluca Gregori. They informed me that the publication of this inscription is forthcoming in an article by G. Gregori, E. Lippolis and A. Lepone in a volume edited by E. Lippolis

Figure 7. Photograph of an inscription dedicated to Gaius Vibius Postumus. The inscription reads: C(aio) Vibio C(aii) [f](ilio) | Postumo | pr(aetori) proco(n)s(uli) | municipes et | incolae. A later inscription was added in 1836. This reads: Lapidem hunc | prope veterum thermarum puder[e] | effossum | io Dom{i}enico{us} Magliano | emendo servavi{t} | A(nno) D(omi)ni MDCCCXXXVI. Photograph by author.

Figure 8. Photograph of an inscription dedicated to Gaius Vibius Postumus. The inscription reads: C(aio) Vibio C(aii) f(ilio) | Postumo | co(n)s(uli) ((septem)) vir(o) epul(onum) | Colonia Romulensis. Photograph by author.

highly visible display, pointing to his importance in Larinum and in the wider Roman world.

Postumus' brother, Aulus Vibius Habitus, also made it onto the political stage in Rome as suffect consul in AD 8 and proconsul of Africa at a later time. His name appears on a bronze *tessera* of hospitality that dates to AD 16 or 17.[29] The *tessera* is a copy of an agreement between Aulus Vibius Habitus and the *colonia Iulia Assuritana*, probably located in northern Africa. Habitus' connections with Larinum are enforced by the fact that a copy was kept there as a record of his patronage relationship.

---

and A. Lepone containing the proceedings of a conference on ancient fora. I have not read the forthcoming article, but I am grateful to the authors for sharing this information with me.

[29] AE 1913, 40; Stelluti 1997a, number 79.

Within only a few generations of Larinum's incorporation into the Roman state this family produced two consuls. This required maintenance of the family's local political status, in addition to political support in Rome. The fact that two members of the family achieved this honor suggests that the Vibii were highly successful at navigating the transition into the Roman political system, and that integration into the Roman state was a priority for their family and possibly for others in the town, as well.

The influence of these two brothers extended beyond Italy, as their careers in the provinces show. This is reflected in two Greek inscriptions: one from Teos and one from Magnesia on the Maeander.[30] Both thank Gaius Vibius Postumus for his benefactions and explore the possibility of further gifts from his connections. The Vibii thus used the new contacts, prestige, and wealth that they had gained from their political success at Rome to make links across the Adriatic and the Mediterranean and to earn favor in provincial cities around the Empire. The access that the municipal elite gained to new commercial and financial opportunities via Rome was presumably an important motivating factor for their participation in the politics of the wider Roman Empire.

The careers of the first five families

The examples of the Cluentii, the Didii and Paquii, the Papii, and the Vibii indicate that the aristocrats of Larinum, many of whom belonged to prominent local Oscan families before the town was adopted into the Roman state, successfully used their new Roman citizenship to navigate the transition from local- to state-level politics. They continued to hold power and maintain prominent positions in Larinum while also looking toward Rome and the rewards that might come from affiliation with the political elite of the capital. By making the right connections locally through intermarriage and in Rome through political links to Octavian, they were able to become part of the Roman political scene, taking full advantage of the opportunities afforded by their political status, holding offices in the provinces and even acting as benefactors in the East. They and other local families continued to exist in the area of Larinum for several centuries, even if their survival in later periods might have been largely through their freedmen.

---

[30] For these inscriptions seeHiller von Gaertringen 1894, number 17; Kern 1900, number 152; Lafaye 1927, number 1564; Le Bas and Waddington 1870 volume 3, number 103; and Robinson 2013: 890.

Newly prominent families under the Roman Empire

The story of the families discussed above who found success in the late Republic and early Empire contrasts with the evidence of other families that do not seem to have been among the nobility at this early time but instead rose to prominence later under the Empire. These families include the Raii, the Coelii and the Gabbii. Whether these three families had always been participating in the leadership of the city but only came to be represented in the epigraphic and historical record under the Empire, or whether they only managed to obtain success at a later time, they played a large role in the political and religious life of the community of Larinum from the middle of the 1st century AD onward. Some of them also used their local power to make connections in the neighboring territory for the advancement of themselves, their families and their hometown. This is a phenomenon that also occurred frequently among the five previously mentioned families.

The Raii

The Raius family formed part of the group of aristocrats in central-southern Italy that backed Octavian during the time of the battle of Actium and shortly afterward.[31] Its members seem to have enjoyed a prestige at Larinum from the 1st century AD onward, as seen in an honorary inscription dedicated to Gaius Raius Capito (Figure 9).[32] He held the offices of *praefectus fabrum*, aedile, *quattuorvir iure dicundo* twice, and *quattuorvir quinquennalis*. It is likely, but impossible to prove that Capito was a Roman *eques*.[33] His holding of multiple juridical offices and local magistracies points to his elevated status and shows that he participated in local politics at a high level. He was honored for his achievements by the *municipium* of Larinum and its inhabitants.

As happened with the Cluentii, the freedmen of the Raii attained a high status within the town of Larinum. A funerary stele dedicated by Gaius Iulius Epaenitus to himself and to Lucius Raius Felix, a *sacerdos matris deum*, emphasizes this point (Figure 10).[34] The stele likely dates to the late 2nd or 3rd century AD, and thus shows the continuity of this local *gens* into the middle and later Empire.[35] It attests to the rank of Lucius Raius Felix as a priest of the cult of Mater Deum, one that was very popular in the Roman world at this time. Here in Larinum this

---

[31] Castrén 1983: 93, note 26.
[32] Castrén 1983: 93. CIL IX 736; Stelluti 1997 number 12. For the date of this inscription see Cerva 2000, *passim* and Stelluti 1997: 96, although this inscription is strangely not mentioned anywhere in the former article.
[33] Cerva 2000: 185-187; Liebenam 1922: 18.
[34] CIL IX 734; Stelluti 1997, number 10.
[35] This date is based on the formula *b(ene) m(erenti) p(osuit)*.

Figure 9. Photograph of an honorary inscription dedicated to Gaius Raius Capito. The inscription reads: C(aio) Raio M(arci) f(ilio) | Capitoni | praef(ecto) fabr(um) aed(ili) | ((quattuor))vir(o) i(ure) d(icundo) | iter(um) ((quattuor))vir(o) quin(quennali) | municip(es) et | incol(ae). Photograph by author.

Figure 10. Photograph of an inscription dedicated by Gaius Iulius Epaenitus to himself and to Lucius Raius Felix. The inscription reads: C(aius) Iulius Epae | nitus religi | osus sibi et L(ucio) | Raio Felici | sacerdoti | matris deum | b(ene) m(erenti) p(osuit) | posterisq(ue) | suis. Photograph by author.

cult may have been linked, at least initially, with the highly important local cult of Mars.[36] Gaius Raius Capito's status as a priest of this cult shows that the *Raius* name still carried weight in the town even in this later period.

The inscriptions pertaining to this family suggest that a local branch of it had a fairly strong influence on politics within the town of Larinum and its surrounding territory. Yet their political ambitions may not have extended much beyond that scale, since the highest known office to be achieved by a family member is that of *praefectus fabrum*.

The Coelii

The family of the Coelii appears in seven inscriptions from Larinum that span the time period from the first half of the 1st century AD to at least the 2nd century AD.[37] What makes them stand out from the other families previously discussed is that the women seem to have been much more successful locally than the men. Perhaps the most important member of the family lived in the middle of the 1st century AD: Coelia Tertulla, a priestess of the cult of Divine Livia (Diva Augusta). Coelia Tertulla appears in three inscriptions from the site of Larinum, indicating that she was an influential figure in the town and received several honors there.

The first inscription to mention her, found on a statue base placed in a public space within the town, likely dates to the AD 40s.[38] It reads: *Coeliae M(arci) f(iliae) Tertullae | sacerdoti divae Augustae | Gabbia M(arci) f(ilia) Tertulla | avia pos⸢u⸣it | huic primae omnium | in municipio annorum VII | decurionum decreto sacer | dotium datum est*. It states that the statue on it was dedicated to Coelia Tertulla, priestess of Diva Augusta, and was set up by Gabbia Tertulla, her grandmother.[39] The inscription notes that Coelia became the priestess of the cult by decree of the *decuriones*, and was the first woman in the *municipium* to hold this honor, despite being only seven years old.[40] Since Livia's cult was officially established only in AD 41, this inscription proves that Larinum quickly adopted and organized the imperial cults.[41] The choice of Coelia Tertulla as priestess of Diva Augusta at such a young age and so soon after the establishment of the cult testifies to her family's standing within the *municipium* of Larinum, and to Larinum's standing

---

[36] Robinson and Sironen 2013.
[37] Calabi Limentani 1968: 158; De Caro 1991: 268; Stelluti 1997: 128, 197.
[38] *AE* 1991, 514a; De Caro 1991: 268; Stelluti 1997, number 123a. This statue base was later reworked for a new statue in the 4th century AD (De Caro 1991: 269).
[39] De Caro 1991: 268.
[40] De Caro 1991: 268; Stelluti 1997: 196.
[41] De Caro 1991: 268.

Figure 11. Photograph of an honorary inscription for Gaius Paccius Priscus. The inscription reads: C(aio) Paccio C(aii) f(ilio) Cor(nelia tribu) | Prisco Aed(ili) ((duum))viro | quinq(uennali) i(ure) d(icundo) patrono | coloniae Venafr{o}⌐i¬ | Coelia M(arci) f(ilia) Ter | tulla testamen(to) | poni iussit | l(oco) d(ato) d(ecreto) d(ecurionum). Photograph by author.

within the broader Roman world.[42]

The second inscription mentioning Coelia Tertulla is an honorary inscription for Gaius Paccius Priscus, arranged for in Coelia's will (Figure 11).[43] This inscription links the *gens Raia* and the *gens Paccia*. Paccius was the patron of Venafrum and enrolled in the Cornelia tribe, suggesting that he may not originally have been from Larinum. Yet he may have been related to Coelia, and she may have used her local prestige to advance the standing of this individual from another *gens* of Oscan origin.[44] The inscription would thus provide further evidence of the municipal elite of Larinum mixing with high-ranking citizens of other towns.[45] It probably dates to the late 1st century AD, after her death, and it shows that she maintained a privileged status and considerable wealth up to her death.[46]

The inscription mentioned above in connection with Marcus Paquius Aulanius acting as *actor municipii Histoniensium* around AD 70 in a boundary dispute attests to the prominence of a member of the Coelius family, as well.[47] It refers

---

[42] De Caro 1991: 268.
[43] CIL IX 735; Stelluti 1997, number 11; Tria 1744: 49.
[44] De Caro (1991: 268-269) suggests that Coelia Tertulla married into the family and that Gaius Paccius Priscus might even be her son.
[45] The tribe of Venafrum is typically given as Teretina (Taylor 1960: 275). This suggests that C. Paccius Priscus was not originally from Venafrum. Venafrum was located about 115km from Larinum.
[46] De Caro 1991: 269, note 7; Stelluti 1997: 94-95.
[47] AE 2000, 68; AE 2006, 54; CIL IX 2827; De Caro 1991: 269, note 10; ILS 5982; Stelluti 1997, number 161.

to a certain Quintus Coelius Gallus who had acted as a judge (*arbiter*), a position of local importance and respect, in an earlier boundary dispute in AD 19.[48] It thus provides evidence of another member of this family, in addition to Coelia Tertulla, who obtained prestige locally and participated in activities involving neighboring communities.

The Gabbii

The inscription on the statue base for Coelia Tertulla contains information about another local family from Larinum and provides important information about the political and social mechanisms active in the town in the 1st century AD. Gabbia Tertulla, Coelia's grandmother, belongs to a *gens* that has so far been found only at Larinum: *Gabbia*.[49] The Gabbii appear in seven inscriptions from Larinum, two of which are on tile stamps. Since the manufacturers of tiles and bricks tended to be wealthy, and since this manufacture most often took place locally, it is very likely that the Gabbii were a wealthy local family.[50]

An inscription that further points to the prestige of this family is a fragmentary building inscription mentioning a woman from the *gens*.[51] The inscription reads: [---*Iuno*]*nis Reginae* | [--- *co*]*llapsam Ga*[*b*]*bia* | [---] *sacerdos divae* | [---*refici*] *unda*[*m*] *cura*(*vit*) [*-3-*]*tis*. It seems to refer to a rebuilding undertaken by Gabbia, a priestess of a female imperial cult, of a structure that must be a feminine noun, likely a religious building dedicated to Juno.[52] She most likely paid for the repairs herself, since as a woman she cannot have held any magistracy and therefore was not acting in any official capacity. It is clear that she was wealthy enough to undertake these repairs, and that she held a position of prestige in the town, as shown by her priesthood. She certainly would have gained renown from her restoration of the building, which may even have used bricks and tiles from her family's own brickyard. The inscription dates to the late 1st or early 2nd century AD, after the family's marriage with the Coelii, at a time when its prestige still seems to have been on the rise.

---

[48] Stelluti 1997: 240. For the dating of this boundary dispute based on the consulship of M. Iunius Silanus and L. Norbanus Balbus, see RE volume 10.1, columns 1098-1099, number 175; and RE volume 17.1, columns 931-932, number 8, respectively.
[49] A search of the Clauss-Slaby epigraphic databank (http://www.manfredclauss.de/gb/index.html) reveals only seven examples of this gentilician, all from Larinum.
[50] Frank 1940: 207-209. This does not exclude the possibility that they may originally have come from outside Larinum
[51] AE 1997, 343; Stelluti 1997, number 114; Stelluti 1997: 187, claims that this was a funerary or sacred inscription, but he must be mistaken, since even the way he has expanded it shows that it refers to the rebuilding of a structure.
[52] In the online Clauss-Slaby database (http://www.manfredclauss.de/gb/index.html), the search 'llapsam' reveals 17 possibilities that include: *aedicula, via, aedes, cella, porticus* and *quadriga*.

It is interesting that it was the women of the Coelii and the Gabbii, in particular, who seem to have had the most ambition in these families. They participated in the imperial cults in the 1st century AD and may have seen the offer of these priesthoods as a vehicle to promote themselves.[53] It goes without saying that women who held this priesthood had to be citizens,[54] and therefore this is yet another example of the ways that the people of Larinum seem to have embraced their Roman citizenship and the opportunities that it offered. Regardless of whether or not it brought success for the men in their family, the women took advantage of this opportunity.[55] As a result, the women seem to have surpassed the prestige of the men in their family, and to have made use of their families' wealth for their own benefit. Among the possible motivations for women seeking priesthoods,[56] the desire for personal prestige and gain must have been quite prominent; this element is echoed in funerary monuments such as the one that Didia Decuma's two daughters erected for her already in the late 1st century BC in Larinum.

The careers of the last three families

The *gentes Raia*, *Coelia* and *Gabbia* thus provide examples of local families whose members came to the forefront only in the 1st century AD, at least 100 years after Larinum became a *municipium*. They gained significant local prestige that lasted for only a century or so, and they seem never to have aspired to offices or magistracies in Rome, or at least they never succeeded in gaining access to them. They and their freedmen flourished and died out on the local level without ever experiencing the larger-scale successes of the Cluentii, the Papii, the Didii, the Paquii and the Vibii.

Conclusions

Despite their less illustrious careers, the families of the Raii, Coelii and Gabbii nevertheless took over some power in Larinum from the other seemingly more ambitious and successful families. The men of the Raii, in particular, held

---

[53] On this office as the principal means for women to act publicly, see Bielman 2012: 247.
[54] Hemelrijk 2005: 159.
[55] It certainly seems to have benefited Gaius Paccius Priscus, if he was indeed related to Coelia Tertulla. Otherwise, apart from Quintus Coelius Gallus, the men of the Coelii and the Gabbii are largely politically untraceable in the epigraphic record.
[56] For possible motivations, see Cenerini 2013: 17-18; Donahue 2004: 889-890; Hemelrijk 2006: 90-93; Hemelrijk 2012: 480, 483-484; Hemelrijk 2013: 76-77, 79-80; Meyers 2012a: 463-465; Meyers 2012b: 157-158. For a general discussion of female benefactors, see Bielman 2012.

multiple local offices, while the women of the Coelii and Gabbii participated in important priesthoods. Such a transition of power from one group of local families to another reflects a natural cycle of power struggles in the town: as one family loses its importance or its financial stability or simply dies out, other local families will step in to take its place. The important result of this study is the realization that from the time of the Social War onward the older aristocratic families were being replaced not by Romans or outsiders, but by other locals. This proves a continuity of local power long into the time of the Empire without significant intervention or migration from the capital or from other distant places. While initially some prominent local families took advantage of the new opportunities made available to them through Roman political networks to advance their standing, others later seem to have preferred to participate in politics within the *municipium* alone. It is possible that by the time that the Roman Empire had become well-established and Larinum's role within it had been fixed, the local aristocracy of the town focused less on connections with Rome and political success there. In the Empire the families of Larinum spent more energy building and maintaining local relationships and local power networks, particularly through the strategy of intermarriage among elites in the region. Although each family had its own trajectory, their various tactics led to the significant stability of the local Oscan aristocratic families after the Roman conquest.

The results of this prosopographical analysis of the leading families of Larinum indicate that the town's transition into the Roman state was a smooth one, effected in part by local aristocrats, both men and women, who were vying with each other and with their contemporaries in order to participate in the political arena both at Rome and at home. The larger study, of which these results represent only a part, tells a new story of the aristocracy of Larinum that differs from the previously published histories. It restores agency to the citizens of the newly-Roman *municipium* who took advantage of the opportunities that their recently acquired Roman citizenship afforded to them. Throughout Italy other families were making the same sorts of decisions to participate in politics or to remain on the sidelines. The successes of those who participated contributed to the success of their towns and of the Roman Empire, as well. While Roman authors point out the significant contributions of people from the capital, the epigraphic evidence greatly enriches the histories of towns like Larinum by providing information about the participation of local families in the municipal politics and religious life of Italy after the Roman conquest.

References

Bielman, A. 2012. Female Patronage in the Greek Hellenistic and Roman Republican Periods. In S. L. James and S. Dillon (eds.), *A Companion to Women in the Ancient World*: 238-248. Malden, MA, Wiley-Blackwell.

Birley, E. 1951. The prefects and their altars. In I. A. Richmond and J. P. Gillian (eds), *The Temple of Mithras at Carrawburgh. Archaeologia Aeliana* 29: 45-51.

Buonocore, M. 1997. I Cluentii Larinates: le testimonianze epigrafiche. In N. Stelluti (ed.), *Pro Cluentio, di Marco Tullio Cicerone: atti del convegno nazionale: Larino, 4-5 dicembre 1992*: 45-51. Larino, L'Amministrazione comunale.

Calabi Limentani, I. 1968. *Epigrafia Latina*. Varese-Milano, Istituto editoriale cisalpino.

Camodeca, G. 1982. Italia: Regio I (Campania, esclusa la zona di Capua e Cales), II (Apulia et Calabria), III (Lucania et Bruttii). *Tituli* 5: 101-163.

Castrén, P. 1983. Cambiamenti nel gruppo dei notabili municipali dell'Italia centro-meridionale nel corso del I secolo a.C. In *Les 'Bourgeoisies' Municipales Italiennes au IIe et Ier Siècles av. J.-C.*: 91-97. Naples, Centre Jean Bérard.

Cenerini, F. 2013. The Role of Women as Municipal *Matres*. In E. Hemelrijk and G. Woolf (eds.), *Women and the Roman City in the Latin West*: 9-22. Leiden, Brill.

Cerva, M. 2000. La Praefectura Fabrum: Un'Introduzione. In M. Cébeillac-Gervasoni (ed.), *Les Élites Municipales de l'Italie Péninsulaire de la Mort de César à la Mort de Domitien entre Continuité et Rupture*: 177-196. Rome, Ecole française de Rome.

Claridge, A. 2010. *Rome: An Oxford Archaeological Guide*. New York, Oxford University Press.

Collingwood, R. G. and Wright, R. P. 1965. *The Roman Inscriptions of Britain*. Oxford, Clarendon Press.

Corbier, M. 1974. *L'aerarium Saturni et l'aerarium militare*. Paris, Diffusion de Boccard.

De Benedittis, G., Gaggiotti M. and Matteini Chiari, M. 1984. *Saepinum: Guida agli Scavi Archeologici*. Campobasso, Edizioni Enne.

De Caro, S. 1991. Base di statua con iscrizione opistografa da *Larinum*. In S. Capini and A. Di Niro (eds.), *Samnium. Archeologia del Molise*: 268-270. Rome, Quasar.

De Felice, E. 1994. *Forma Italiae, 36: Larinum*. Firenze, L. S. Olschki.

Di Niro, A. 2007. *Il Museo sannitico di Campobasso: catalogo della collezione provinciale*. Pescara, Carsa.

Donahue, J. F. 2004. Iunia Rustica of Cartima: Female Munificence in the Roman West. *Collection Latomus* 283: 873-891.

Frank, T. 1940. *An Economic Survey of Ancient Rome, volume 5: Rome and Italy of the Empire*. Baltimore, The Johns Hopkins Press.

Gerding, H. 2002. *The Tomb of Caecilia Metella: Tumulus, Tropaeum and Thymele*. Lund, H. Gerding.

Hemelrijk, E. A. 2005. Priestesses of the Imperial Cult in the Latin West: Titles and Function. *L'antiquité classique* 74: 137-170.

Hemelrijk, E. A. 2006. Priestesses of the Imperial Cult in the Latin West: Benefactions and Public Honour. *L'antiquité classique* 75: 85-117.

Hemelrijk, E.A. 2012. Public Roles for Women in the Cities of the Latin West. In S. L. James and S. Dillon (eds.), *A Companion to Women in the Ancient World*: 478-490. Malden, MA, Wiley-Blackwell.

Hemelrijk, E. 2013. Female Munificence in the Cities of the Latin West. In E. Hemelrijk and G. Woolf (eds.), *Women and the Roman City in the Latin West*: 65-84. Leiden, Brill.

Hiller von Gaertringen, F. 1894. Ausgrabung enim Theater von Magnesia am Maiandros. I. Inschriften. *Mittheilungen des Kaiserlich Deutschen Archäologischen Instituts, Athenische Abteilung* 19: 1-53.

Keppie, L. 1984. *The Making of the Roman Army: From Republic to Empire*. London, Batsford.

Kern, O. 1900. *Die Inschriften von Magnesia am Maeander*. Berlin, W. Spemann.

La Regina, A. 1991. C. PAPIVS C. F. MVTILVS IMP. In S. Capini and A. Di Niro (eds.), *Samnium. Archeologia del Molise*: 149-152. Rome, Quasar.

Lafaye, G. 1927. *Inscriptiones Graecae ad Res Romanas Pertinentes*. Paris, E. Leroux.

Le Bas, P. and Waddington, W. H. 1870. *Inscriptions grecques et latines, recueillies en Grèce et en Asie Mineure*. Paris, F. Didot.

Levick, B. 1983. The senatus consultum from Larinum. *Journal of Roman Studies* 73: 97-115.

Liebenam, W. 1922. Fabri: Praefectus fabrum. In E. De Ruggiero (ed.), *Dizionario Epigrafico di Antichità Romane*, volume 3: 14-18. Roma, Pasqualucci.

Malavolta, M. 1978. A proposito del nuovo S.C. da Larino. *Sesta Miscellanea Greca e Romana*. Roma: 347-382.

Meyers, R. 2012a. Female Portraiture and Female Patronage in the High Imperial Period. In S. L. James and S. Dillon (eds.), *A Companion to Women in the Ancient World*: 453-466. Malden, MA, Wiley-Blackwell.

Meyers, R. 2012b. Reconsidering Opportunities for Female Benefactors in the Roman Empire: Julia Antonia Eurydice and the *Gerontikon* at Nysa. *L'Antiquité Classique* 81: 145-159.

Ricci, C. 2006. *Gladiatori e Attori nella Roma Giulio-Claudia. Studi sul Senatoconsulto di Larino*. Milan, LED.

Robinson, E. C. 2013. Local Power Networks at Larinum Before and After its Integration into the Roman State. In L. Bombardieri, A. D'Agostino, G. Guarducci, V. Orsi and S. Valentini (eds.), *SOMA 2012 Identity and Connectivity: Proceedings of the 16th Symposium on Mediterranean Archaeology, Florence, Italy, 1-3 March 2012*: 887-894. Oxford, Archaeopress.

Robinson, E. C. and Sironen, T. 2013. A New Inscription in Oscan from Larinum: Decisive Evidence in Favor of a Local Cult of Mars and Mater (Deum?). *Zeitschrift für Papyrologie und Epigraphik* 185: 251-261.

Silvestrini, M. 1996. Dalla nobilitas municipale all'ordine senatorio: esempi da Larino e da Venosa. *Cahiers du Centre Gustave Glotz* 7: 269-282.

Stelluti, N. 1997. *Epigrafi di Larino e della bassa Frentania*. Campobasso, Editrice Lampo.

Syme, R. 1939. *The Roman Revolution*. Oxford, Oxford University Press.

Taylor, L. R. 1960. *The Voting Districts of the Roman Republic: The Thirty-Five Urban and Rural Tribes*. Rome, American Academy.

Torelli, M. 1982. Italia: Regio IV (Samnium). *Tituli* 5: 165-199.

Torelli, M. 1996. Industria laterizia e aristocrazie locale in Italia: appunti prosopografici. *Cahiers du Centre Gustave Glotz* 7: 291-296.

Torelli, M. R. 1973. Una nuova iscrizione di Silla da Larino. *Athenaeum* 51: 336-354.

Tria, G. A. 1744. *Memorie storiche civile ed ecclesiastiche della città e diocesi di Larino, metropoli degli antichi frentani*. Rome.

Wiseman, T. P. 1971. *New Men in the Roman Senate 139 B.C. - A.D. 14.* London, Oxford University Press.

The kindred dimension of the Black Sea associations: between fictive and real meaning

(3rd century BC – 3rd century AD)

Annamária–Izabella Pázsint[1]

The uttermost important goal of this paper is to provide an outlook on the familial vocabulary and composition of the private associations from the Greek colonies of the Black Sea. More precisely, the paper will bring forward information regarding the vocabulary of belonging used in the inscriptions to name the members of the associations, correlated to the members who sometimes come from the same family.

Due to its character, the paper will have a dual approach, the first part will focus on the fictive familial language used in inscriptions, and the second will focus on the actual familial component of associations, providing a number of examples.

Fictive familial language

The fictive kinship terminology used within Christianity has been thoroughly studied,[2] but this was not the case for the associations of the Greek and Roman world, which have been much more neglected.[3] Moreover, a certain denial is present in the works of some researchers of the private associations, who consider that except for the associations in Tanais, this terminology was almost not in use in the Greek associations.[4]

Several other scholars have risen against this perspective, showing that the evidence we encounter when speaking of Greek associations is much greater and reliable than previously thought.[5]

In this context, the paper will evaluate the existing epigraphical evidence corresponding to the private associations from the Greek colonies of the Black

---

[1] This work was supported by a grant of the Romanian National Authority for Scientific Research, CNCS-UEFISCDI, project number PNII-RU-TE-2014-4-0488.
[2] Schäfer 1989; Sandnes 1994; Burke 2003.
[3] Among researchers, only Philip Harland has thoroughly tackled this subject 2005, 2007.
[4] Poland 1909: 54-55.
[5] Nock 1924: 105; San Nicolo 1972: 33-34; Harland 2005; Harland 2007.

Sea area, in order to distinguish the significance of such terminology in an associative setting.

The evidence for this type of familial language and for this communal identity is present in a wider geographical area than the one which will come into our attention. More precisely, the evidence comes from Asia Minor, Greece, Macedonia, the Danubian area, the Bosporus, and Egypt.[6]

The terminology of belonging is explicitly expressed through the titles: *mater, pater, adelphos*, two of them (*mater*, and *pater*), corresponding to honorific rather than functional positions[7] inside the associations. Both the title father and mother were encountered in associations devoted to Dionysos, Cybele, Sarapis, and Theos Hypsistos,[8] while the title brother is present in two associations which do not preserve the name of the worshipped divinity.

As the chronology indicates, the titles *mater, pater*, and *adelphos* appear mostly late in this associative *milieu*, being characteristic for the 2nd and 3rd century AD,[9] long after the first mentions and development of the private associations in the Greek colonies, but during the zenith of the associative life. Poland[10] and Jaccottet[11] mention the fact that the title *pater* may come from a Roman influence of the *pater collegii* but the evidence from Tanais,[12] as well as that from Egypt[13] points to a Hellenistic origin.

The inscriptional evidence provides us, on the one side fictive kinship terminology, and on the other side real kinship engagement in the associative life. When it comes to individuals who are given the title *mater, pater*, or *adelphos*, the sources point out that these are not titles given as a consequence of the real familial connections between individuals. As a matter of fact, these titles rather express honorific positions, and the wider concept of belonging. On the other side, real kinship is attested, even though in some cases we cannot be sure that certain individuals (who bear a common patronymic) are related or not.

---

[6] Harland 2005: 497.
[7] Avram 2015: 127.
[8] In this case only the title of *pater* and *adelphos*.
[9] See Table nr. 1.
[10] Poland 1909: 372.
[11] Jaccottet 2003: 65-66.
[12] Avram 2015: 125; Ivantchik 2008: 94-95, n. 1 = SEG 58 782; Ivantchik 2008: 96-100, n. 2 = SEG 58 783; Ivantchik 2008: 100-103, n. 3 = SEG 58 784.
[13] Harland 2005: 505.

Mater

Women are a light presence on the associative scene, and when we find them, they usually are priestesses, and some benefactresses.[14] In three epigraphic instances they also bear the title of *mater*, with its different variants.[15] The title appears in two associations dedicated to Cybele (a *collegium dendrophorum*[16] and a *sacratus dumus*[17]) and in an association which dedicated an inscription to the Thracian Horseman (*collegium Romanorum*[18]). In this latter case, the Thracian Horseman was probably not the main divinity of the association (the text does not mention it), but considering this title, we might be facing another association worshipping Cybele. In the *collegium dendrophorum*, mothers and fathers were subordinate to the high priest, but they occupied a higher position than the *archidendrophoroi*.[19]

The title appears to be of honorific nature, and as evidence from Italy shows it, women were probably granted the title of mother due to their financial capacity and availability and to their social status; overall the title boosted their reputation.[20] At Tomis, the *mater* Flavia Nona was among the few members who donated and dedicated a monument to their fellow-members.[21] In what concerns their social origin, it is assumed that women bearing this title come from the same social-category as the other members of the association, and in some cases they might be the relatives of certain members[22] (but not real mother). Such titles were not used only in *alba* which recorded the internal hierarchy of an associations, they appear also in votive inscriptions, making room for self-representation, and showing that the title brought a certain social status and prestige[23] by displaying it.

Pater

The title of father,[24] is the most frequently used and it is widespread especially on the northern shore of the Black Sea, in associations dedicated to Theos Hypsistos. In these associations the title of mother has not been attested,[25] but

---

[14] Pázsint 2017: 159-173.
[15] See Table nr. 1.
[16] ISM II 83 = IGR I 614 = Tacheva-Hitova 1983: 93-94, n. 48 = SEG 27 399.
[17] ISM II 160 = Tacheva-Hitova 1983: 78-80, n. 14 = CCCA VI 454.
[18] CIL III 7532 = ILS 4069 = CCET IV 48 = ISM II 129.
[19] Tacheva-Hitova 1983: 149.
[20] Hemelrijk 2008: 140.
[21] ISM II 160.
[22] Hemelrijk 2008: 137.
[23] Hemelrijk 2008: 128.
[24] See Tabel I.
[25] Considering the preponderance of associations dedicated to Theos Hypsistos, the lack of the title mother is explained through the male composition of such associations.

instead we have the title of brother, which does not appear in any other Greek colonies from our area of interest.

Inscriptions from Tanais[26] and Pantikapaion[27] point to the fact that the *pater synodou* comes always after that of the *hiereus*, these two being probably the highest-ranking members of the association.[28] The hierarchy enlisted in inscriptions indicates that most probably one of the position was functional (*hiereus*), while the other was honorific (*pater*), situation which corresponds to the case of the *speira* from Histria, where we find a duality at the head of the association dedicated to Dionysos:[29] besides a *mater* or a *pater*, there is also a *hiereus/ archiereus*.

In one instance at Tomis,[30] and one at Pantikapaion,[31] an individual has not only the title of *hiereus*, but also that of *pater* (Marcus Antonius Marcianus and Papas, son of Pannuchos), which indicates according to Avram[32] the functionality of the first position, and the honorific meaning of the second, here both are held by the same individual. Therefore, as Avram points out, the title of *pater* could have been given to a former priest which occupied the leading position.[33]

An interesting case comes from Histria and Tomis, where Achilleus son of Achillas was *pater* both in an association dedicated to Dionysos[34] and in one dedicated to Cybele.[35] The individual therefore had the same honorific title in two different associations from two cities, each association being created around the most important local deity, ensuring therefore the same distinction to our individual.[36]

At Histria, a private association for Mithras records among its members several local personalities, like the pontarch M. Ulpius Artemidoros,[37] which is also a member of the *speira Dionysiaston*.[38] Inside this association we also have a *pater*,

---

[26] CIRB 1261; 1263; CIRB 1277; CIRB 1282; CIRB 1288.
[27] CIRB 96; CIRB 98; CIRB 99; CIRB 100; CIRB 104; CIRB 105.
[28] Avram 2015: 127.
[29] Suceveanu 2007: 144-153.
[30] Bărbulescu-Câteia 2007: 248 = AE 2007 1231 = SEG 57 680 = Conrad 2004: 160-161, n. 132.
[31] CIRB 95.
[32] Avram 2015: 128.
[33] Avram 2015: 128.
[34] ISM I 99 = SEG 19 477; ISM I 100 = SEG 17 342.
[35] ISM II 83 = IGR I 614 = Tacheva-Hitova 1983: 93-94, n. 48 = SEG 27 399.
[36] Ruscu 2014: 147.
[37] ISM I 137 = CIMRM II 2296.
[38] ISM I 207 = SEG 48 970.

which in the hierarchy of Mithraic cults was the highest grade,[39] the father being the head of the group.[40]

At Dionysopolis,[41] the priest (M. Aurelios Koures, son of Hestiaios) of an association of Attiastai was not only the first archon of the city, but also *hieronomos* of the local *Asianon speira*.[42] Among his colleagues we find a certain Piaitralis, son of Silanos, a *pater tes thynes*, who therefore fulfilled the position of president of the feast.

Overall, the title *pater* is, except in the case of cult association dedicated to Mithras, a secondary position, which implies an honorific component.

Adelphos

Besides these two titles, one can also find at Pantikapaion,[43] an inscription where the term *adelphos* is recorded, and is given to regular members of associations devoted to Theos Hypsistos. In this geographical area, from using the familial term of 'brother', for denominating its regular members, we find later on associations which bear as title fraternal names (i.e. 'the adopted brothers'). It is the case of an association from Sinope[44] and one from Tanais,[45] dedicated to Theos Hypsistos; the members of the first describe themselves 'the vowing brothers', while those of the latter as 'the adopted brothers who revere'. At Tanais each inscription which uses this expression records different lists of members, but considering their date (210-227 AD, 228 AD, 230 AD, 210-234 AD, and 220-240 AD), we can probably safely assume that they register members of the same associations.

An obvious question which arises is why did these associations have such titles for their members? One answer could be that these denominations expressed the idea of a community, community which was sometimes bound by real kinship, but more frequently by fictive kinship. The fictive kinship could create an inner connection among the members, a familial bound, which made the associations to become an extension of the real family, and of the local society they lived in. Basically, a certain recreation of the domestic sphere can be distinguished, even though to a smaller scale. In this respect we also find

---

[39] Vermaseren 1960: 115-126.
[40] Clauss 2001: 138.
[41] SEG 60 768.
[42] IGBulg I 23.
[43] CIRB 104.
[44] Doublet 1889: 303-304.
[45] CIRB 1281 = IGR I 918; CIRB 1283 = IGR I 920; CIRB 1284; CIRB 1285 = IGR I 919; CIRB 1286.

offices such as *oikonomos*,[46] or *nomophylax*,[47] and we have certain associations which imply the idea of home, i.e. '*oikos* ton Alexandreon',[48] '*oikos* ton en Tomei naukleron',[49] '*oikos* ton naukleron'.[50]

Therefore, besides being 'des cités en miniature',[51] associations were also 'des familles en miniature', which, even though did not imitate so closely the structure of the family and its role, it did create a sense of familial belonging.

Familial engagement in associations

Besides using a familial terminology and sometimes having also a familial structure, associations could also comprise, among its ranks, real family members, or even more, its membership could have been exclusively composed of family members, and their co-dependents (slaves, freedmen). From the overall number of members attested in the inscriptional records of the Greek colonies coming from the Black Sea, 15 % of them provide reliable evidence for blood kinship,[52] but many other familial connections are possible, but disputable due to the character of the sources.

In the envisaged geographical area we do not encounter 'exclusive' associations, which are comprised solely of real family members, but as already stated, we do encounter associations which comprise several family members at the same time, or associations which comprise family members in different periods.

Family life in an associative context is not surprising;[53] it is common for individuals, especially for those who come from an upper social stratum, to perpetuate a certain social behaviour, behaviour which helped increase the visibility, status and engagement one has inside society.

Such examples are relatively frequent in this geographical area, and several family trees were reconstructed based on the epigraphical evidence at our disposal. In most cases, due to the fragmentary state of the inscriptions, or due to the poor prosopographical information which the inscription offers, we cannot tell much on the exact kinship between family members. Most often, we can identify members of the same family only through their patronymic,

---

[46] CIRB 1130; CIRB 1134.
[47] ISM II 17.
[48] ISM II 53 = IGR I 604.
[49] ISM II 60 = IGR I 610.
[50] ISM II 132, which might be the same association as the previous.
[51] Baslez 1988: 139-158.
[52] Based on internal statistics.
[53] Poland 1909: 87-88.

which sometimes might mislead us. In the following lines, some examples will be given of the cases which surely provide familial connections.

Tanais certainly offers the most prolific evidence for this topic, and this is mostly due to the fact that demographic studies have been carried out and that there are over 20 inscriptions (many being *alba*) which emanate from associations. Based on the patronymic of the individuals, and on their prosopographical data provided by the sources, we can tell that a large number of members (male) are related, even though we usually can only trace members of the nuclear family, and much rarer of the extended family. Ustinova also sustains the fact that in Tanais a large sector of the free men were members of these associations,[54] at least between 225 and 230 AD, therefore it gives credit to the idea that familial engagement (of men) was a reality in that area.

Except for Tanais, in other parts of the Bosporan area, the familial engagement in associations is sometimes difficult to distinguish, due to the fact that the individuals' names and patronymic are very common (i.e. Dionysos), and to the fact that they appear in roughly the same period. However, as mentioned above, a decent percentage of interrelated individuals have been identified. As example we bring forward a case from Pantikapaion,[55] where real brothers are recorded inside the same association: the sons of Chophranos I, Papias, Chophranos II and Herakleides.

From Byzantion we have six stelae[56] which record an association dedicated to Dionysos Kallon.[57] Most of the members of this association seem to be interrelated, but here references do not necessarily lead to the association being a household association.[58]

This association dedicated to Dionysos Kallon embodies the highest number of women among its members, women who occupy positions of great significance, these are not only religious positions, but also administrative and honorific functions, which are usually the attribute of men.

---

[54] Ustinova 1999: 184.
[55] CIRB 36.
[56] IKByzantion 30 = SEG 18 278 = Jaccottet 2003: 78, n. 38.1; IK Byzantion 31 = SEG 18 280 = Jaccottet 2003: 79, n. 38.2; IK Byzantion 32 = SEG 19 282 = Jaccottet 2003: 81, n. 38.5; IK Byzantion 33 = SEG 18 282 = Jaccottet 2003: 80, 38.4; IK Byzantion 34 = SEG 18 284 = Jaccottet 2003: 81, 38.6; IK Byzantion 35 = SEG 18 281 = Jaccottet 2003: 79, n. 38.3.
[57] The title Kallon might have a philosophical meaning, or a geographical origin (Callum). Jaccottet 2003: I 82.
[58] See Stemma nr. 1.

Among these cases we mention Lollia Katylla, daughter of Quintus (and probably the wife of Gaius Iulius Italicus), she occupied the position of *hieropoios*, but she was also a benefactress, and priestess of the imperial cult. She was honoured for her benefactions in private settings, but also in public ones, because she also offered public sacrifices on behalf of the city on two occasions. From this profile we may assume that she and her family were wealthy and had a respectable social status, as the reference to the imperial cult indicates.

The brother (Diodorus son of Quintus) and the sister-in-law (Stallia Prima) of Lollia Katylla, were also active members of the association; the couple jointly occupied the position of gymnasium-director 'in an extravagant and noble manner'. If in this case we deal with a joint position, in the case of Crispina, daughter of Aischylos, the situation is different: she was the member of the same association, but she occupied the position of gymnasium-director alone. In this case we cannot rule out the possibility that Crispina was the daughter of a former gymnasium-director, who received a hereditary title.[59] Overall, the epigraphic evidence points to the existence of 41 cases across the ancient world, where woman occupy the position of gymnasium-director,[60] therefore we are facing a rather rare case, especially since all these women come from the same association. This rarity supports the idea that women could play a non-religious role in an association if well financially placed.

Another distinguishable case of familial engagement comes from Olbia,[61] where we have an association which records members coming from two families: seven of the members are the sons of Leokrates, while other four individuals are relatives (son and grandsons) of Leoprepes.[62] The evidence comes from a fourth century statue dedicated to Zeus Soter, while the associations seem to worship a local hero named Heuresibios, who is said to have liberated Olbia from a tyrant.[63] The family members are priests among the *thiasos*, but they probably did not occupy the position simultaneously.[64]

At Histria the association of Dionysos was among the most popular, and it also had among its members representatives of the elite.[65] In this association, the family of Eleis[66] stands out for their engagement (Aurelios Eleis, Aurelios Ailianos Eleis, Aurelios Alexandros Eleis, Aurelios Satourneilos Eleis), one of its

---

[59] Casarico 1982: 123.
[60] Casarico 1982: 118-122.
[61] SEG 18 304 = IOlbia 71 = IGDOlbia 11.
[62] Stolba 2013: 293-302. See the stemma of these two families at page 299.
[63] Stolba 2013: 299.
[64] Stolba 2013: 300.
[65] Like the pontarch M. Ulpius Artemidoros, or T. Cominius Euxenides.
[66] ISM I 100 = SEG 17 342.

Table 1. Titles which express familial belonging.

Personal name/ cognomen	Father	Position	Divinity	Period	Ref.
Nanas	Theadon	*mater dendrophoron?*	Cybele	199-201 AD	ISM II 83
Menia Iuliane	such	*mater Romanorum*	Thracian Horseman, maybe also Cybele	before 165 AD	ISM II 129
Flavia Nona	such	*mater*	Cybele	2nd/3rd C AD	ISM II 160
Achilleus	Achillas	*pater*	Dionysos, Cybele	199-201 AD	ISM I 99, ISM I 100, ISM II 83
Aurelius Valerianus		*pater*	Cybele	2nd/3rd C AD	ISM II 160
Meniskos	Noumenios	*pater*	Mithras	159/160 AD	ISM I 137
Piaitralis	Silanos	*pater tes thynes*	Attis, Pontic Mother of Gods	215-235 AD	SEG 60 768
Silanos	Antrophion	*maybe a pater*	Pontic Mother of Gods	after 212 AD	SEG 60 767
Marcus Antonius Marcianus	-	*pater nomimos*	Hekate	2nd C AD	AE 2007 1231
such	Menekrates	*pater ton pastophoron*	Isis	2nd/3rd C AD	ISM II 98
Antisthenes	Herakleides	*pater*	?	204 AD	CIRB 96
Agathous	Zenon	*pater synodou*	?	173-211 AD	CIRB 77+1136
such	such	*pater synodou*	?	2nd C AD	CIRB 95
Iulius Sambion	such	*pater synodou*	?	214 AD	CIRB 98
Seitalkes	Seitalkes	*pater synodou*	?	221 AD	CIRB 99
such	Dionysios	*pater synodou*	?	221 AD	CIRB 100
Phidas	such	*pater synodou*	?	3rd C AD	CIRB 102
such	such	*pater synodou*	Dionysos?	Hellenistic	SEG 58 782
Kallistos	Kallistos	*pater synodou*	?	c. 200-250 AD	CIRB 104, CIRB 105
Antimachos	such	*pater synodou*	Theos Hypsistos	131-154 AD	CIRB 1261
such	such	*pater synodou*	Theos Hypsistos	c. 100-150 AD	CIRB 1263
Chorouathos	such	*pater synodou*	Theos Hypsistos	173-211 AD	CIRB 1277
Phazinamos	Ar[---]damos	*pater synodou*	Theos Hypsistos	220 AD	CIRB 1278
Nibloboros	Dosumoxarthos	*pater synodou*	Theos Hypsistos	228 AD	CIRB 1282
such	Atamazas	*pater synodou*	Theos Hypsistos	227-234 AD?	CIRB 1288
such	such	*pater synodou*	?	2nd/3rd C AD	Saprykin, Maslennikov 1999: 194, n. 2
Symphoros	Philippos	*adelphos*	?	c. 200-250 AD	CIRB 104

members (Aurelios Alexandros Eleis)[67] being recorded also in an association from Tomis devoted to Cybele.

Other familial connections can be traced through the specific mentioning of the type of relationship between various characters, and sometimes through their names and patronymic if they are easily discernible. From this data we can tell that familial involvement in an associative context is a fact, which can be explained, among others, also through the desire of individuals to act, and have a say in their community, irrespective of their origin and status.

Conclusions

The nature of the sources and the contexts in which we have found a parental and fraternal language gives credit to the idea that its use was underestimated in most of the previous works, nonetheless their use was rather marginal in inscriptions.

As we have seen, the familial component of associations was not limited to the vocabulary used, which could be applied to any member, but it was also represented by an integration of real family members among their elements.

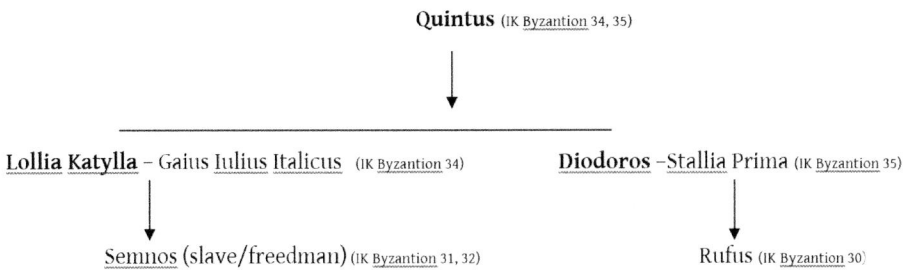

Figure 1. Stemma of Quintus' family.

---

[67] ISM II 83 = IGR I 614 = Tacheva-Hitova 1983: 93-94, n. 48 = SEG 27 399.

References

Avram, Al. 2013. *Prosopographia Ponti Euxini Externa*. Leuven-Paris, Peeters.

Avram, Al. 2015. Newly Published Documents Concerning Cult Associations in the Black Sea. Some Remarks. In V. Gabrielsen, Ch. A. Thomsen (eds.), *Private Associations and the Public Sphere*: 122-135. Copenhagen, The Royal Danish Academy of Sciences and Letters.

Baslez, M.-Fr. 1988. Les communautés d'orientaux dans la cité grecque. Formes de sociabilité et modèles associatifs. In Raoul Lonis (ed.), *L'Étranger dans le monde grec. Actes du colloque organisé par l'Institut d'études anciennes*: 139-158. Nancy, Presses Universitaires de Nancy.

Bărbulescu, M., Câteia, A. 2009. Pater nomimos în cultul Hecatei la Tomis. *Pontica* 40: 245-253.

Burke, T. 2003. *Family Matters. A Socio-Historical Study of Kinship Metaphors in 1 Thessalonians*. London, T&T Clark International.

Casarico, L. 1982. Donne ginnasiarco (A proposito di P. Med. inv. 69.01). *ZPE* 48: 117-123.

Chiekova, D. 2008. *Cultes et vie religieuse des cités grecques du Pont gauche (VIIe – Ier siècles avant J.-Chr.)*. Bern, Peter Lang.

Clauss, M. 2001. *The Roman Cult of Mithras. The God and His Mysteries*. New York, Routledge.

Cojocaru, V. 1966. Onomastikon. Aspects démographiques dans les villes ouest-pontiques de la province Moesia Inferior. *Arheologia Moldovei* 19: 135-149.

Cojocaru, V. 2004. *Populația zonei nordice și nord-vestice a Pontului Euxin în secolele VI – I a. Chr. pe baza izvoarelor epigrafice*. Iași, Editura Universității Alexandru Ioan Cuza.

Cojocaru, V. 2007. L'histoire par les noms dans les villes Grecques de Scythie et de Scythie Mineure aux VIe – Ier Siècles av. J.-C. In: V. Grammenos, E. K. Petropulos (eds.), *Ancient Greek Colonies in the Black Sea 2*. Vol. I: 383-433. Oxford, British Archaeological Reports.

Conrad, S. 2004. *Die Grabstelen aus Moesia Inferior*. Leipzig, Casa Libri.

Craco-Rugini, L. 1976. La vita associative nelle città dell'Oriente greco. Tradizioni locali e influenze romane. In D. M. Pippidi (ed.), *Assimilation et résistance à la culture gréco-romaine dans le monde ancien. Travaux du VIe Congrès International d'Études Classiques*. Bucarest – Paris, Editura Academiei Române – Les Belles Lettres.

Doublet, G. 1889. Inscriptions de Paphlagonie, *Bulletin de Correspondance Hellénique* 13/1: 293-319.

Gabrielsen, V. 2009. Brotherhoods of Faith and Provident Planning. The Non-public Associations of the Greek World. In I. Malkin, C. Constantakopoulou (eds.), *Greek and Roman Networks in the Mediterranean*: 176-203. London/New York, Routledge.

Harland, Ph. A. 2005. Familial Dimensions of Group Identity: 'Brothers' in Associations of the Greek East, *Journal of Biblical Literature* 124: 491-513.

Harland, Ph. A. 2007. Familial Dimensions of Group Identity (II): 'Mothers' and 'Fathers', in Associations and Synagogues of the Greek World, *Journal for the Study of Judaism* 38: 57 – 79.

Ivantchik, A. 2008. Greeks and Iranians in the Cimmerian Bosporus in the Second/First Century BC. New Epigraphic Data from Tanais. In S. M. R. Darbandi, A. Zournatzi (eds.), *Ancient Greece and Ancient Iran. Cross-cultural Encounters*: 93-107. Athens, National Hellenic Research Foundation.

Jaccottet, A.-Fr. 2003. *Choisir Dionysos. Les associations dionysiaques ou la face cachée du dionysisme. Vol. 1 Text, Vol. 2 Documents*. Zürich, Akanthus Verlag.

van Nijf, O. 1997. *The Civic World of Professional Associations in the Roman East*. Amsterdam, Gieben.

Nock, A. D. 1924. The Historical Importance of Cult-Associations. *The Classical Review* 38: 105-109.

Pázsint, A.-I. 2017. It's a man's world: a gender perspective on the private associations from the Black Sea area (3rd C BC – 3rd C AD). In Dániel Bajnok (ed.), *Alia Miscellanea Antiquitatum. Proceedings of the Second Croatian-Hungarian PhD Conference on Ancient History and Archaeology*: 159-173. Budapest-Debrecen, Kódex.

Poland, Fr. 2007. *Geschichte des griechischen Vereinswesens*. Leipzig, B. G. Teubner.

Schäfer, K. *Gemeinde als Bruderschaft. Ein Beitrag zum Kirchenverständnis des Paulus*. Bern, Peter Lang.

San Nicolò, M. 1972. *Ägyptisches Vereinswesen zur Zeit der Ptolemäer und Römer. 1.* München, C. H. Beck.

Sandnes, K. O. 1994. *A New Family. Conversion and Ecclesiology in the Early Church with Cross-Cultural Comparisons*. New York, Peter Lang.

Shelov, D. B. 1971. *Tanais I Nizhnii Don v pervye veka nashei ery*. Moscow.

Stolba, V. 2013. A Prosopographical Note on IOlbia 71 (Dubois IGDOlbia 11), *Mnemosyne* 66: 293-302.

Suceveanu, Al. *et al.* 2007. *Histria XIII. La basilique épiscopale*. Bucarest, Editura Academiei Române.

Tacheva-Hitova, M. 1983. *Eastern Cults in Moesia Inferior and Thracia (5th century BC – 4th century AD)*. Leiden, Brill.

Ustinova, Y. 1999. *The Supreme Gods of the Bosporan Kingdom. Celestial Aphrodite and the Most High God*. Leiden-Boston-Cologne, Brill.

Vermaseren, M. J. 1960. *Mithra, ce dieu mystérieux*. Paris – Bruxelles, Sequoia.

Tarraco. Town and society in a 2nd–century AD Roman provincial capital

Diana Gorostidi, Ricardo Mar and Joaquín Ruiz de Arbulo

In the forum of the small *Colonia Barcino* in the early second century AD, at least 22 different preserved pedestals were dedicated to L. Licinius Secundus.[1] This simple but exceptional freedman was *accensus* or administrator for the extremely powerful L. Licinius Sura, three-times consul of Rome and a friend of the emperors Trajan and Hadrian. The texts are almost identical: expressions of gratitude for his favours and largesse from the *ordo* and *seviri* of Barcino, the *ordo* of Auso (Vic), the *ordo* of Iamo (Ciutadella on the island of Menorca), and up to four different examples from the *seviri* of Tarraco (IRC IV 83-104). This accumulation of statues dedicated to a single person is rather surprising in a town as small as Barcino, whose urban area covered a mere 12 hectares, most of which was occupied by the large public forum complex and its gigantic temple dedicated to the deified Augustus. The population of Barcino could not have been more than 2,500, but of course some of its most important families could have amassed enormous wealth and prestige.

In comparison, the neighbouring *Colonia Tarraco*, provincial capital of Hispania Citerior, also known, according to the Baetican geographer Pomponius Mela, as Hispania Tarraconensis, was one of the largest towns in Hispania. It was only smaller than Emerita, which covered more than 100 hectares, and was similar in size to Corduba, Hispalis and Clunia, all estimated to have been around 70 hectares (Carreras 1996). However, this was not a particularly impressive size, being only slightly larger than an average Italian town. Pompeii, for example, covered 66 hectares, had a walled area of 3.2 km and a population estimated by different experts to have been between 8,000 and 20,000 (probably closer the upper figure). At the other extreme of urban magnitude, we know that the walls Aurelian built around the city of Rome between 271 and 282 AD were 19 km long and enclosed an area of 1,386 hectares and even so did not include all the 14 urban regions established by Augustus.

Historical demography is a difficult science to apply to the study of ancient societies.[2] In reality, we do not know how many people lived in Rome itself, the *Urbs*, during the different periods of its history. However, thanks to Livy, we do

---
[1] Rodà 1970.
[2] Bellancourt-Valdher and Corvisier eds. 1999.

Figure 1. Plan of the colonia Tarraco with the situation of the main buildings, public complexes and known archaeological remains superimposed on the urban layout of Tarragona (according to Mar, Ruiz de Arbulo, Vivó, Beltran 2012).

know the number of Roman citizens registered on the census over the several centuries of the Republic and also in the three censuses taken by Augustus. We also know exactly how many citizens of Rome went to collect their share of the grain distributed under Caesar and Augustus.[3]

The case of Hispania is no different.[4] The only specific numerical data we have on the population of Roman Hispania throughout its history is Pliny's precise reference to the population of the three *conventus* of north-western Iberia that he visited in person when he was provincial procurator, shortly before the large census in the year 74. There were 240,000 free individuals in the *conventus Asturum*, 166,000 in the *conventus Lucensis* and 285,000 in the *conventus Bracarum*. It is truly unfortunate that Pliny, who even noted the size of *Hispania Citerior* province measured in paces (Plin. *HN*, III, 3, 29), did not transcribe in his book the population data that would also have been available in the public records and that he also no doubt included in some of his innumerable files.

Scholars of ancient demography, such as Pierre Salmon (1974), Carmen García Merino (1974), F. A. Hassan (1981) and J.N. Corvisier (2000),[5] have also compiled the data available for the Roman world. These have been cross-referenced to

---

[3] Pieri 1968; Lo Cascio 2001.
[4] Gozalbes 2007.
[5] Salmon 1974, García Merino 1974, Hassan 1981, Corvisier 2000.

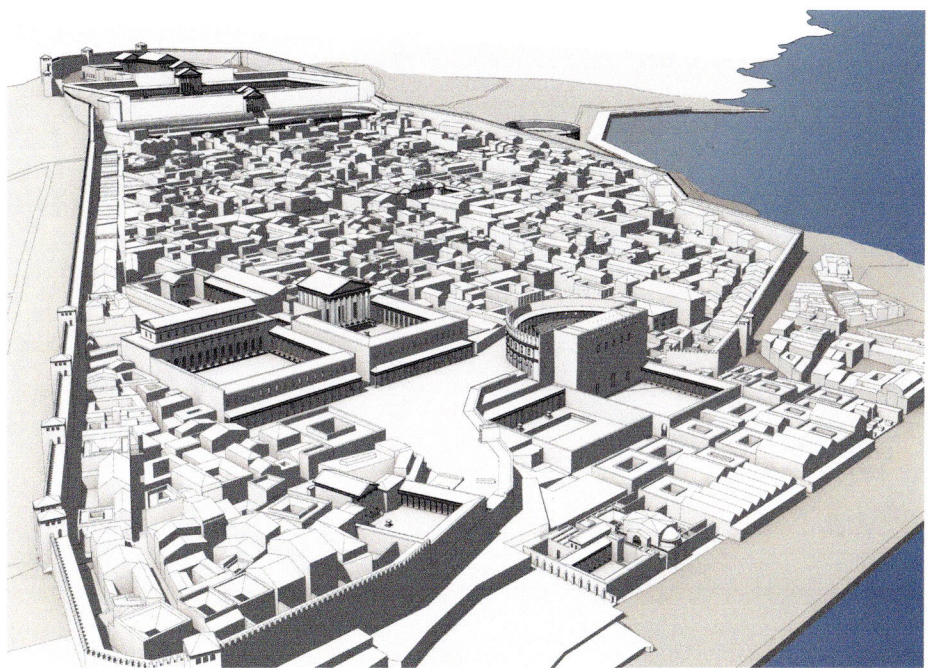

Figure 2. A. Reconstruction of the colonia Tarraco in the second and third centuries AD according to R Mar and A Beltrán.

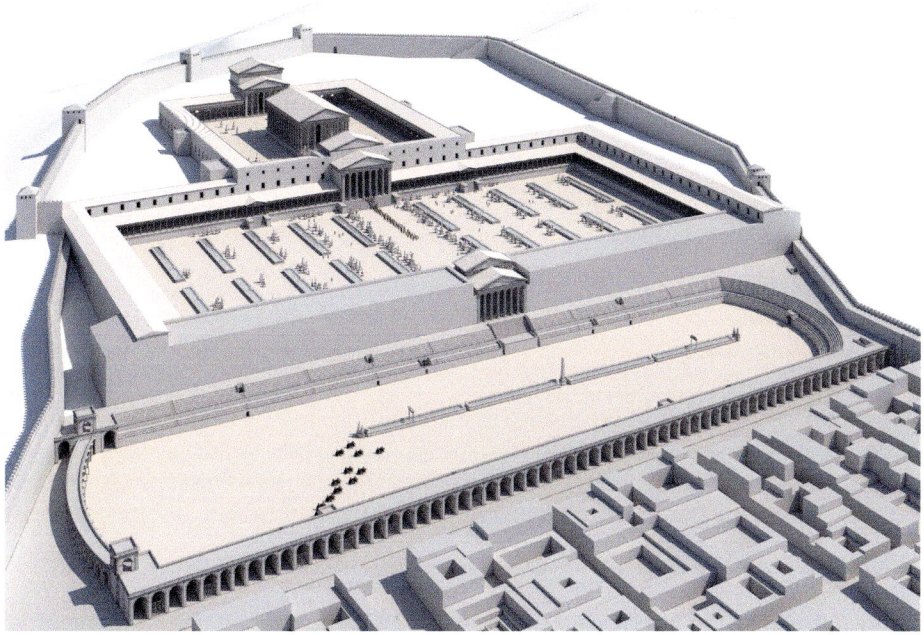

Figure 2. B. Reconstruction of the provincial forum and circus in the second and third centuries AD according to R. Mar and F. Gris.

Figure 3. Honorific pedestal of the provincial flamen C. Fabius Silo (CIL II²/14, 1135. Photo: MNAT.

provide at least approximate population figures, although there is a considerable disparity in criteria when it comes to accepting them and they should be thought of as for 'guidance purposes' only. Overall summaries of Roman social history, such as that of Géza Alföldy (2012),[6] consider that the Roman Empire had more than a thousand large towns and that, in general, the populations of these would have been between 10,000 and 15,000. Only large cities such as Antioch, Alexandria, Carthage and Pergamon would have had populations estimated in the hundreds of thousands. Rome, the *Urbs caput mundi*, may have had a million inhabitants.

But this does not mean that the majority of the possible 50 to 80 million inhabitants of the Roman world lived in the country.[7] The situation was quite the opposite. In fact, a large part of the population of the Roman Empire depended in all aspects of their lives on the nearby towns. In a well organised *Imperium*, these towns acted as administrative, religious, political, social and commercial centres for the populations of the *pagi, vici et villae* scattered across their respective *territoria*. Therefore, we have to be aware that the size of Roman towns should not be the only criterion taken into account when studying their populations. An early Roman town was above all a service centre for its *territorium* and not necessarily a place of habitation. This is the explanation that allows us to understand the huge size of the public buildings in early Roman towns compared to the rest of its urban uses: residential, productive and commercial.

---

[6] Alföldy 2012.
[7] Corvisier 2000.

The area of the *pomerium* in Tarraco during the early Roman period did not reflect the actual size of the inhabited town (nor did it in any other town). We have to take into account, on one hand, the size and density of the suburban port district, the *emporium*, and, on the other hand, the residential neighbourhoods located near the town. Suburban *villae*, workshops, warehouses and *vici* were dotted along the different roads into the town, sharing space with the various necropolises.

Calculating that Tarraco's amphitheatre would have held approximately 14,000 spectators shows us that it was relatively small, if we compare it to the amphitheatre of Nemausus (Nîmes) that held 21,000 or the gigantic Colosseum or Flavian Amphitheatre in Rome, which could accommodate 50,000 people. However, this figure does not help us with the urban population, as it is evident that the audiences for the performances also came from the suburbs and, of course, from the rest of the colonial *territorium*.

Figure 4. Inscription of Staberius Felix (CIL II2/14, 1062). Photo: MNAT.

Even so, the estimated population of Tarraco was calculated by Alberto Balil (1968)[8] at around 16,000 inhabitants. For his part, Simon J. Keay,[9] using F.A. Hassan's (1981) population calculations based on the average number of inhabitants per hectare, places it at between 9,500 and 15,000, while Alföldy follows the opinion of Josep Maria Recasens, calculating a population of 20,000 to 30,000 for Tarraco, in keeping with its importance as a provincial capital. We

---

[8] Balil 1968.
[9] Keay 1981.

repeat that these data can only be considered as a rough guide, a reasonable approximation based on the documentation we currently possess.

The city of Tarragona, together with some of the nearby towns such as Altafulla, Constantí and Roda de Bará, preserve important vestiges from the Roman period. This concentration of monuments makes Tarragona's heritage so exceptional that it was included in UNESCO's World Heritage List in 2001. The buildings of ancient Tarraco represent the universal value of all that a Roman provincial capital signified in antiquity: a symbol of the civic and ideological values of the community of peoples and cultures that came to be the Roman Empire.

Tarraco in the 2nd century AD

Emperor Hadrian visited Tarraco in the winter of 122-123 AD, at a time when the town had reached its full urban development. After centuries of a complex town planning situation, it finally presented a unitary image. The construction of the main public monuments had been completed, the port supported an intensive trading activity and Tarraco was consolidated as the grand capital of one of the most important provinces in the *Imperium*.[10]

For the traveller arriving by sea, Tarraco appeared lofty and dominating. *Hispanae pete Tarraconis arces,* 'reach the citadels of Hispanic Tarraco', was the phrase used by Martial (X, 104) on describing the arrival in Hispania by sea of one of his little books on its journey from Rome to his beloved Bilbilis. In the fourth century AD, the poet Ausonius (XXIII, 12) described the town in a similar way in one of his verses praising his beloved Hispalis and saying that with it they could not compete either with Corduba or 'the powerful citadel of Tarraco' (*Corduba non, non arce potens tibi Tarraco certat*). Paulinus of Nola (XX, 233) also defined the town in the same way in the fourth century AD in one of his letters to Ausonius. He reproached his friend for having only spoken in a letter of Hispanic towns in ruins, failing to mention those that were still active, such as Caesaraugusta, the beautiful Barcino 'and Tarraco, that contemplates the sea from its high rock' (*et capite insigne despectans Tarraco pontum*). These enthusiastic descriptions would have resulted from the visual impact of viewing the monumental urban configuration of Tarraco on its successive monumental terraces from the sea.[11]

But it would be the daily activities of a large metropolis, in other words, the residential and commercial areas and those devoted to artisanal production, that would form the definitive urban image of the town. The basic indicators

---

[10] Ruiz de Arbulo 1993; 1998.
[11] Mar 1993; Ruiz de Arbulo, Mar, Domingo and Fiz 2004.

that allow these formal features to be identified are the layout of the streets with the façades that define them, the drainage and sewage system, the shape and structure of the blocks or plots (*insulae*) delimited by the streets, the system of division into plots that defined the properties within the blocks, and the types of buildings that occupied them. In the case of Tarraco, the study of these categories allows us to clearly differentiate as many as five different urban fabrics, all well to characterise them from a morphological point of view.

The highest part of the Tarraco hill would have presided over the urban landscape of the grand provincial worship area located in the centre of the circuit delimited by the Republican walls. This consisted of the large provincial imperial cult temple surrounded by a sacred porticoed area, a second plaza of huge proportions –the largest known to date in the entire Roman world– and the adjoining circus.[12] The provincial forum must have been a spectacular sight when viewed from the sea, with its summit presided over by the eight white Luni-Carrara marble columns of the grand temple of Augustus, its two large plazas superimposed on terraces at different levels, and the circus at its feet.

The Flavian reforms would have profoundly reconfigured the upper plaza around the large temple of Augustus with new porticos and a large axial hall for ceremonial use. During Hadrian's visit, his biographer in the *Historia Augusta* (HA, *Hadr*. XXII, 3-4) stated that the emperor agreed to pay for the restoration of the temple of Augustus: 'he then left for the *Hispanias* and spent the winter in Tarraco, where at his expense he restored the temple of Augustus, and called all the *Hispanos* to come together in an assembly' (*Post haec Hispania petit et Tarracone hiemavit, ubi sumptu suo aedem Augusti restituit. Omnibus Hispanis Tarraconem in conventum vocatis*).

The iconic cycles of the *divi imperatores* displayed in the provincial forum were no doubt enriched by new images dedicated to the deified Trajan and Hadrian and their respective empresses, Plotina and Sabina. It is probable that the number of additional statues became quite overwhelming. The new provincial flamen, *C. Numisius Modestus* (CIL II^2/14, 1155), a native of Carthago Nova, was specifically appointed by the *concilium pHc* to be 'in charge of the gilded bronze statues of the divine Hadrian' (*electo a concilio provinciae ad statuas aurandas Divi Hadriani*). As would happen in Athens, it is possible to imagine that the towns of the provincial assembly of Hispania Citerior, including the rich conventual capitals, would have made specific statuary offerings to commemorate the Emperor's visit.

---

[12] Mar 1993; Ruiz de Arbulo 2007.

Throughout the second century AD, Tarraco's grand 'plaza of representation' housed the statues of the provincial *flamines* and *flaminicae*, who, at the end of their one-year mandate, were awarded a statue in the plaza recording their merits. Thanks to Géza Alföldy's brilliant epigraphic studies, we know of 75 statues of *flamines* and 12 of *flaminicae* from the Flavian and Antonine dynasties.[13] Other important personages were honoured in the provincial plaza by their communities of origin. They included M. Fabius Paulinus (CIL II²/14, 1026) from Ilerda, who was appointed a knight by Hadrian; his fellow citizens thus wished to express their gratitude for his munificence towards the town, but to erect the statue they would have needed the permission of the province (*loco a prouincia [imp]etratus*). Other expressions on the epigraphs, such as *consensus concili pHc* in the case of a dedication to the *flaminica* Sempronia Placida by her husband, C. Cornelius Valens, (CIL II²/14, 1184) or *consentiente pHc* in a similar case in which the Vaccaean, L. Antonius Modestus, wished to honour his wife, the *flaminica* Paetinia Paterna, a native of Cantabria (CIL II²/14, 1180), clearly refer to the explicit authorisation of the council for the placement of the statues.

The most indicative case regarding the distribution of the statues in the great provincial plaza is from the pedestal of a statue dedicated to C. Valerius Arabinus (CIL II²/14, 1194). Its text first mentions that the *concilium* was paying homage to this person for his care of the provincial census and goes on to specify that his image was placed 'among the statues of the *flamines*', which we should understand as an exceptional honour (*ob curam tabulari / censualis fideliter administr(atam) statuam inter flaminales viros positam*).

Filled to the brim with statuary homages, Tarraco's 'provincial forum' reveals itself as the true *locus celeberrimus* of the province, the grand scenographic centre of the annual Imperial cult festivities, a monumental setting at the service of the judicial tasks of the governor and his *iuridicus* legate and, finally, the archive for the immense amount of documentation generated by the provincial administration and the place where the various provincial taxes were collected.[14]

Soldiers and civil society: the veterans of the VII Gemina legion settled in Tarraco

Tarraco was the site of the provincial *officium*, in which a permanent contingent of men from the *Legio VII* was stationed. They were employed in the tasks of archiving, correspondence, policing, as bodyguards and messengers and

---

[13] Alföldy 1973, 1975, 1981; RIT and CIL II²/14.
[14] Ruiz de Arbulo 2008.

often opted to stay in the town as *veterani* once they had completed their years of service. The official period of active service in the early Roman period was 25 years, although statistical studies of the funerary epigraphs of the soldiers of the VII legion shows the average time served (*stipendium*) to have been around 15.5 years. According to the statistical studies made by Juan José Palao (2006),[15] the life expectancy of a soldier on active service was around forty years and those who had been discharged as veterans lived to 64.5 years.

In the early third century AD, the veteran Q. Caelius Felix celebrated his *honesta missio* having been *commentariensis praesidis pHc*, in other words, head of the provincial archive and the oral judicial sessions of the provincial governor

Figure 5. Pedestal of C. Caecilius Quartus, from Sicca (CIL II²/14, 1050). Photo: CIL/BBAW.

(*praeses*) (CIL II²/14, 836). Fulfilling a promise made on his arrival in Tarraco years earlier as a simple *speculator*, Caelius, together with Jupiter Optimus Maximus, dedicated an altar in the provincial enclosure to the *Genius* of the Legion VII Gemina Pia Felix and to *Fortuna Redux*, the goddess Fortuna 'of the good return'. In this case, it is obvious that our veteran, following his discharge and having made this offering, intended to return to his community of origin. However, this was not the usual case. Normally, having finished their military service, soldiers preferred to stay in the area to which they had become accustomed and in the company of their comrades in arms. Most of them settled near where they had spent their final years of military service. Established in Tarraco with their families, veterans could look for a small farm on the outskirts of the capital

---

[15] Palao 2006.

or seek employment in the speciality they had acquired during their years of active service.

This could be the reason Tarraco has the largest number of epigraphic testimonies of VII Legion veterans in the whole of Hispania. It is followed by Emerita, the other provincial capital, with presence of soldiers in the government *officium*, Asturica Augusta, capital of a *conventus* and seat of the mining procurator from where the main gold mines in north-western Iberia were managed, and in fourth place, the zone of Tritium Magallum, in La Rioja, an important centre for industrial pottery production that attracted a good number of veterans thanks to the high quality of the land and the good communications.

Life in Tarraco for these soldiers was marked by obligations and destinations that distanced them from civil society, strengthening the corporative ties and feelings of brotherhood they maintained after they were discharged and became *veterani*. Many of them had their parents with them, were married or owned properties and slaves in Tarraco. Their tombstones were dedicated by their parents, wives, children, freedmen or slaves who had been liberated in compliance with clauses in wills. In the cases of the *beneficiarii* T. Cornelius (CIL II²/14, 1051) and Valerius Atticus (CIL II²/14, 1057), we know that both lived as guests (*hospites*) in private houses in the town and were buried by their respective matrons. If the soldiers were unmarried, their epitaphs were normally written by their comrades, either because they had been named as heirs (CIL II²/14, 1072) or for corporative or collegial reasons. This was the case, for example, of the *speculator* Q. Annius Aper, who died in Tarraco without making a will (*intestato defuncto*) and whose burial and funerary altar were paid for by seven of his comrades (*collegae eius*) (CIL II²/14, 1043). Other cases are those of the *beneficiarius consularis* of African origin, L. Aufidius Felix, buried by his fellow townsman (*municeps*); the *speculator* Gargilius Rufus of the VII legion (CIL II²/14, 1047); and a soldier from the same legion, *Staberius Felix*, a weapons instructor (*discens armaturae*), who was buried in Tarraco by his comrades, *commilitoni et contubernali*, at the end of the second century AD (CIL II²/14, 1062).

Immigrants in Tarraco: the epigraphic evidence of *Africani*

As a large town and provincial capital, Tarraco was, without doubt, a place in which individuals from all over the province could seek promotion. We know of the presence in the town of important persons from the neighbouring regions and towns, such as Barcino (Barcelona), Ilerda (Lleida), Iluro (Mataró), Sigarra (Prats del Rei) and Auso (Vic), or from more distant Hispanic towns such as Complutum (Alcalá de Henares), Uxama (Burgo de Osma, Soria), Bracara Augusta (Braga, Portugal), Italica (Santiponce, Seville) and Palma (Mallorca, Balearic

Islands). There were also immigrants from Italy, southern Gaul, Aquitania, Narbonensis, Dalmatia, Pannonia, Greece, Asia Minor, Egypt and, above all, North Africa[16].

Among the people documented in the epigraphy of *Tarraco*, Géza Alföldy points out eleven Africans, four of them soldiers, either from the explicit mention of their *origo* or because they had characteristic Roman African names.[17] Among the former, L. Caecilius Porcianus, *ex prov[inc(ia)] Africa*, was admitted to the ranks of the *decuriones* and honoured with a statue for having been an aedile and perhaps also a duumvir (CIL II²/14, 1204). Aufidia Prima, who died in Tarraco and was commemorated by Florentinus (CIL II²/14, 1296), was from Cirta. The husband and wife Valeria Meletina and [---]mmius Saturninus recalled on the funerary epitaph of their monumental sepulchre (CIL II²/14, 1306) that they were both natives of Mauritania Caesarensis. The *beneficiarius* C. Caecilius Quartus (CIL II²/14, 1050) was from Sicca, near Zama. Also of African origin was the young rhetor, Florus, who bequeathed us the only description we have of life in Tarraco at the beginning of the second century AD. Personages such as Firmidius Caecilianus (CIL II²/14, 1052), Gavidius Primulus (CIL II²/14, 1286), Silicius Donatus (CIL II²/14, 1271), Bennius Hermes (CIL II²/14, 1012), Satrius Felix (CIL II²/14, 1316) or the fellow *municipes* Aufidius Felix and Gargilius Rufus (CIL II²/14, 1047) had names that were well attested in Roman Africa.[18]

On the other hand, the logic of this intensity of trading relations was due to the role Tarraco would have played as a redistribution hub for African products destined for the Ebro Valley and inland Iberia. The importance and stability of the maritime route between Carthage and Tarraco also allowed the arrival in the town in the late period of mosaic laying patterns and sarcophaguses from the workshops of Carthage.[19]

The urban society of Tarraco: some given names

The honorary-type statues, funerary epitaphs and votive offerings provide us with an extensive selection of examples from the different social classes present in the *colonia tarraconense*. Thanks to Géza Alföldy's epigraphic studies (RIT, 1993, 2002, 2011, 2013 and CIL II²/14), we know by name more than a thousand inhabitants of the ancient town during the first three centuries of our Era. The inscriptions also show the family relations and obligations of the heirs.

---

[16] For a more exhaustive list, cf. the indices of Volume CIL II²/14, fasc. 4 (2016) (*IX. Geographica*).
[17] Alföldy 2002.
[18] Cf., however, the considerations regarding the *cognomina* said to be 'African' in Le Bohec 2005.
[19] On the presence of African sarcophaguses in the town, cf. Rodà 1990.

Considering as separate the list of provincial *flamines*[20] and soldiers, we know approximately 900 names of Tarraco residents over a period of three centuries, which represents an average of only 90 - 100 names per generation in intervals of 30 years. This figure is clearly insufficient in statistical terms, but the wise epigraphist was able to extract many useful observations from it.[21]

The *nomina* Aemilius, Caecilius, Cornelius, Fabius and Valerius are the most common, with more than 30 mentions, followed by Antonius, Atilius, Clodius, Domitius, Fulvius, Iunius, Licinius, Pompeius, Porcius, Sempronius and Sulpicius. All these are also the most common names in Roman Hispania[22]. Latin names account for 70% of the *cognomina*, compared to 30% Greek names, the latter being of liberated slaves who became freedmen. Among the 112 bearers of Greek *cognomina* in the first and second centuries AD, 54 are expressly cited as slaves, freedmen or *seviri augustales*. The early Romanisation of the town means that very few *cognomina* of Iberian or Celtiberian origin are found during the Imperial period.

Town and territory: Tarraco society in its suburban villas

The territory of the ancient capital of Hispania Citerior was very large compared with other towns in the province and even in comparison to the rest of the provincial capitals. We do not know its exact limits, but it has been calculated to have had an area of some 4,400 km². To the south, it bordered on the *ager Dertosanus* and the *ager Illerdensis* in the area of Montblanc. To the north, it bordered, on the one hand, with the *ager Sigarrensis* and, on the other, towards the east, with the *ager Barcinonensis*, at the point where the Roman bridge of Martorell crosses the River Llobregat, the ancient *Rubricatus*, where the *statio ad fines*, that recalls the ancient itineraries, has been identified.[23]

The Roman epigraphy found in this vast territory is a privileged source of information for our knowledge of the population that occupied, lived in or depended on the numerous villas and rural establishments. The preserved texts have allowed us the locate in the rural area persons known from the town's epigraphy and, thanks to these coincidences, we know that some of them were the owners of the residential villas dispersed throughout the suburbs.[24] Some of these persons have been identified as high-ranking magistrates and civil servants of the *colonia*. Others, however, were small landowners, some of

---

[20] Alföldy 1973.
[21] Alföldy 2002.
[22] For a quick comparison, J. M. Abascal's repertory (1994) continues to be extremely useful.
[23] Alföldy 1990: 50-51.
[24] Gorostidi 2010; Gorostidi *et al.* 2013.

them wealthy freedmen or slaves who may have been looking after the villas or the numerous wine and olive oil exploitations that carpeted the ancient *ager Tarraconensis*.[25]

Given the quantity and quality of most of the preserved inscriptions from the territory, we can state that they mainly illustrate the upper classes of society and, therefore, reflect their privileged status. Their most likely purpose was to be seen by a private sector, close to their owners. However, it should also be highlighted that Roman monumental epigraphy has always had a clear aim of potential public exhibition; in other words, for a possible anonymous spectator from outside the most intimate, restricted circle[26]. This is also evident in the large funerary mausoleums, but is especially true of the honorary pedestals destined to decorate the *pars urbana* of the leisure villas. The idea was to reproduce in the private sphere the aesthetics and iconography of the public recognition found in the monumentalised spaces of the town.[27]

An exceptional case is the large inscription over the Arch of Berà (CIL II²/14, 2332). Following a bequest in the will of L. Licinius Sura, this grand arch was built 14 miles from Tarraco, probably on the spot where the Via Augusta crossed his properties.[28] This person has been identified as an ancestor of the same name from the time of Augustus of the three-times consul, whose freedman and *accensus*, L. Licinius Secundus, to whom we referred in the introduction to this paper, exercised a more than notable influence in the period of Trajan, both in Tarraco and Barcino. The arch was consecrated to Augustus, which shows the penetration in Tarraco of the Augustan precepts for channelling the elites' political propaganda through monumental epigraphy, as well as in the private sphere.[29]

Based on the monumental inscription on the Arch of Berà, we can state that the Augustan period marked the beginning of the presence of epigraphy in the territory that, as in the town, would reach its peak in the late first and early second centuries AD. In the second half of the first century, two senators are documented in their respective villas in the territory. One of them was Senator Q. Gargilius Q. f. Macer Aufidianus, *legatus Augusti iuridicus provinciae Hispaniae citerioris* under the Flavians (CIL II²/14, 982), who lived in the villa with his wife, Apronia L. f. Iusta. The other villa was very close to the Via Augusta and was the

---

[25] Regarding the exploitation of the territory of the ancient *colonia*, cf. the volumes resulting from the ICAC *Ager Tarraconensis* research project.
[26] In this regard, cf. the observations of Donati, Susini 1986.
[27] Gorostidi 2010: 44-46.
[28] Dupré 1993.
[29] Alföldy 1991b.

Figure 6. Reconstruction of Arch de Berà and its inscription according to F. Gris, J. Ruiz de Arbulo and R. Mar.

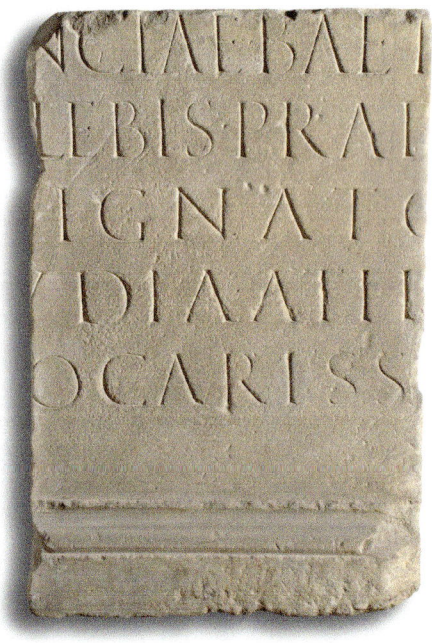

burial place of a young *ignotus*, whose funerary monument was dedicated to him by his wife, Claudia Atiliana (CIL II²/14, 2289), a member of an important Tarraco family. A third senator found in the territory was M. Fabius Priscus, a member of the personal circle of the future Emperor Galba, who appears on a pedestal dedicated to C. Apronius *Secundus*, probably in the villa belonging to the latter, in an area farther from the coast (*CIL* II²/14, 2291).

Figure 7. Monumental inscription of an ignotus senator dedicated by his wife Claudia Atiliana (CIL II²/14, 2289). Photo: MNAT.

Figure 8. Inscription dedicated to the Genius Coloniae by L. Minicius Apronianus (CIL II²/14, 819). Photo: MNAT.

Also documented in the territory are magistrates linked to the colonial administration. The most emblematic case is that of the duumvir C. Valerius Avitus (CIL II²/14, 2308-2309), the owner of the lavish villa of Els Munts during the time of Antoninus Pius,[30] although there were other magistrates of the time who followed the Roman custom according to which illustrious members of the administration had a house in town and a residence for relaxation and leisure on the outskirts. For example, in the period between Hadrian and Antoninus Pius, L. Minicius Apronianus (CIL II²/14, 2293), who held all the posts

Figure 9. Pedestal of the sevir Augustal C. Fulvius Musaeus (CIL II²/14, 2283). Photo: MNAT.

---
[30] Ruiz de Arbulo 2014.

of the municipal *cursus honorum* until he reached the flaminate of the Emperor Trajan, was probably the owner of a villa in the nearby suburb. Similar cases are those of L. Aemilius Sempronius (CIL II²/14, 2305), another magistrate, whose pedestal was also found in a villa on the outskirts, and C. Clodius Aemilianus (CIL II²/14, 2353), from farther away, in the Garraf area, identified in the capital thanks to an honorary inscription discovered in the colonial forum (CIL II²/14, 1015).

The finds have also allowed us to identify private citizens who the prosopography tells us had links with the high political spheres of second-century Tarraco. This is the case of P. Furius Montanus (CIL II²/14, 2248), documented in the central dado of a small tripartite funerary pedestal that reminds us he was the husband of Numisia Victorina, the sister of a provincial flamen. A similar case is that of the Calarii (CIL II²/14, 2260), an otherwise unknown native family who can be associated with the various C. Lutatii, who are better documented in the town (e.g. CIL II²/14, 1055, 1149).

From Flavian times, we also see in various villas important freedmen who had good connections with members of the local aristocracy. A good example is the honorary pedestal of the *sevir Augustal* C. Fulvius Musaeus, a freedman of the important *flaminica* Fulvia Celera (CIL II²/14, 1179), dedicated to him by his wife Sutoria Surilla, who was without doubt the owner of the famous villa of Centecelles in its early Roman phase (CIL II²/14, 2283). Both Musaeus and Surilla are also documented on various pedestals of similar characteristics found in the town, those of the woman dedicated by their own freedmen (CIL II²/14, 1347).

L. Bennius Primigenius was another wealthy freedman who merited a large funerary monument dedicated by his wife, Quintia Procula, near the Via Augusta, on the land of the suburban villa located at Mas Sardà (CIL II²/14, 2290). Primigenius had not held any post nor had any honour that was worthy of recording on his tombstone. However, this family may have been related in some way to the officials of the treasury through one Bennia Venustina located in the town, who was the wife of an *arcarius pHC* (CIL II²/14, 1098)[31].

From the area farthest from the urban centre, in the present-day county of El Penedès, near the *ager Barcinonensis*, we know more names of persons who, if we believe their inscriptions, enjoyed a certain prestige among their fellow citizens, although we have not been able to link them to anybody in the town. This is the case of C. Farronius Quietus, probably of a family from Hasta (*Gallia*

---

[31] In fact, we know of another woman who was the wife of a provincial *arcarius*: Quintilia Procula (CIL II²/14, 1099), who may perhaps have been related to Quintia Procula and Bennius Primigenius.

Figure 10. Monumental inscription of L. Bennius Primigenius (CIL II²/14, 2290). Photo: MNAT.

Cisalpina), who was buried on his own land (CIL II²/14, 2341), and C. Caecilius Inparatus, probably the first owner of the large villa of El Vinyet in Sitges (CIL II²/14, 2355). On the other hand, the enormous size –compared to the average of those found in the territory– of the funerary monument of one Bassus suggests that he also attained considerable social prestige, or at least the financial means to maintain it (CIL II²/14, 2335). The same can be inferred from the remains of the monumental inscription corresponding to the mausoleum of an unknown person found in the area of Castellet i la Gornal castle (Les Massuques) (CIL II²/14, 2350). Both cases document the more than likely presence in the Alt Penedès area of landowners whose wealth was reflected in the size of their funerary monuments.

The epigraphy of the territory also commemorates persons of servile status. This is the case of the funerary inscriptions of two men, both with the formula *hic situs est*: the tombstone of Primus, servant of Cornelia Optata, was dedicated by his children, probably wealthy freedmen, judging by the quality of the piece and the presence of a brief *carmen epigraphicum* (CIL II²/14, 2301). In contrast, the plainer monument to Cladus, a slave belonging to one Lucretius, was dedicated by a woman, Prima, probably his mother (CIL II²/14, 2346). Finally, the large number of fragments of little significance, but of notable quality, attest the continuity of the epigraphic practice in the rural areas and the presence of a population with sufficient means to maintain certain standards of quality throughout the first two centuries of the Empire.

Figure 11. Funerary inscription of Primus, servant of Cornelia Optata (CIL II²/14, 2301). Photo: D. Gorostidi.

The inscriptions discovered and the analysis of their media have allowed us to establish the presence of this aristocracy in the rural environment. Moreover, among the scarce archaeological remains preserved, the finds of prestige epigraphic elements, such as pedestals or monumental funerary epigraphy, allow us to sketch out propaganda scenario outside the town. Some of the persons identified have indications of Italian origins, possibly descendants of the first Roman colonists who settled in the territory and, therefore, importers of an epigraphic praxis that was not only transferred to the public posts, but also found its correspondence in the private sphere and, therefore, in its rural residences.

References

Abascal, J. M. 1994. *Los nombres personales en las inscripciones latinas de Hispania*, Murcia.
Alföldy, G. 1973. *Flamines prouinciae Hispania citerioris*. Anejos de AEspA, 6, Madrid.
Alföldy, G. 1975. *Die römischen Inschriften von Tarraco*, 2 vols., Berlín.
Alföldy, G. 1981. Bildprogramme in den römischen Stadten des Conventus Tarraconensis. Das Zeugnis der Statuenpostamente. *Homenaje a García y Bellido, Revista de la Universidad Complutense de Madrid*, 18-4: 177-277.

Alföldy, G. 1991a. *Tarraco*, Forum, 8, Tarragona. Traducción revisada con actualización bibliográfica de la voz Tarraco, *Paulys Real-Encyclopädie der classischen Altertumswissenschaft*, Suppl. XV, cols. 570-643, Munich, 1978.

Alföldy, G. 1991b. Augusto e le iscrizioni: tradizione ed innovazione. La nascita dell'epigrafia imperiale. *Scienze dell'Antichità*, 5: 573–600.

Alföldy, G. 1993. Tarraco y la Hispania romana, cultos y sociedad. In M. Mayer (ed.), *Religio Deorum. Actas del Coloquio Intern. de epigrafía, culto y sociedad en Occidente* (Tarragona 1992), Sabadell: 7-26.

Alföldy, G. 2000. Wann wurde Tarraco römische Kolonie?. In G. Paci (ed.), *Epigraphai. Miscellanea epigrafica in onore di Lidio Gasperini*, Tívoli: 3-22.

Alföldy, G. 2002. Desde el nacimiento hasta el apogeo de la cultura epigráfica en Tarraco, en: L. Hernández Guerra, L. Sagredo san Eustaquio and J.M. Sainz Solana, (eds.), *Actas del I Congreso Internacional 'La historia antigua hace 2000 años'* (Valladolid 23-25 de Noviembre 2000), Valladolid 2001 [2002]: 61-74.

Alföldy, G. 2007. El ejército romano en Tárraco. In A. Morillo (ed.), *El ejército romano en Hispania. Guía arqueológica*, León: 503-521.

Alföldy, G. 2011. Tausend Jahre epigraphische Kultur im römischen Hispanien: Inschriften, Selbstdarstellung und Sozialordnung. *Lucentum* 30: 187-220.

Alföldy, G. 2012. *Nueva historia social de Roma*, Sevilla.

Alföldy, G. 2013. El Imperio Romano durante los siglos II y III: continuidad y transformaciones. IN J. M. Macias and A. Muñoz (eds.), *Tarraco christiana civitas*, Tarragona: 13-30.

Andrés, F. J. Poderes jurisdiccionales del gobernador provincial en la Hispania de los Antoninos. In L. Hernández (ed.). *Actas del II Congreso Internacional de Historia Antigua. 'La Hispania de los Antoninos (98-180)'* (Valladolid, 2004). Valladolid: Universidad. Secretariado de Publicaciones e Intercambio Editorial, 2005: 11-20.

Aquilué, X., Dupré, X., Massó, J., Ruiz de Arbulo, J. 2000. *Tarraco. Guías del Museu d´Arqueologia de Catalunya*, 2ª Ed., Tarragona.

Arrayas, I. 2005. *Morfología histórica del territorio de Tarraco (ss. III-I aC.)*, Barcelona: Unversidad de Barcelona.

Bejor, G. 1999. Vie Colonnate, paesaggi urbani del mondo antico. *Rivista di Archeologia*, Supplementi 22, Roma.

Bellancourt-Valdher, M., Corvisier, J.N. 1999. *La demographie historique antique*, Arras.

Bringmann, K. 2008. *Augusto*, Barcelona: Ed. Herder.

Caballos, A. 1990. *Los senadores hispano-romanos y la romanización de Hispania (siglos I-III d.C.)*, Sevilla.

Carreras, C. 1996. Una nueva perspectiva para el estudio demográfico de la Hispania romana, *BSAA* 62: 95-12.

CIL II^2/14, 2: Alföldy, G. (ed.) 2011. *Corpus Inscriptionum Latinarum. Pars XIV. Conventus Tarraconensis. Fasc. Secundus. Colonia Iulia Urbs Triumphalis Tarraco*, Berlín: De Gruyter.

CIL II^2/14, 3: Alföldy, G. (ed.) 2012. *Corpus Inscriptionum Latinarum. Pars XIV. Conventus Tarraconensis. Fasc. Tertius. Colonia Iulia Urbs Triumphalis Tarraco*, Berlín: De Gruyter.

CIL II²/14, 4: Alföldy, G. (ed.) 2016. *Corpus Inscriptionum Latinarum. Pars XIV. Conventus Tarraconensis. Fasc. Quartus. Colonia Iulia Urbs Triumphalis Tarraco,* Berlín: De Gruyter.

Corvisier, J.N. 2000. *La population de l'Antiquité Classique,* Paris.

Donati, A., Susini, G. 1986: La scrittura esposta: i modi della scrittura romana. In G.R. Cardona (ed.), *Sulle tracce della scrittura,* Bologna: 65-78.

Dupré 1993. *L'arc romà de Berà (Hispania Citerior),* Roma.

Garcia Merino, C. 1974. *Análisis sobre el estudio de la demografía de la Antigüedad y un nuevo método para la época romana,* Valladolid.

Gorostidi, D. 2010. *Ager Tarraconensis 3. Les inscripcions romanes* (Instrumenta 16), Tarragona.

Gorostidi, D., López Vilar, J., Prevosti, M., Fiz, I. 2013. Propietaris de vil·les de l'*ager Tarraconensis* (meitat occidental del Camp de Tarragona). Proposta per a un catàleg. IN M. Prevosti, J. López Vilar and J. Guitart (eds.), *Ager Tarraconensis 5. Paisatge, poblament, cultura material i historia. Actes del Simposi internacional* (Documenta 16), Tarragona: 401-424.

Gozalbes, E. 2007. La demografía de la Hispania romana, tres décadas después. *HAnt.* 31: 181-208.

Guitart, J., Prevosti, M. (coord.). 2010-2013. *Ager Tarraconensis* (*Instrumenta* 16) (1-5 vol.). Tarragona.

Haensch, R. 1997. *Capita provinciarum. Statthaltersitze und Provinzialverwaltung in der römischen Kaiserzeit.* Mainz am Rhein: P. von Zabern.

Hassan, F.A. 1981. *Demographic archaeology,* Cambridge.

IRC IV: Fabre, G., Mayer, M. y Rodà, I. 1997. *Inscriptions Romaines de Catalogne, IV, Barcino,* París: Diffusion De Boccard.

Koppel, E. M. 1988. *La schola del collegium fabrum de Tarraco y su decoración escultórica,* Faventia Monografies, 7, Bellaterra.

La Torre; G.F. 1988. Gli impianti comerciali ed artiglianali In L. Franchi dell'Orto (ed.), *Pompei. L'informatica al servizio di una citta antica,* Roma: L'Erma di Bretschneider: 75-102.

Le Bohec, Y. 2005. L'onomastique de l'Afrique romaine sous le Haut-Empire et les cognomina dits ' africains '. *Pallas* 68: 217-239.

Le Roux, P. 1982. *L'armée romaine et l'organisation des provinces ibériques d'Auguste à l'invasion de 409 (Publications du Centre Pierre Paris 8).* Paris.

Le Roux, P. 1998. Ejército y sociedad en la Tarraco romana. *Butlleti Arqueologic* 19-20: 83-107.

Lo Cascio, E. 2001. Il census a Roma e la sua evolzuione da eta serviana alla prima età imperiale. *MEFRA* 113: 563-603.

Macías, J.M., FIZ, I. (Dirs.) 2007. *Planimetria Arqueològica de Tàrraco.* Serie Documenta 5 / Atles d'Arqueologia Urbana 2 / Treballs d'Arqueologia Urbana 1. Tarragona: Institut Català d'Arqueologia Clàssica. http://oliba.uoc.edu/icac/llibres/tarraco/.

Mar, R. (ed.). 1993a. *Els monuments provincials de Tàrraco. Noves aportacions al seu coneixement,* Documents d'Arqueologia Clàssica, 1, Tarragona: Univ. Rovira i Virgili.

Mar, R., Pensabene, P. 2009. Financiación de la edilicia pública y cálculo de los costes del material lapídeo. El caso del foro superior de Tarraco. In In J. Lopez and O. Martin (eds.), *Congres Internacional en Homenatge a Th. Hauschild (Tarragona 2009). Butlleti Arqueologic* 3: 345-409.

Mar, R., Pensabene, P. 2010. Il tempio di Augusto a Tarraco. Gigantismo e marmo lunense nei luoghi di culto imperiale in Hispania e Gallia. *Archeologia Classica* 61: 243-307.

Mar, R., Ruiz de Arbulo, J. 2011. Tarragona romana. Republica i Alt Imperi (anys 218 aC- 265 dC), en: *Història de Tarragona*, vol. 1, Lleida: Pagès Ed.: 205-538.

Mar, R., Ruiz de Arbulo, J., Vivó, D. 2010. El foro de la colonia Tarraco entre la República y el Imperio, en: *Simulacra Romae II* (Reims 2008). *Bulletin de la Societé Archeologique Champenoise*, 19, Reimsî; 39-70.

Mar, R., Ruiz de Arbulo, J., Vivó, D. 2011. Las tres fases constructivas del Capitolio de Tarragona. In J. Lopez and O. Martin (eds.), *Congres Internacional en Homenatge a Th. Hauschild (Tarragona 2009). Butlleti Arqueologic* 3: 507-540.

Mar, R., Ruiz de Arbulo, J., Vivó, D., Beltran, A. 2012. *Tarraco. Arqueologia y urbanismo de una capital provincial romana*, Vol. 1, Documents d'Arqueologia Classica, 5, Tarragona: Univ. Rovira i Virgili / Institut Català d'Arqueologia Clàssica.

Mar, R., Ruiz de Arbulo, J., Vivó, D., Beltran, A., GRIS, F. 2015. *Tarraco. Arqueologia y urbanismo de una capital provincial romana*, Vol. 2, Documents d'Arqueologia Classica, 6, Tarragona: Univ. Rovira i Virgili / Institut Català d'Arqueologia Clàssica.

Palao, J.J. 2006. *Legio VII Gemina (Pia) Felix. Estudio de una legión romana*. Salamanca: Ediciones de la Universidad de Salamanca.

Palet, J.M. 2003. Estructuras agrarias en el territorio de Tarraco (Tarragona): organización y dinámica del paisaje en época romana. In A. Bouet, F. Verdin (dirs), *Territoires et paysages de l'Age du Fer au Moyen Âge- Melanges offerts à Ph. Leveau*, Bordeaux : Editions Ausonius : 213-226.

Palet, J.M. 2009. Formes del paisatge i trames centuriades al camp de Tarragona : aproximació a l'estructuració del territori de Tarraco. In J. A. Remola (ed), *El territori de Tarraco: villes romanes del Camp de Tarragona, Forum, 13*, Tarragona: Museu Nacional Arqueologic de Tarragona: 49-64.

Panciera, S. 2000. Netezza urbana a Roma. Organizzazione e responsabili In X. Dupre and J. A. Remola (eds.), *Sordes Urbis. La eliminacion de residuos en la ciudad antigua* (Roma 1996): 95-106.

Pieri, G. 1969. *L'Histoire du Cens jusqu'à la fin de la Repubique romaine*, Paris.

Rankov, B. 1999. The governor's men: the officium consularis in provincial administration. In A. Goldsworth And I. Haynes, I. (eds.). *Roman Army as a community*. Portsmouth (Rhode Island): Journal of Roman Archeology, Supplementari series 34: 15-34.

Remola, J.A. (ed.). 2009. *El territori de Tarraco: vil.les romanes del Camp de Tarragona, Forum, 13*, Tarragona: Museu Nacional Arqueologic de Tarragona.

RIT: Alföldy, G. 1975. *Die römischen Inschriften von Tarraco*, 2 vols., Berlín.

Roda, I. 1970. Lucius Licinius Secundus, liberto de Lucius Licinius Sura. *Pyrenae* 6 : 167-183.

Rodà, I. 1990. Sarcofagi della bottega di Cartagine a Tarraco. *Atti del VII Convegno di Studio sull'Africa Romana* (Sassari 1989), Sassari : 727-736.

Roddaz, J.M., Hurlet, F. 2001. Le gouverneur et l'image du pouvoir imperial. Recherches sur la diffusion de l'ideologie dynastique en Occident su Ier siecle ap.J-C. In C. Evers And A. Tsingarida (ed.). *Rome et ses Provinces. Genèse et diffusion d'une image du pouvoir. Hommages à Jean Charles Balty*. Bruselas: Le Livre Timperman (Lucernae Novantiquae) : 153-166.

Rodriguez Neila, J.F., Navarro, F.J. 1999. *Elites y promoción social en la Hispania romana*, Pamplona: Eunsa Ed.

Ruiz de Arbulo, J. 1993. Edificios públicos, poder imperial y evolución de la élites urbanas en Tárraco, (s. II - IV d.C.), en: *Ciudad y comunidad civica en Hispania (s. II-III d.C.)*, (Madrid 1990), Madrid: Casa de Velazquez / CSIC: 93-114.

Ruiz de Arbulo, J. 1998. Tárraco. Escenografía del poder, administración y justicia en una capital provincial romana (s. II aC- II dC). *Empúries* 51: 31-61.

Ruiz de Arbulo, J. 2000 (ed). *Tarraco 99. Arqueología de una capital provincial romana* (Tarragona 1999), Tarragona.

Ruiz de Arbulo, J. 2002. La fundación de la colonia Tárraco y los estandartes de César, en: J. L. Jimenez and A. Ribera (coords.), *Valencia y las primeras ciudades romanas de Hispania*, Valencia: 137-156.

Ruiz de Arbulo, J. 2007. Las murallas de Tarraco de la República al Bajo Imperio. In A. Rodriguez Colmenero and I. Roda (eds.), *Murallas de ciudades romanas del Occidente del Imperio. Lucus Augusti como paradigma*, Lugo: Diputación Provincial: 567-592.

Ruiz de Arbulo, J. 2007. Bauliche Inszenierung und literarische Stilisierung: das Provinzialforum von Tarraco. In S. Panzram (ed.). *Städte im Wandel* (Hamburg 2005). Munster: LIT Verlag: 149-212. Trad. Castellana: Nuevas cuestiones en torno al foro provincial de Tarraco. *Butlleti Arqueologic*, Ep. V. 29, Tarragona, 2008: 4-66.

Ruiz de Arbulo, J. 2008. La legio Martia i la fundació de la colonia Tarraco, en: *Tarraco. Pedra a Pedra*, Catál. Expos.. Tarragona. MNAT: 36-56.

Ruiz de Arbulo, J. 2009a. El altar y el templo de Augusto en la colonia Tarraco. Estado de la cuestión. In J. M. Noguera (ed.), *Fora Hispaniae. Paisaje urbano, arquitectura, programas decorativos y culto imperial en los foros de las ciudades hispano-romanas* (Lorca 2002), Murcia: 155-190.

Ruiz de Arbulo, J. 2012. La dedicatoria a Mars campester del centurión T. Aurelius decimus y el campus de la guarnición imeprial de tarraco en el siglo II d.C. Algunas reflexiones sobre la topografía militar de la capital provincial. *CuPAUAM* 37: 499-515.

Ruiz de Arbulo, J. 2014. El *signaculum* de *Caius Valerius Avitus*, duoviro de *Tarraco* y propietario de la villa de Els Munts (Altafulla). *Pyrenae* 45: 125-151.

Ruiz de Arbulo, J., Mar, R. Domingo, J., Fiz, I. 2004. Etapas y elementos de la decoración arquitectónica en el desarrollo monumental de la ciudad de Tarraco. In *La Decoración Arquitectónica en las ciudades romanas de Occidente* (Cartagena 2003), Murcia: 115-152.

Salmon, P. 1974. *Population et dépopulation dans l'Empire Romain*, Col. Latomus, 137, Bruselas.

Taller Escola d'Arqueologia (TED'A) 1987. *Els enterraments del Parc de la Ciutat i la problemàtica funeraria de Tarraco.* Tarragona.

Taller Escola d'Arqueologia (TED'A) 1989. *Un abocador del segle V dC en el fòrum provincial de Tarraco*, Tarragona.

Taller Escola d'Arqueologia (TED'A) 1990. *L'Amfiteatre Romà de Tarragona. La basílica visigòtica i l'església romànica.* Tarragona.

Tarraco i l'aigua 2005. Tarragona: Museu Nacional Arqueològic de Tarragona.

Tarraco. Capitale de l'Hispania citerior 2006. Toulouse: Musée Saint-Raymond.

Tarraco pedra a pedra 2009. Tarragona: Museu Nacional Arqueològic de Tarragona.

Soldiers and their monuments for posterity: manifestations of martial identity in the funerary iconography of Roman Dacia

Monica Gui, Dávid Petruț

Most of the studies concerned with the funerary monuments from Roman Dacia were centred on matters of style and typology, with the ultimate purpose of establishing the provenance of certain iconographic models and discerning local workshops.[1] Whenever iconography was discussed in depth, the emphasis was placed either on the ethnic origin of the deceased, or on tracing elements connected to specific cults. Recent works in this field of study, some of which will be cited below, bring valuable information regarding the preference of military men from various places for a certain type of monument or motif. However, their scope is usually limited to a site or a small number of sites, or refers to specific kinds of monuments. Our approach intends to be complementary, as the focus is reversed: starting from a distinct segment of the provincial population, i.e. the soldiery, we will attempt to outline its manifestations in the field of funerary iconography. This will be done within the limits enforced by the sparse nature of the evidence and by the publication of the material. Accordingly, we will turn our attention to the provinces of Dacia Porolissensis and Superior. Although due to space limitations the present study cannot be exhaustive, hopefully it will provide an overview of how this very well-defined socio-professional group from Dacia looked upon itself and projected its identity through the funerary monuments of choice.

At the level of the entire Empire, one can notice right away the great variety encountered amongst the soldiers' funerary representations, a fact determined by chronological, cultural and geographic or local factors.[2] Generally, the picture derived from preserved 1st century AD monuments is that of a more 'warlike' army: the men were featured in full battle gear, sometimes involved in standard fighting scenes, although this is also seen in later centuries. However, especially during the 3rd century, military men were mostly depicted in 'camp' dress, displaying just a bare minimum of elements (nonetheless significant) that

---

[1] Țeposu Marinescu 1982 remains one of the most geographically comprehensive studies of this sort.
[2] Coulston 2007; see also Coulston 2014.

could identify them as soldiers, such as the sword, belt, baldric or cloak.[3] The message is clear in these two situations (i.e. status display), but less so when it comes to symbolic representations that do not include explicit martial elements, although they appear to be characteristic for the military (e.g. funerary banquet scenes, a specific type of garment like the *paenula* etc.). There are a number of potential causes for these gradual shifts: perhaps veterans wished to be seen as more peaceful; maybe active soldiers and veterans alike wanted to be regarded foremost as Roman citizens and family men.[4] This, in turn, can be linked to the overall transformation of the army at a moment in time when it became more stationary and the military more integrated into the provincial society.

Returning to Dacia, the number of active military personnel and veterans must have been high and a somewhat proportional representation within the funerary figural *corpus* was to be expected. However, in many cases of surviving monuments the figural component is divorced from its original epigraph, resulting in uncertainties concerning the identity of the persons they illustrate. Furthermore, iconographic elements that undoubtedly point to a military identity appear tobe underrepresented when compared to the ratio of soldiers in the provincial society. The purpose of this paper is to draw attention to a significant number of definite or possible representations associated to active or retired soldiers. The underlying assumption is that, to a certain degree, they reflect the social and professional category of those who commissioned them and were not solely determined by what the local workshops had on offer. The investigation aims to uncoverthe themes and motifs preferred by the military and the reasons behind them, and thus to determine if there is a noticeable common representational 'language'. If so, then the iconographic *corpus* can be further refined, including information that goes beyond the purely descriptive and typological, and the attestations of soldiers can also be increased. For this purpose, the available material was divided into six more or less clear-cut figural categories which will be detailed and exemplified in what follows. These categories are mainly based on the strength and range of martial identifiers and will be discussed, wherever possible, in the wider context of funerary military iconography.

Cuirassed representations

As mentioned above, there are just a handful of funerary reliefs and statues of armoured soldiers in the province; indeed, throughout the empire their numbers have declined drastically following the end of the 1st century AD, being mostly replaced by un-armoured representations. Among this category,

---

[3] Speidel 2009: 235–239.
[4] Speidel 2009: 237.

the so-called cuirassed statues probably represent the most conspicuous cases displaying the grandeur of the parade armour together with its accessories. H. Devijver has argued that a vast number of reliefs and statues depicting standing soldiers in a parade posture and armoured in breastplate (*thorax*; *lorica*), *pteruges* and long cloak (*paludamentum*) belonged to the funerary monuments of equestrian rank officers who have performed certain stages of the *militia equestris*. Accordingly, each *militia* was represented by a specific set of insignia: members of the first militia (usually *praefecti cohortes*) were featured in an undecorated cuirass, *pteruges* and cloak, lacking any additional attributes; the second militia (legionary tribunes) additionally displayed the *parazonium*, the officer's long dagger, while members of the third militia (*praefectialae*) and possibly also the *a militiis* displayed the officer's sash, the *cinctorium,* as well, tied around their breastplate between the abdomen and the chest.[5] Although one might argue that they cannot be viewed as soldierly representations in a strict sense, but rather as symbolic manifestations of a social élite,[6] the fact that the members of the equestrian order were commemorated in this way, directly alluding to their former military career,[7] should mean that we can view them as *de facto* military representations. The evidence so far indicates that cuirassed representations, statues and statuesque reliefs were restricted to the upper echelons of Roman society, specifically the equestrian order and indeed the emperor. While this seems to be generally true, some counterexamples did in fact emerge, as is the case with a legionary centurion commemorated with a cuirassed relief in Britain during the mid-1st century AD, namely M. Favonius Facilis of the *legio XX*.[8]

With regard to the material from Roman Dacia, a detailed discussion concerning the iconography and its wider symbolic implications, especially in terms of the expression of certain ranks within the militia is to be found in a relatively recent comprehensive analysis by A. Diaconescu[9] rendering such an enquiry unnecessary here. The corpus of cuirassed statues in the province comprises a series of marble statues from Apulum and Ulpia Traiana Sarmizegetusa. Although the possibility that we might be dealing with imperial representations has initially arisen– especially in the case of a high quality and well preserved piece from Apulum (Figure 1) associated with the figure of Emperor Pertinax– this assertion was later dismissed by Diaconescu[10] and Noelke,[11] who saw in

[5] Devijver 1989: 444–446.
[6] Diaconescu 2012: 146
[7] Devijver 1989: 422
[8] Phillips 1975: 102–105, plate IX.
[9] Diaconescu 2012.
[10] Diaconescu 2005; 2012.
[11] Noelke 2012.

Figure 1. Cuirassed marble statue of an equestrian officer from Apulum, kept at the National Museum of Unification, Alba Iulia (photo: http://www.ubi-erat-lupa.org/monument.php?id=19304).

them the funerary statues erected for persons of equestrian rank. Belonging originally to complex funerary monuments, these statues are disassociated from their accompanying epitaphs, hindering their unequivocal identification as products of funerary sculpture. The number of such statues in Dacia is quite low: in total, five pieces are accounted for at the moment, the majority coming from Apulum,[12] the most important military centre of the province, reuniting probably a considerable number of equestrian rank officers. Only one such statue was discovered outside the aforementioned city, in Ulpia Traiana Sarmizegetusa.[13]

One quite surprising case is that of the funerary relief belonging to an *aedicula* from Brâncovenești,[14] which features a very similar representation with the abovementioned statues (Figure 2). The statuesque representation displays an individual wearing a thick cloak fastened on his right shoulder with a T-shaped brooch, covering completely his left shoulder and partially

---

[12] Diaconescu 2012: cat. M 28–30; Lupa 23326.
[13] Diaconescu 2012: cat. M 20.
[14] Diaconescu 2012: 151; Petruț 2015.

Figure 2. Funerary relief (aedicula hind wall) containing the cuirassed representation of an equestrian (?) officer from Brâncovenești, kept at the Mureș County Museum, Târgu-Mureș (photo: D. Petruț).

his torso while hanging down from his left hand. The cloak in question can most likely be identified with a *sagum*, although the possibility that we might be dealing with a *paludamentum* cannot be ruled out entirely given the variety of ways this garment was represented on statues: most often around the shoulders (as in this case) or lying casually over one shoulder. The parade posture is clear from the raised right hand and the left hand resting on the grip of the sword with an elaborately rendered pommel in the shape of an eagle's head. Based on analogies the weapon might either be a *parazonium* or a *spatha* worn by cavalrymen as part of their gala equipment.[15] The weapon is fastened on a wide baldric (*balteus*) further suggesting that we are dealing with a *spatha*.[16] Probably the most conspicuous element is found on the breastplate of the soldier in the area of the abdomen and is most likely a rather poor attempt of rendering a double *cinctorium* with its upper strap missing from the depiction, typical for cavalry prefects.[17] A comparison with the funerary relief of T. Flavius Mikkalus from Perinthos in Thrace[18] may indicate that in fact a double *cinctorium* was intended for the relief from Brâncovenești. Furthermore, *pteruges* appear to be represented on the right shoulder. All facts appear to indicate that the

---

[15] Speidel 1994b: 106–107.
[16] Fischer 2012: 193.
[17] Diaconescu 2005: 412.
[18] Devijver 1989: 436, fig. 9.

individual is wearing a muscle cuirass, although some features which are normally consistent with cuirassed representations cannot be accounted for, e.g. the lack of anatomic features on the breastplate, which prompted Diaconescu[19] to consider the possibility of a leather cuirass. It is also important to point out that the officer is portrayed with the shortened form of the breastplate worn usually by cavalrymen, also encountered on the abovementioned cuirassed statue from Ulpia Traiana Sarmizegetusa (Figure 3). In fact, further analogies with the respective statue can be invoked, as apart from the short breastplate and the double *cinctorium*, both display similar eagle-head swords, suggesting that we might be dealing with officers of the same rank.[20] Considering that the garrison of the fort from Brâncovenești comprised of the *ala I Numeri Illyricorum*, the representation of a cavalry prefect would make sense, although the nature of the monument could also point to a cenotaph or a funerary monument erected by one of the prefect's freedmen.

Figure 3. Marble cuirassed statue of an equestrian officer from Ulpia Traiana Sarmizegetusa, kept at the Museum of Dacian and Roman Civilization, Deva (photo: Al. Diaconescu).

A further case somewhat connected to this category is a relief from Napoca[21] featuring a young man in 'heroic nudity', with a *paludamentum* and a *parazonium*. Based on analogies, also highlighted by Devijver,[22] Diaconescu[23] considered

---

[19] Diaconescu 2012: 151.
[20] Petruț 2015.
[21] Lupa 15344.
[22] Devijver 1989: 429.
[23] Diaconescu 2005: 414; 2012: 152–153.

this to be the representation of a young equestrian officer passed away during military service in the *militiae*.

Soldiers in battle gear

Evidently, soldiers in full battle gear are easy to identify. However, this type of imagery is rare in Dacia, possibly because, among other reasons, the majority of the material dates from a time when it was no longer fashionable for soldiers to be represented as such. The most notable exception is the probably funerary high-relief from Apulum dated to the Severan period that depicts a legionnaire (Figure 4).[24] The soldier is gripping a sword in one hand and a curved rectangular shield with a *gorgoneion* boss in the other. He is equipped with *manica* and segmental armour also combined with scales in

Figure 4. Funerary relief of a legionary soldier from Apulum, kept at the National Museum of Unification, Alba Iulia (photo: M. Gui).

the shoulder area, the so-called Alba-Iulia type of '*lorica segmentata*' seen only on the monument in question.[25] Although this kind of armour has not been archaeologically identified so far, it is quite specific, making it hard to believe that it was just the figment of the craftsman's imagination.

Another rather peculiar piece is an altar from Transylvania kept in Cluj-Napoca, said to represent a soldier (Figure 5).[26] The frontal personage is dressed with a short-sleeved tunic apparently ending with *pteruges*, but this has to be a simplification of the intended costume and we must also take into account the possibility that some elements could have been only painted. Turning to

---

[24] Diaconescu 2012: 185, cat. M 38, fig. 38 = Lupa 19233.
[25] Bishop 1999: 33–37.
[26] Țeposu Marinescu 1982: 165, no. A 21, pl. XX = Lupa 12379.

Figure 5. Funerary altar from Transylvania, kept at the National History Museum of Transylvania, Cluj-Napoca (photo: S. Odenie).

the equipment, the man is wearing a somewhat curious helmet and holding a pair of lances in his right hand, while with his left he appears to be making an offering on a small altar. Furthermore, he is carrying a sword on a narrow baldric. Notwithstanding the crude artistic execution, one can notice that the man's *balteus* does not seem to be the usual 3rd century broad type used in conjunction with the *spatha,* and the rest of his attire also suggests a rather earlier date. Except for the offering gesture, the man strikes a pose quite typical for soldier representations.[27] However, we cannot completely rule out the possibility of it actually depicting a martial deity, similar, for instance, to the Mars in full panoply figured on an altar from Housesteads.[28] At any rate, the attire and posture of the individual from Dacia does liken him to the series of standing soldier monuments.

Apart from these, we only know of two other representations of equipped soldiers, ready for battle,

---

[27] Ubl 2013: Kat. Nr. 4, Taf. 2/6, 7 = Lupa 2706 – 1st century; Kat. Nr. 6, Taf. 3/11= Lupa 3598; Kat. Nr. 91, Taf. 32/127 – 3rd century = Lupa 3844

[28] RIB I1596; for some examples of deities wearing contemporary military equipment, see Coulston 2014: 72–73.

both found at Apulum. Since they present cavalrymen, the monuments will be discussed in the next section of our paper.

Riders

The rider in his many variants is a frequently encountered theme in the funerary repertoire of Dacia Porolissensis and Superior,[29] appearing on numerous *stelae* and *aediculae* walls, but the question that arises is how many of these riders can be safely equated with the self-image of cavalry soldiers? A few figured monuments preserved together with their epigraphic field can point to the type of imagery employed by mounted soldiers and thus aid in the possible identification of further such monuments even when missing an inscription. Sadly, most of the complete examples disappeared and survive only in the form of sketchy illustrations or notes.

One notable monument is the complete *stela* of a *duplicarius al(a)e (milliariae)* from Sutoru: in the upper field, above the inscription, a clumsily rendered male figure (*calo*) is holding the reins of the two horses flanking him (Figure 6).[30] Based on this, and on

Figure 6. Funerary stela of a duplicarius from Sutoru, kept at the National History Museum of Transylvania, Cluj-Napoca (photo: S. Odenie).

---

[29] Nemeti and Nemeti 2014: 241–244.
[30] CIL III 7644; Țeposu Marinescu 1982: 129, S no. 112, pl. XI = Lupa 12307.

numerous complete monuments presenting similar images[31] there is no doubt that the fragmentary *aedicule* lateral wall from Gherla illustrating on one side the very same scene[32] belonged to a *duplicarius*or *sesquiplicarius*, probably from the resident *ala II Pannoniorum*, as these ranks were entitled to a pair of war horses and they frequently illustrate their superior status in this manner. It is noteworthy that the same scene appears on two different types of monuments. There are records of other cavalrymen's *stelae* depicting a rider in various stances above the inscription. Monuments of this kind surfaced in places like Ilișua,[33] Gherla[34] or Apulum[35] but today they are lost and further information is unavailable. On *stelae,* the rider can also appear beneath the inscription, as on a lost example from Micia[36] or on a fragmentary piece from Apulum.[37] Many horsemen's *stelae* of various types, with the rider as the main image above or below the inscription, usually (but not always) illustrating the 'triumphant rider', are known from across the Empire and date from the 1st to the 4th centuries AD.[38] However, they are much less common in the Danube regions and in the East, where the armed rider appears more often only as a secondary image.[39]

A richly decorated *stela* from Gherla, intended for an *imaginifer* of the aforementioned *ala*, displays two registers above the inscription: in the upper one a couple of busts, male and female, are rendered in a medallion niche, while in the lower one, a saddled horse carrying two spears and a shield stands beside a peacock.[40] This goes to show that even though the rider and his mount are not the central focus of the monument, they can be inserted among other representations, as an indication of the deceased's profession. Thus, a *stel a*from Gilău with a funerary banquet scene in the upper register and a horseman together with an individual holding a spear in the lower one (Figure 7),[41] although different in details, appears similar in intent and should likely be attributed to a cavalryman, probably from the *ala Siliana* garrisoned there.

---

[31] Ubl 2013: Kat. nos. 63–66, Taff. 24–25/90–96; Speidel 1994a: 131–132, no. 14; 285–286, no. 524; 513, no. 570.
[32] Țeposu Marinescu 1982: 204, AE no. 27, pl. XXXIX = Lupa 12536
[33] CIL III 800–802 = Gaiu and Zăgreanu 2011: 85–86, nos. I.3.b.10–12, pl. VIII.
[34] Zăgreanu 2014: 145, gr. S23, pl. IV.
[35] CIL III 1200 = IDR III/5 2, 601 = Lupa 11663.
[36] CIL III 1381 = IDR III/3, 169 = Ciongradi 2007, 196, S/M 20, Taf. 39.
[37] IDR III/5-2, 632 = Țeposu Marinescu 1982: 148, no. S 195 = Ciongradi 2007, 161, S/A 12, Taf. 39 = Lupa 13028.
[38] Schleiermacher 1984.
[39] Schleiermacher 1984: 51.
[40] Zăgreanu 2014: 139–140, Gr.S1, pl. I = Lupa 11349.
[41] Țeposu Marinescu 1982: 128–129, S no. 109, pl. X = Lupa12393.

Figure 7. Funerary stela from Gilău, kept at the National History Museum of Transylvania, Cluj-Napoca (photo: S. Odenie).

The type of monument on which horsemen are illustrated most frequently appears to be the *aedicule* with multiple registers, but, unlike some of the *stelae* mentioned above, the *aedicule* walls bear no textual indication about the identity of the deceased. Nevertheless, a few are more informative. For instance, the early 2nd century piece from Șeica Mică is regarded as an example of merger between two iconographic types.[42] The upper register is occupied by a rider, while the lower two display agricultural and domestic activities. The horseman's posture, the fallen enemy trampled by the horse, all point to the 'triumphant rider', whereas the fluttering cloak and the lack of any military equipment other than the spear resemble the man to the *heros* rider. Such imagery seems rather specific to a military mind-set and there is little doubt that the monument belonged to a

---

[42] Țeposu Marinescu 1982: 214, AE no. 74, pl. XXXVIII; Schleiermacher 1984: 54, 328, Kat. 115; Bianchi 2015: 174–178, Fig, 8; Lupa15085.

cavalryman. Apparently, this iconographic type is also exhibited by an *aedicula* wall from Cristeşti and a *stela* from Târnăveni.[43] However, the pieces are so worn and badly illustrated, that a hunting scene also seems plausible, such as the one seen on a fragmentary *aedicula* from Micia.[44] But even in this case a military connection should not be ruled out. An *aedicula* wall from Sângătin[45] featuring a hunting scene is considered by L. Bianchi[46] as an instance in which a former cavalryman intended to be immortalised in a loftier stance. He is betrayed by the pair of javelins carried by his horse. In fact, M. P. Speidel has pointed out that the hunting theme is frequently employed by the *equites singulars* in Rome to epitomise their *virtus* and skills, so it proves to be a popular theme amongst the Danubian armies.[47] A. Busch goes even further, convincingly challenging the idea that the 3rd century boar hunting scenes appearing on the monuments of the *equites singulares* derive directly from Thracian models.[48]

There is quite a number of other walls or fragments originating from Dacia Porolissensis and Superior featuring plain, less personalised riders, most, though not all, unarmed and simply standing. Most were found at Apulum,[49] Gherla, Sutoru and Gilău,[50] but examples are also known at Potaissa, Napoca, Porolissum,[51] Şoimeni,[52] Sarmizegetusa or Micia.[53] These are the most problematic, their fragmentary state making them hard to interpret. To take an example, in her work centred on the Roman cavalrymen's funerary monuments of the 'triumphant rider' type, M. Schleiermacher excluded those illustrating hunters and 'Thracian' riders, as these reflected the image of the *heros*. The rider-hero does not have mandatory military implications, even though some cavalry soldiers, especially from the Danubian provinces, did choose the theme for their gravestones, modelled on the Thracian rider's iconography.[54] However, this reasoning does not necessarily apply to Dacia Porolissensis and Superior, where numerous mounted or half-mounted troops were garrisoned. As mentioned in the previous paragraph, some images like the boar hunting,

---

[43] Nemeti and Nemeti 2014: 242, note 9.
[44] Ţeposu Marinescu 1982: 209, AE no. 51, pl. XL; Ciongradi 2007: 221, Ae/M11, Taf. 76; Lupa15088.
[45] Lupa 17356.
[46] Bianchi 2015: 178.
[47] Speidel 1965:81–82; see also Busch 2011: 133–134; Speidel 2009: 236.
[48] Busch 2011, 133.
[49] Ciongradi 2007: 161, S/A 11, Taf. 39, 184, S/A 89, Taf. 57, 185, S/A 96, Taf. 58, 215, Ae/A 3, Taf. 77; = Lupa 13044, 19235, 19431, 11358.
[50] Nemeti and Nemeti 2014: 252–253, nos. 13, 14, 16, 17, pl. I/6, II/6, III/2, II/1; 250–251, nos. 7–8, 10, pl. I/1–3; 249–250, nos. 4, 6, Pl. II/2, I/4 = Lupa 12537, 12538, 12284, 12317.
[51] Nemeti and Nemeti 2014: 248–249, nos.1–2, pl. III/1, 3; 254, no. 18, pl. I/5.
[52] Nemeti and Marcu 2014: pl. I-II.
[53] Ciongradi 2007: 214 Ae/S 3, Taf. 80; 223 Ae/M 20, Taf. 79 = Lupa 18558, 15074.
[54] Schleiermacher 1984: 51–59.

although apparently evoking the Thracian rider, have in fact strong military associations. Furthermore, the rider monuments, including those rendering men simply standing, tend to cluster in places where cavalry troops were stationed.[55] Consequently, although not all of the funerary monuments from Dacia Porolissensis and Superior depicting a rider unquestionably reference a mounted soldier, there are fairly good chances that in fact they do so, even if the man appears in a more peaceful stance and irrespective of the origin and initial meaning of the motif. Indeed, for horsemen it was particularly important to be recognised as such, given their superior status and prestige compared to the infantry.[56]

The relatively large number of monuments and fragments from this category appearing at Apulum can be linked either to the *equites legionis XIII Geminae* and officers, or to the governor's mounted guards, since, apart from the legionary fortress, the large and complex site also housed the *praetorium* of the consular governor of the three Dacian provinces. Two further figured fragments from Alba county undoubtedly illustrate cavalrymen, because both characters are fully equipped for battle, a rare sight in the funerary iconography of Roman Dacia. The first, found at rural Răhău, wears a 'parade' helmet with a high crest and a sword. He also carries a pair of javelins and appears to be dressed in scale armour.[57] The second was found in a funerary context from Apulum and was summarily described as a typical *heros* (Figure 8).[58] However, this rider is armed, equipped, and engaged in battle, but he is neither *heros*, nor 'triumphant rider'. His enemy has not fallen under the horse, but is attacking from behind with a weapon (sword? spear?), forcing the horseman to turn backwards, away from the galloping direction, counter-attacking with his spear and defending himself with a small round shield. Thus, it becomes a rather dynamic composition. The details are also significant. For instance, one can notice the multiple, decorative straps included in the harness and such multi-straps (more or less skilfully executed) appear on other examples from Dacia and from elsewhere. The most striking, however, is the soldier's helmet, which can be tentatively identified as a helmet of the Heddernheim - G type, used by both cavalry and infantry during the 3rd century, characterised by the raised crest, the lack of mobile cheek pieces and mask, and by the way the face-piece leaves open a T-shaped slot.[59] Although the representation is of much lesser quality, the same type of helmet is probably represented on the previously discussed monument as well. According to H. Ubl, the only funerary representation of a soldier wearing

---

[55] Nemeti and Nemeti 2014: 248.
[56] Coulston 2007: 546–547; Speidel 2009: 236.
[57] Miles 1997, 15, no. 68, Pl. I/68 = Lupa 19236.
[58] Moga 2008: 478–480, no. 3, fig. 3 = Lupa 19234.
[59] Robinson 1975: 128–129, figs. 376–383.

128 Social Interactions and Status Markers in the Roman World

Figure 8. Funerary relief from Apulum, kept in the National Museum of Unification, Alba Iulia (photo: http://www.ubi-erat-lupa.org/monument.php?id=19234).

a Heddernheim helmet is that seen on a mid-3rd century sarcophagus of a legionary centurion from Brigetio,[60] but the list should now be supplemented with the two from Alba.

Soldiers in camp dress

Especially during the 3rd century AD, but even before this period, many soldiers chose to be represented in a less combative attitude, leaving out the armour. However, they retained a limited number of pieces of equipment that would make their profession obvious for the onlooker. The main and most important difference between a soldier wearing the 'camp' attire and a civilian

---

[60] CIL III 4315 = Lupa 3243; Ubl 2013: 21–22, Kat. 37, Taf. 14/53.

is that the former carries a sword and the appropriate sword belt, either a waist belt – *cingulum,* or a baldric – *balteus,* dress item which thus gains a symbolic value.[61] An example of this kind from Dacia is the centurion represented on a funerary block from Micia dated after the middle of the 2nd century AD.[62] The man wearing a belted tunic and a cloak fastened with a circular brooch on the right shoulder is holding a *volume* in his left hand and a *vitis* in his right, the last element clearly pointing to his rank. The fact that he is a soldier is further stressed by the specific sword he is carrying.

Starting with the 3rd century, military men begin to be depicted with a broad belt with circular fastener, the *Ringschnallen cingulum*, whilst the long sword was now hung on an equally broad baldric.[63] The ring-buckle became a signifier for the soldiery, being worn by cavalry and infantry alike. However, most of the figured pieces bearing an inscription belong to legionnaires and praetorians and the 'ring-buckle monuments', although spread throughout the Empire, tend to concentrate in the Middle Danube area and in Rome, undoubtedly connected to the Illyrian armies.[64] Such a *stela* from Rome, for instance, was set up for a praetorian originating from Dacia.[65] Despite the fact that the iconographic evidence from this province is rather limited, it is not without importance. From the two major cities of the province, Apulum and Ulpia Traiana Sarmizegetusa, there are a total of four funerary statues and one relief illustrating soldiers wearing baldrics and tunics belted with *Ringschnallen cingula*, all dating from the Severan period to the middle of the 3rd century. The pair of statues from Sarmizegetusa is of a lesser quality and not so well preserved[66] and the relief from Apulum is worn down.[67] However, the two nearly life-size marble statues from Apulum (Figure 9)[68] render the men's attire in more detail, the scabbarded *spathae* with circular chapes being diagnostic for their profession. The fact that the illustrated belt and baldric fittings (grooved ring-buckle, domed studs, *balteus phalera* and terminal pendant) are actually confirmed by grave inventories from Apulum and from elsewhere in Dacia and even beyond[69] is not without significance, nor is the fact that most of the iconographic and artefact evidence,

---

[61] Hoss 2011.
[62] Ciongradi 2007: 213 Pf/M 3, Taf. 69 = Lupa 19172.
[63] Coulston 1987; Coulston 2007.
[64] Coulston 1987: 145–146.
[65] IDRE I, no. 30, pl. III.
[66] Alicu et al. 1979: 127, no. 297, pl. XLIX/297 = Diaconescu 2012: 181, Cat. M 21, Fig. 32a = Lupa 21953; Alicu et al. 1979: 127, no. 295, pl. XLIX/295 = Diaconescu 2012: 181, Cat. M 22, Fig. 32b = Lupa 17644.
[67] Ciongradi 2007: 231, Sc/A 5, Taf. 85/a-b = Lupa 19414.
[68] Diaconescu 2012: 183–184, Cat. M 31, Fig. 30 = Lupa 15334; Diaconescu 2012: 184, Cat. M 32, Fig. 31 = Lupa 19305.
[69] Ciugudean 2011; Gui 2015.

admittedly limited, is connected to *legio XIII Gemina*. In this context, it is worth mentioning a 'ring-buckle gravestone' from *Doliche* set up by a soldier of this troop for his colleague who had died during one of the 3rd century eastern campaign.[70]

Another interesting piece from Dacia is a fragmentary funerary high relief found at Napocawhich illustrates a man wearing a tunic and cloak, as well as a sword hanging from a baldric (Figure 10).[71] Although his clothing is not very skilfully rendered, care was taken to represent the baldric *phalera* fastener, the ornate terminal and strap, and also the decoration on the sword grip. However, the *balteus* terminal and fastener are in an unusual position, in the centre, whereas they should normally rest on the side of the figure. Perhaps the situation was determined by the nature of the monument or by the sculptor's lack of competence, but it could also signal an attempt to draw attention to this particular item.

The funerary banquet scene (*Totenmahl*)

Either directly or indirectly the depictions of the funerary banquet (*Totenmahl*) on gravestones is by and large associated with elements of the military in frontier provinces, and not only. They are among the most popular funerary representations

Figure 9. Marble statue of a legionary soldier from Apulum, kept at the National Museum of Unification, Alba Iulia (photo: M. Gui).

---

[70] Facella and Speidel 2011.
[71] Diaconescu 2012: Cat. M 41, Fig. 32c = Lupa 20983.

employed by soldiers of the Rhineland armies starting with the early Flavian period[72] and spreading throughout the next decades to the military environments of the Danubian provinces, Britain[73] and the *equites singulares Augusti* in Rome.[74] Putting aside some uncertainties regarding its emergence and later development, the motif is most certainly of Greek origin with Middle-Eastern roots.[75] Still it is hitherto unclear how it made its way to the Rhine towards the end of the 1st century AD, although some scholars have traced its point of departure to Northern Greece and Thrace.[76]

Although there is no recent synthesis to provide a general picture in this regard, based on a survey of the published material it can be said that in Roman Dacia the *Totenmahl* reliefs are concentrated in the northern, more militarised part of the province, Dacia Porolissensis, with over 30 examples, while to the south in Dacia Superior *c.* eight such reliefs can be accounted for. In Dacia Inferior on

Figure 10. Funerary relief from Napoca, kept at the National History Museum of Transylvania, Cluj-Napoca (photo: S. Odenie).

---

[72] Gabelmann 1972: 70, 116–122.
[73] Hope 1997, 253–254
[74] Speidel 1994a: 4–5; Busch 2011: 131-132.
[75] Dana 2014: 345–346.
[76] Speidel 1994a: 5, note 26.

the other hand there is virtually no trace of this motif on local funerary monuments.[77] Depictions of waiting servants[78] were not considered in this survey as their relevance in this matter is doubtful. With only a few exceptions,[79] instances of *Totenmahl* representations in Dacia Porolissensis are connected to military sites, around half of the total number coming from the legionary base of Potaissa and the auxiliary bases from Gilău and Brâncovenești, while further pieces coming from Ilișua-Arcobadara, Cășeiu, Gherla, Porolissum and Dej. Due to the fragmentary state of the material and the fact that a large proportion of the reliefs are comprised of disjointed *aedicula* walls, and thus separated from their inscriptions, there are only eight instances in which the identity of the deceased or commemorator can be established from the epitaph. Among these a direct link with military personnel or veterans, either as the commemorated or the commemorators is possible in seven cases: Iulius Crescens, *veteranus*[80] and Aurelius Respectus, *miles* of the *cohors I Britannica*[81] both from Cășeiu; Meatinus Birsi, *veteranus* of the *cohors I Batavorum*[82] and Aelius Bolhas Bannaei, *veteranus* of the *Numerus Palmyrenorum*,[83] both from Potaissa; Aurelius Carinus from Gilău, *cornicularius* of the *ala I Siliana*[84] (Figure 11); Mucapor, from the *ala Frontoniana*;[85] Aurelius Valens, *sesquiplicarius* in the *ala Illyricorum*.[86] The only exception is the *stela* of Valeria Dula[87] from Potaissa, where none of the persons mentioned in the epitaph convey any affiliation with the military. The distribution of the *Totenmahl* reliefs within Dacia, in conjunction with the few surviving epitaphs, does seem to suggest a connection with the military.

The discussion related to the immediate origin of this motif in Dacia is potentially relevant at this point. There are two principal theories in this regard. According to the assertion of Țeposu-Marinescu[88] the high number of *Totenmahl* reliefs in and around Potaissa must be related to the arrival of the *legio V Macedonica*, transferred from Troesmis in Moesia Inferior during the early stages of the Marcomannic Wars. The fact that around 80% of the *stelae* from the West Pontic area display the funerary banquet[89] seems to corroborate this assertion.

---

[77] Bianchi 1974: 159.
[78] Petruț and Mustață 2010.
[79] Zăgreanu 2015.
[80] ILD 781 = Țeposu Marinescu 1982: 127, nr. S 101, pl. X.
[81] ILD 782 = Isac 2013, pl. III, 2–2a.
[82] CIL III 13766+13767 – Münsterberg and Oehler 1902. 107, fig. 22.
[83] CIL III 907=7693 = Țeposu Marinescu 1982: 130, nr. 115, pl. X.
[84] CIL III 847a=7651.
[85] CIL III 799; Gaiu and Zăgreanu 2011: 81–82, nr. 1.3.b.1, pl. VII.
[86] ILD 440; Protase and Zrínyi 1992: 95, nr. 1+ 105, nr. 36.
[87] ILD 513 = Jude and Pop 1972: 7–8, no. 2, pl. II.
[88] Țeposu Marinescu 1982: 48.
[89] Conrad 2003: 57.

Figure 11. Funerary stela of a cornicularius from Gilău, kept at the National History Museum of Transylvania, Cluj-Napoca (photo: S. Odenie).

However Conrad[90] also noted that this motif is mainly characteristic to the urban environment of the region, being employed only sporadically by the soldiers. Indeed, among the few funerary monuments published from Troesmis there is not one depicting the scene of the banquet.[91] Furthermore, based on the recent additions to the corpus of *Totenmahl* reliefs (and excluding the waiting servant depictions) the distribution pattern of this motif within Dacia Porolissensis seems to be evening up constantly between the military sites of the province. It

---

[90] Conrad 2003: 70–71.
[91] Conrad 2003: 185–186.

is thus more likely that the motif made its way to Dacia from the Rhenish *limes*,[92] probably through Pannonia, being brought by the auxiliary troops transferred here.

Cloaked representations

The portrayal of soldiers clad in tunic and cloak, completely unarmed, in an individual or a family setting, usually with a scroll in one of their hands intended to convey the picture of fellow citizen and family man rather than that of battle-hardened warrior.[93] As shown by Hope[94] the tradition of family representations within the rank and file of the military dated well before the legal right to join in matrimony was granted en masse to active soldiers. Two distinctive types of cloaks are regularly identified on funerary monuments. The *sagum*, a rectangular cloak fastened with a brooch on the wearer's right shoulder, seems to have been ubiquitous during the 1st to the 4th centuries AD.[95] Furthermore, Speidel[96] asserted that such cloaks are a distinctive sign of military service, reflected also in some figures of speech e.g. '*saga sumere*' i.e. 'taking the cloak', with the meaning of 'going to war'. The circular cape (*paenula*) fastened with buttons in the front was worn especially by infantry men until *c.* the late-2nd century AD.[97]

In general terms in Dacia, alongside a few representations of *paenulae*, the corpus of *sagum* representations is quite considerable, accounting for the possibility that this motif, possibly the clothing item itself, may have been adopted in the civilian environment as well. Again, the lack of correlation between the reliefs and their accompanying epitaphs induces a high level of uncertainty with regard to the identity of the persons portrayed. To make matters more complicated, full-figure representations are very rare on the *stelae* from Dacia, being usually confined to *aedicula* walls, further reducing the possibility of correlation between epigraphy ad iconography. Hypothetically, the depiction of individuals in Dacia wearing tunic and *sagum* and conspicuously holding a scroll e.g. in the cases of funerary statues from Ulpia Traiana Sarmizegetusa[98] and Apulum[99] may indicate at a symbolic level the affiliation to the military. Depictions of *paenulae* are considerably rarer most probably due to their

---

[92] Bianchi 1974: 160 163.
[93] Speidel 2009: 237.
[94] Hope 1997: 256.
[95] Coulston 2014: 65.
[96] Speidel 2009: 243.
[97] Coulston 2014: 65.
[98] Lupa 19185.
[99] Lupa 19229.

abovementioned chronological characteristics. In some exceptional cases the surviving epitaph confirms the martial identity of the commemorated person e.g. the *stela* of Caius Valerius Silvanus, veteran of the *legio XIII Gemina* from Apulum.[100] In the case of further fine depictions of *paenulae* e.g. on funerary monuments from Porolissum[101] and Brucla,[102] the lack of epitaph hinders any precise identification with regard to the identity of those commemorated.

Conclusions

The manifestations of martial identity in the funerary iconography of Roman Dacia seem to correspond to a general trend representative for the 'militarised' provinces of the Rhineland, the Upper and Middle Danube region and Britain. In similar fashion, representations apparently devoid of conspicuous military elements from Dacia, such as the funerary banquet, the depiction of unarmed individuals on horseback or of individuals simply wearing one of the two main types of military cloaks, the *sagum* or the *paenula*, in most cases indicate a tight connection to the military either from the side of the commemorator or that of the commemorated. Furthermore the different categories of armed or armoured representations (in cuirass, in battle gear, in 'camp dress', or on horseback), have the potential of revealing important details with regard to the social and cultural background of the respective soldiers, or indeed their place within the military hierarchy.

As mentioned at the beginning of the paper, the main goal of the analysis was to highlight the visual identifiers which allow for both active soldiers and veterans to be singled out even in cases in which the epitaphs were lost. As we can see, in Dacia, as elsewhere, they employed a wide range of such identifiers, depending on their rank, status, period in which they were active and the message they wished to convey. It would of course be interesting to see the overall proportion of soldiers who included iconographic clues regarding their military profession as compared to those who indicated this solely by means of inscriptions. For the moment it is our hope that this analysis can contribute to a better understanding of the funerary iconography connected to the military communities of Roman Dacia.

Acknowledgements

The authors kindly wish to thank Irina Nemeti and the National History Museum of Transylvania, Cluj-Napoca, for providing some of the photographic material featured in the paper, and also the National Museum of Unification, Alba Iulia, for allowing us to include photographs of the pieces kept in their collection.

---

[100] Ciongradi 2007: S/A 20, Taf. 43; Lupa 11636.
[101] Petruț and Zăgreanu 2011:202, no. 1, plate 1/1.
[102] Ciongradi 2007, Taf. 115.

References

Alicu, D., Pop, C. and Wollmann, V. 1979. *Figured Monuments from Sarmizegetusa*. BAR IS 55. Oxford.

Bianchi, L. 2015. Edifici in miniature edesigenze d'apparato: l'edicola funeraria pannonico-dacica: 163-172. In: C.-G. Alexandrescu (ed.), *Cult and votive monuments in the Roman provinces: proceedings of the 13th International Colloquium on Roman Provincial Art, Bucharest, Alba Iulia, Constanţa, 27th of May - 3rd of June 2013 : within the framework of Corpus Signorum Imperii Romani*. Cluj-Napoca. Mega Publishing House.

Bianchi, L. 1974. Rilievi funerari con banchetto della Dacia romana (I). *Apulum* 12: 159–181.

Bishop, M. 1999. The Newstead 'loricas egmentata'. *Journal of Roman Military Equipment Studies* 10: 27–43.

Busch, A. 2011. Militär in Rom: militärische und paramilitärische Einheiteinem kaiserzeitlichen Stadtbild. Wiesbaden. L. Reichert.

Ciongradi, C. 2007. *Grabmonument und sozialer Status in Oberdakien*. Bibliotheca Musei Napocensis 24. Cluj-Napoca. Mega Verlag.

Ciugudean, D. 2011. 'Ringschnallen cingulum'-type Belts from Apulum: 99–113. In: I. Piso, V. Rusu-Bolindeţ, R. Varga, S. Mustaţă, E. Beu-Dachin, L. Ruscu (eds.), *Scripta Classica. Radu Ardevan sexagenario dedicata*. Cluj-Napoca. Mega Publishing House.

Conrad. S. 2003. *Die Grabstelen aus Moesia Inferior. Untersuchungen zu Chronologie, Typologie und Ikonografie*. Leipzig. Casa Libri.

Coulston, J. 1987. Roman military equipment on 3rd century tombstones: 141-156. In: M. Dawson, (ed.), *Roman Military Equipment. The Accoutrements of War. Proceedings of the Third Roman Military Equipment Seminar*. BAR IS 336. Oxford.

Coulston, J. 2007. Culture and Service: the Depiction of Soldiers on Funerary Monuments of the 3rd century AD: 529-561. In: L. de Blois, E. Lo Cascio (eds.), *The Impact of the Roman Army (200BC - AD 476). Economic, Social, Political, Religious and Cultural Aspects*. Leiden/ Boston. Brill.

Coulston, J. 2014. Monumentalising military service: Soldiers in Romano-British sculpture: 68-78. In R. Collins, Fr. McIntosh (eds.), *Life in the Limes: Studies of the people and objects of the Roman frontiers*. Oxford. Oxbow Books.

Dana, M. 2014. 'Le banquet des sophistes': représentation funéraire, représentation sociale sur les stèles de Byzance aux époques hellénistique et impériale. In *Banquets of gods, banquets of men. Conviviality in the Ancient World. Studia Universitatis Babeş-Bolyai, Historia* 59/1: 345–371.

Devijver, H. 1989. Equestrian officers and their monuments. In: H. Devijver (ed.), *The Equestrian Officers of the Roman Imperial Army*: 416–449. Mavors Roman Army Research 6. Amsterdam. Brill.

Diaconescu, A. 2005. *Statuaria majoră în Dacia romană*. Cluj-Napoca. NereaMia Napocae.

Diaconescu, A. 2012. Male and female funerary statues from Roman Dacia. *Acta Musei Napocensis* 47–48/I, 2010–2011: 125–203.

Facella, M. and Speidel, M. A. 2011. From Dacia to Doliche (and back). A new Gravestone for a Roman Soldier: 207-218. In: E. Winter (ed.), *Von Kummuḫnach Telouch. Historische und archäologische Untersuchungen in Kommagene.* Bonn. R. Habelt.

Fischer, Th. 2012. *Die Armee der Caesaren, Archäologie und Geschichte.* Mit Beiträgen von Ronald Bockius, Dietrich Boschung, Thomas Schmidts. Regensburg. Verlag Friedrich Pustet.

Gabelmann, H. 1972. Die Typen der römischen Grabstelen am Rhein. *Bonner Jahrbücher* 172: 65–140.

Gaiu, C. and Zăgreanu, R. 2011. *Inscripţii şi piese sculpturale din castrul roman de la Ilişua.* Cluj-Napoca. Accent.

Gui, M. 2015. How to wear the Ringschnallen cingulum in Dacia: 175-189. In: S. Cociş, V.-A. Lăzărescu, M. Gui, D.-A. Deac (eds.), *Ad finem Imperii Romani: studies in honour of Coriolan H. Opreanu.* Cluj-Napoca. Mega Publishing House.

Hope, V. M. 1997. Words and Pictures: the Interpretation of Romano-British. *Britannia* 28: 245–258.

Hoss, S. 2011. The Roman Military Belt: 29-44. In: M.-L. Nosch (ed.), *Wearing the cloak: dressing the soldier in Roman times.* Oxford. Oxbow Books.

Isac, D. 2003. *Castrul roman de la SAMVM-Căşeiu / The Roman auxiliary fort SAMVM-Căşeiu.* Handbook of archaeological monuments from Dacia Porolissensis 9 / Ghid al monumentelor arheologice din Dacia Porolissensis 9. Cluj-Napoca. Napoca Star.

Jude, M. and Pop, C. 1972. *Monumente sculpturale romane în Muzeul de Istorie Turda.* (no further information).

Miles 1997. Miles Romanus in provincia Dacia: catalogul expoziţiei naţionale. Muzeul Naţional de Istorie a Transilvaniei.

Moga, V. 2008. Monumente inedite de la Apulum. *Apulum* 45/1: 477–482.

Münsterberg, R. and Oehler, J. 1902. Antike Denkmäler in Siebenbürgen. *Jahreshefte des Österreichischen Archäologischen Instituts* 5: 94–135.

Nemeti, S. and Marcu, F. 2014. A funerary *aedicule* wall from Şoimeni (Cluj County). *Dacia N. S.* 58: 231–239.

Nemeti, S. and Nemeti, I. 2014. Heros equitans in the funerary iconography of Dacia Porolissensis. Models and workshops. *Dacia N. S.* 58: 241–255.

Noelke, P. 2012. Mars oder Offizier? Eine Kölner Panzerstatue und die Gattung der Ehrenstatuen in den nördlichen Grenzprovinzen des Imperium Romanum. *Jahrbuch des Römisch-Germanischen Zentralmuseums* 59: 391–512.

Petruţ, D. 2015. Military dress or parade armour? A roman officer represented on a funerary relief from Brâncoveneşti. In C. Höpken, Sz. P. Pánczél (eds.), *Introduction to the Eastern Limes of Roman Dacia.* Târgu Mureş. Mega Publishing House. (forthcoming).

Petruţ, D. and Mustaţă, S. 2010. The iconography of the waiting servants depicted on funerary reliefs from Roman Dacia. *Revista Bistriţei* 24: 171–202.

Petruţ, D. and Zăgreanu, R. 2011. *The Funerary Stelae from Porolissum. Typological, Iconographical and Epigraphic Aspects.* Marisia. Studii şi Materiale arheologie 31: 189–218.

Phillips, E. J. 1975. The gravestone of M. Favonius Facilis at Colchester. *Britannia* 6: 102–105.

Protase, D. and Zrínyi, A. 1992.Inscripții și monumente sculpturale din castrul roman de la Brâncovenești (jud. Mureș). *Ephemeris Napocensis* 2, 95–110.

Robinson, H. R. 1975. The armour of imperial Rome. London. Arms and Armour Press.

Schleiermacher, M. 1984. Römische Reitergrabsteine: kaiserzeitlichen Reliefs des triumphierenden Reiters. Bonn. Bouvier.

Speidel, M. P. 1965.*Die Equites singulars Augusti. Begleitruppe der römischen Kaiser deszweiten und dritten Jahrhunderts.* Antiquitas 1/11. Bonn. Rudolf HabeltVerlag.

Speidel, M. P. 1994a. *Die Denkmäler der Kaiserreiter Equites Singulares Augusti.* Beihefte der Bonner Jahrbücher 50. Köln, Bonn. Dr. Rudolf Habelt GMBH.

Speidel, M. P. 1994b. *Riding for Caesar. The Roman Emperors' Horse Guards.* London. B. T. Batsford.

Speidel, M. A. 2009. Dressed for the occasion. Clothes and context in the Roman army. In M. A. Speidel (Hrsg.), *Heer und Herrschaft im Römischen Reich der Hohen Kaiserzeit*: 235–248. Stuttgart. Franz Steiner Verlag.

ȚeposuMarinescu, L. 1982.*Funerary Monuments of Dacia Superior and Dacia Porolissensis.* British Archaeological Reports International Series 128. Oxford.

Ubl, H. 2013.*Waffen und Uniform des römischen Heeres der Prinzipiatsepoche nach den Grabreliefs Noricums und Pannoniens*: Dissertation zur Erlangung des Doktorgrades an der philosophischen Fakultät der Universität Wien Juni 1969. Austria Antiqua3. Wien. UniPress.

Zăgreanu, R. and Gaiu, C. 2011. *Inscripții și piese sculpturale din castrul roman de la Ilișua.*Cluj-Napoca. Accent.

Zăgreanu, R. 2014.The Roman funerary *stelae* from Gherla. *Revista Bistriței* 28: 131–152.

Zăgreanu, R. 2015. The funerary stelae from the rural settlements of Dacia Porolissensis. In A. Gavrilaș, D. L. Vaida, A. Onofreiu, G. G. Marinescu (eds.), *Trecutul mai aproape de noi. Omagiu profesorului Gheorghe Marinescu la 70 de ani.* Cluj-Napoca. Editura Mega.

Origo as identity factor in Roman epitaphs

Tibor Grüll

One of the most decisive factors of a person's identity is his/her origin, which can be defined on the basis of an ethnic group, nationality, citizenship, town/country of birth etc. Paul, the apostle, identified himself to a Roman officer with the following phrase: 'I am a Jew, from Tarsus in Cilicia, a citizen of no ordinary city' (ἐγὼ ἄνθρωπος μέν εἰμι Ἰουδαῖος, Ταρσεὺς τῆς Κιλικίας, οὐκ ἀσήμου πόλεως πολίτης, Acts 21:39 NIV).[1] Three hundred years later, a man called Aurelius Aeliodorus—who died at Tarragona at the age of 80—identified himself as 'by nationality Greek, citizen of Tarsus (of) Cilicia' (*natione Graeca civis Tarsus Cilicia*, RIT 958).[2] As a matter of fact, Roman epitaphs often use the terms *natione, civis, patria, domo,* which are usually accompanied with the name of a province, settlement (*colonia, municipium, civitas, vicus*), or tribe. In the Epigraphische Datenbank Heidelberg we find more than 800 inscriptions referring to someone's origin with the above mentioned phrases. On the basis of this database I was investigating how the place of origin, ethnic affiliation, occupation or nationality affect the choice of which *origo* is emphasized on the epitaph. Is ethnic origin, place of birth, or provincial identity the stronger marker—and can we find a pattern in the use of these terms?

Civis

Let us start with phrase ***civis*** (n=65). It is self-evident that the most important component of the identities in the Roman Empire was the Roman citizenship.[3] In spite of this, we rarely find the term *civis Romanus* on the epitaphs, perhaps because it was obvious from somebody's name (*tria nomina*) or from the representation of the deceased, at least in the Danubian provinces, where tombstones often portray the deceased with a scroll—definitely the diploma of his citizenship—in his hand.[4] In the 65 cases examined in the EDH the

---

[1] I do not treat here the controversial question of Paul's Roman citizenship, see *contra* Stegemann 1987 and *pro*: Van Minnen 1995.
[2] The fourth-century epitaph is evidently Christian, therefore we cannot rule out that the *ordinator* of the inscription deliberately alluded to the New Testament, see Gorostodi Pi 2013: 50, #23.
[3] A strongly selected bibliography for this wide-ranging topic: Sherwin-White 1973; Nicolet 1976; Hope 2000 (a); Laurence Berry 2001; Mathisen 2006; Garnsey 2008.
[4] There is an ongoing debate about the function and meaning of the *rotuli* in the right hand of the deceased. László Borhy explained this phenomenon as follows: 'the scroll is intended to

civis did not refer to Roman citizenship. It is interesting, however, that in opposition of the terms *natione* and *domo* here the civilians (50 cases = 77%) are in the majority against soldiers (14 cases = 23%). On the basis of the literary sources we should suppose that the use of *civis* is mostly related to the citizenship of *coloniae* and *municipia*. But the situation is more complex. In the examined epigraphic material we find 22 cities, 16 tribal names, 15 *civitas* centers, 9 provinces and 3 peoples. For me the biggest surprise was the relatively high number of provinces, although the *Afer* (African), *Arabus*, *Dalmata*, *Thracus/Thrax* or *Surus* (Syrian) can also be interpreted as collective ethnical names. Notwithstanding, the terms *Saviensis* [Pannonia Savia], *Bithynus, Raeta, Norici,* and perhaps the *Pannonius* too are definitely referring to provinces. Among the tribal names we find the *Annaunus* [an African tribe], *Aeduus, Batavus, Bellovacus, Bessus* [a Thracian tribe], *Biturgis Cubi, Eravisca, Frisiavus, Germaniceus, Leucus, Lingonus, Nemes, Senonus, Sequanus, Thracus (Thrax)* and *Trever* seven times altogether. All these tribes lived in *civitates*, thus the phrase *civis* + tribal name (in the ablative) can be explained with strong *civitas*-consciousness. Another fine example of this is the famous building inscription of the Alcántara bridge, where eleven *civitates* from Lusitania occur as dedicators.[5] This *civitas*-mindedness is also manifest in the relatively high number of references to municipal citizenship. The man who calls himself *civis Petr(ucorii)* was a citizen of *Vesunna Petrucoriorum* (Périgueux) in Aquitania (AE 1911, 238). The phrase *civis Belalitanus* refers to *Belalis Maior* in Africa (Henchir El Faouar, Tunesia) (AE 1961, 80; 1978, 848); and the *civis* of the *res publica Uchitanor(um) Maior(um)* was the citizen of Uchi Maius (Henchir Douamis, Tunisia) (CIL VIII 26239, 26255, 26275). Some more examples: the *civis Tolosianus* belonged to *Tolosa* (Toledo, Spain) (AE 1978, 422); the *civis Dunnonia* comes from *Dumnonia* (Devon, Great-Britain) (CIL III 9515 = AE 1973, 403 = ILCV 185); the *civis Mediom(atricus)* originates from *Divodurum Mediomatricorum* in Belgica (Metz, France) (CIL XIII 7369; AE 1907, 110); and the *civis Remus* was the citizen of *civitas Remorum* also in Belgica (Reims, Germany) (ILS 5435 = RIB 103). The most important citizenship, after that of the Roman of course, was the Alexandrian.[6] We did not find, however, any *civis Alexandrinus*, among the Latin epitaphs. Among the larger cities we find *Antiochia* (Syria) (SEG LVII, 995 = AE 2007, 994), *Carthago* (Africa) (AE 1993, 1066), *Puteoli* (Italy) (AE 1978, 500),

---

emphasize the erudition of the deceased' (Borhy 2006: 14, translation is mine G. T.). The author refers an outdated scholarly article from Brein 1973. As far as I am concerned, these scrolls (*rotuli*) generally refer to the Roman citizenship of the deceased, although there were exceptions to this rule.

[5] The authenticity of the Alcántara bridge-inscription (CIL II 760-762) was hotly debated in the 1970's, but it has been eventually defended by Hoyos 1978. As to the other philological and historical problems of the inscriptions see Carbonell I Manils 2007.

[6] On the Alexandrian citizenship see: El-Abbadi 1962; Delia 1991; Bagnall 1993; Whitehorne 2001.

together with the much smaller Perusia (AE 1993, 1584) and Urbs Salvia (CIL XIII 6538). In the East we find a civis Tomitanus from Tomis, Ovid's famous place of exile (CIL III 7466); Tarsus of Cilicia mentioned in the introduction. In the west the Spanish Emporiae (Ampúrias) (AE 1969/70, 287), and Colonia Claudia Ara Agrippinensium (Köln) (CIL III 6570), capital city of Germania Inferior are mentioned.

Domo

Regarding the phrase ***domo*** we are in possession of a significant number of epigraphic evidence (n=397).[7] The majority of the inscriptions belong to the military (301 cases = 76%), the other 90 inscriptions (23%) is civilian, and the *dubia* is only six (1%). It is conspicuous that the overwhelming majority of the phrases beside the *ablativus originis* (*domo*) are names of cities (320 cases = 80%), other expressions can be considered as exemptions. But let us first examine these exemptions. In most cases these are tribal names, such as domo *Batavus, Bessus, Dalmata, Serdus* etc. (26 = 6.5%).[8] There are some Hispanic tribes among them which occur only in this epigraphic material.[9] Probably the most known examples of this phrase are the two Jewish inscriptions found in 2009 at Carnuntum (Petronell, Austria).[10] Both epitaphs—dated roughly to the age of Marcus Aurelius—contain the phrase *domo Iudaeus* or in the plural *domo Iudaei*. Bearing in mind the above mentioned examples of *domo Batavus, domo Bessus* etc. we can hardly find this expression as an oddity: the expression *domo Iudaeus* simply means 'Jewish in origin' or 'belonging to the people of the Jews'.[11] The second largest group consists of names of provinces (16 cases = 4%). *Africa* occurs four times, *Hispania* and *Thracia* twice, besides these we can find *Asia, Bithynia, Cappadocia, Dacia, Macedonia,*

---

[7] The phrase *domo* + toponym and/or *gentilicium* was investigated by Gonzalez Fernandez and Molina Gomez 2011.

[8] On the basis of Ton Derks' investigations the terms *natione* and *domo* indicate a strong ethnic identity; the use of *civis* and *civitas* are rare amongst Batavians, probably because of their strong military imprint. In fact, they continued using tribal affiliation even after the grant of Roman citizenship, perhaps because of the positive qualities (e.g. strength, bravery) associated with their tribal name (Derks 2009).

[9] The expression *domo Hispanus* has been investigated by Speidel 1985. In general see Yébenes 2007; Lefebvre 2011.

[10] AE 2009, 1051; Beutler and Kremer 2013. For the epigraphic testimonies of the Jews in Pannonia see: Kovács 2010; Grüll 2016.

[11] In this case the expression has nothing to do with the question of re-naming *Iudaea* to *Syria Palaestina* by Hadrian. Notwithstanding, we have another inscription from the time of Hadrian (IGRR IV 1431, line 29 = CIJ II 742 = ISmyrna 697 = IJO II 40), where we cannot tell with certainty if the Greek expression οἵ ποτε Ἰουδαῖοι refers to people from the 'former province of Iudaea' or 'former Jews', see Williams 1997; Wilson 2000.

Mauritania, Numidia and *Sardinia*.¹² Between the cities and the provinces we find some historical regions, such as *Calabria, Ituraea* and *Phrygia*. In 23 cases the names of cities and provinces are connected: six times the provinces are ahead, seventeen times in the back. The provinces attached to cities are multifarious: *Syria* (5 cases), *Africa* and *Mauretania Caesariensis* (3 cases), *Hispania* (2 cases), *Italia* (2 cases), as well as *Galatia, Gallia Narbonensis*, the two *Pannoniae*, and *Moesia Superior*. Let us now turn to the city names of which 80% consist of the *domo* phrase. In most cases only the name of the settlement is placed (in the ablative, locative or—perhaps by the influence of Greek—accusative form), the legal status of the town is rarely attested: we find four *coloniae*, three *municipia*, and two *civitates*. And now, if we consider the settlements themselves, we can realize that out of the 320 names only 10 are unidentifiable (3%). The settlements specified in the epitaphs belonged to 33 different provinces, among which Italy—which is, of course, still not a 'province' at this time—is in absolute majority (119 cases = 37%). Italian cities were followed by the Syrians (35 cases = 11%), and the Pannonians (31 cases = 10%). More than ten cities are only from *Gallia Narbonensis* (11 cases = 3%), but here we must mention *Hispania* (9 cases), *Asia* (9 cases), *Moesia* (8 cases), *Africa* (8 cases), and *Macedonia* (7 cases). It is a point of interest that among the Italian cities, *Roma* most often occurs as the *origo* of the deceased (24 cases = 20%). At this point we can safely assert a kind of pride on behalf of the people who were responsible for formulating the epitaph. In some cases we find the Roman tribal name attached to the city in the following order: *domo* + *tribus* + settlement.¹³ Let us see a few examples:

Table 1. Attestations of the domo + tribus + settlement type

Name	Text	Finding place	Dating	EDH no.
C. Quintius Severus	domo Camilia Ravenna	Cappuck, Britannia	AD 201-300	026425
L. Surius Sabinus	domo Publilia Verona	Roma, Italia	?	014262
Q. Novellius Martialis	domo Fabia Brixia	Roma, Italia	?	014262
L. Pompeius Licetus	domo Pomptina Arretio	Londinium, Britannia	AD 101-300	015612
Valens Iangali	domo Quirina Scupo	Athenae, Achaia	?	063736
P. Maecius Sabinus	domo Sergia	Dozmat, Hungary	AD 71-100	040434
M. Aurelius Emeritus	domo Sergia Karnunto	Brigetio, Pannonia	AD 151-200	039420
Atilius Primus	domo Sergia Marsis	Carnuntum, Pannonia	AD 151-200	072786
Refius Marcellus	domo Sergia Savaria	Carnuntum, Pannonia	AD 151-300	073465
C. Iulius Longinus	domo Voltinia Philippis	Reate, Italia	AD 1-100	051075

---

[12] The expression *domo Dacia* has been investigated by Mrozewicz 1989 and Oltean 2009.
[13] About the *tribus*-names in general see Forni 2006; for the connection of tribal names and the cities in Italy and the provinces see Forni 1977; Tovar 1989.

It turns out from the above mentioned examples that the *tribus* names were used mostly by the citizens of Italian towns (*Arretium, Brixia, Ravenna, Verona*, and the *civitas Marsorum* or *Marruvium*). Beside the Italian towns we find the following colonies: (1) *Colonia Augusta Iulia Philippensis* which was founded in 27 BC (today Philipipi, Greece); (2) *Carnuntum* (*Colonia Septimia Aurelia Antoniniana Carnuntum*) which was elevated to the rank of colony by Septimius Severus in 194 BC (today Petronell, Austria); (3) *Scupi* in Moesia Superior (today Skopje, Macedonia) which was appointed to a colony by the Flavians (*Colonia Flavia Scupi*). We are aware that Scupi's habitants were numbered to the *tribus Quirina* which is the reason why we find the phrase *domo Quirina Scupos* (CIL III 7289) in the epitaph of a soldier deceased in Athens. (4) The expression *domo Sergia Savaria* (CSIR Carnuntum 541) is, however, odd because we know that citizens of *Savaria* (today Szombathely, Hungary) belonged to the *tribus Claudia*. In this case we can assume that this people of *Savaria* were immigrants from a North Italian city.[14]

Natione

As regards the phrase **natione** (n=223), this was also mostly used by military personnel (151 cases = 67%). Civilians represent one-third of the examined material (65 cases = 30%), while the uncertain status is only 3% (7 cases). It is particularly interesting that among the identifiable civilian professions gladiators were the most often mentioned, which points out that these two 'militant' groups of the Roman society were particularly proud of their origin, probably because with their bravery and valor they acquired glory for their homelands as well.[15] Among the civilians—though less frequently—we also find slaves who referred to their origin on their tombstones. The appellation *natione* was attached to the following names and toponyms:

peoples: 84 cases = 35%
tribal names: 58 cases = 25%
town, village, and other toponyms: 23 cases = 10%
province: 53 cases = 23%
other type: 16 cases = 7%

---

[14] Savaria was a colony founded by Claudius in ca. 43 AD (Kiss *et al*. 1998: 31-34). See also Gregoratti 2014.
[15] About the soldiers see Ricci 2000; Speidel 1986; Haynes 2013; some of the gladiators' epitaphs found at Nîmes (Hope 1998) and in Italy (Hope 2000 (b)) were also referring to the ethnic affiliation of the deceased; a few other examples collected from the Inscriptiones Latinae Selectae see Wiedemann 1992: 114.

What did the *natio* mean in the imperial age? This noun, which in modern Indo-European languages usually means 'nation', was either used to denote geographical affiliation (40%) or as a mark of belonging to a group of peoples (60%).[16] Let us look first at the geographical affiliation. Among the toponyms, the provincial names are the most frequently mentioned (23%). In the West the most provincial-minded people were the Pannonians (*Pannonius, Pannonicus*, 14 cases); in the East the Syrians (*Surus*, 11 cases).[17] In the West we find 8 *Norici*, 7 *Dalmatae* or *Dalmatici*, 5 *Raeti*, 5 Thracians (*natione Thracia*), 4 *Corsi* or *Corsicani*, 4 *Hispani* (one *Hispanus Tarraconensis*).[18] In the East quite frequently occur the *Aegyptius* (6 cases) and the *Cilix* (3 cases). In regard to the town names—no wonder—we find most often the mention of *natione Alexandrino* (7 cases) in both military and civilian context. Among these appellations we find either the self-conscious colonies (*Gaditanus, Aquincensis, Nicomedia*) or the humble villages (*Anartia, Balatucelo*). In some cases a kind of hierarchy is also palpable in the references. A 35-year-old soldier who was deceased in Rome (AE 1996, 91), refers to his *origo* as follows: *nat(ione) Mysia superiore / reg(ione) Ratiarese vico C[-]/ nisco*. Thus, the order is *natio > regio > vicus*, it is intriguing, however, that in this case the *natio* did not points to his ethnic affiliation, but his native province. A similar hierarchy can be observed in the *natione > domo* affiliations, e.g. *nati/ one Pannonius / domo Sirmi* (AE 1999, 1555), or *natione / Surus domo Heme/sa* (CIL III 3301 = RIU 1031), although in these cases the *Pannonius* and *Surus* can also be interpreted as a pan-ethnic affiliation. Other types of geographical names are the 'African' (*Afer*), 'Italian' (*Italus* or *Italicus*), 'Rhodian' (*Rhodius*), and the

---

[16] The *natio* was first of all a kin-group in the antiquity: 'The Latin *natio* did not refer to a form of political organization, but rather to a breed, a stock, a kind, a race, a tribe, a people' (Just 1989: 73). About the 'patriotism' in the Roman Empire see Walbank 1972; Bonjour 1975; Thomas 1996; Speidel 2010.

[17] Mark Handley writes about the Easterners' epitaphs in the West which I cannot agree more: 'The epitaphs of many of these Easterners commemorated in the West included unusually detailed information about their origin, often going beyond a reference to a province or city of origin to state the particular village that a person came from. This is most common amongst Syrians in the West, but is also seen amongst people from Asia Minor, Thrace, Egypt, and Arabia. Many other Syrians were simply denoted by *Syrus* or *Syra*, or by the cities of Antioch or Apamea, but those that provided more detail are perhaps indicative of an audience of Syrians at their new hometown for whom the identification of the deceased with a particular village was important. The stress placed upon the identity that was associated with a particular village, rather than with being 'Syrian', is noteworthy, not least because this expression of village identity is probably to be related to the flourishing state of the Syrian villages themselves in the late period; this florescence may have been reflected in the pride with which the inhabitants of these villages viewed their origins, even when so far removed.' (Handley 2011: 87-88). For the Syrians see also Andrade 2013. – As for the Pannonians, were are aware that the Celtic *Boius* tribe was fairly self-conscious, see Kovács 2015.

[18] About the provincial identity of the people originating from Noricum see Hainzmann 2011.

'Pontian' (*Ponticus*). These were regions and not provinces.[19] Of course, *Africa proconsularis* was a province, but here, instead of the properly constructed *Africanus*, we find *Afer*; and *Pontus* was co-governed with *Bithynia*.

Peoples' names are—leastwise as I consider them—comprehensive ethnic names, so-called 'umbrella terms', under which tribal names are classified, e.g. *Gallus, Germanus, Syrus* etc. As I mentioned above, there are peoples' names which tightly adhere to the provinces, because the province itself was named after the peoples living there: e.g. *Raetus, Hispanus, Pannonius, Britannicianus, Armenius, Aegyptius*. (The *Graecus* is an exception because there is no province 'Graecia', only *Macedonia* and *Achaia*.) Notwithstanding, many northern—mostly German and a few Celtic—tribes (e.g. *Bessus, Batavus, Suebus, Tunger, Helvetius, Ubius, Frisavonus* etc.) did not use the ethnic umbrella term but they preserved their peculiar and particular tribal identity. This is most probably tied to the fact that in the Roman army their units were named after their tribal name (*nationes* or *numeri*).[20] The ethnic and tribal names form together 60% in the epitaphs mentioning origins as *natio*.

Conclusions

The above mentioned phrases (*civis, natione, domo*) denoting somebody's origin in the Roman imperial age were thoroughly examined by Michael P. Speidel in relation with the Roman soldiers.[21] He called attention to a Berlin papyrus according to which the Roman soldiers were enlisted 'by consular (years), ethnic affiliation, and home (or province)' ([*milites di*]*gesti per co(n)s(ules) et nationes et* [*patrias* or *provincias*], *P. Berl.* 11596 Ro; ca. 122–145 AD, Philadelpheia).[22] This is quite natural: even today the three most important data beside our names are the year of birth, the ethnic affiliation, and the place of origin (usually the name of the country and the town). My investigation on the use of *civis, natione* and *domo* in non-official, private epitaphs, however, clearly demonstrated that there was a confusion in using these terms, denotations of these terms are overlapping. Eventually, the *civis Batavus, natione Batavus,* and the *domo Batavus* means nothing else but 'Batavian in origin'. It can also be observed

---

[19] As regards to the regional identities, it was recognized by Mark Handley that concerning the Balkans 'unlike some other regions, there was no supra-regional identity such as *Hispanus, Gallus* or *Afer* that could be claimed. All the instances therefore express their identity either by reference to the town (*de civitate Mursese; patris Lypiensium*) or province (*Pannoniis gentius; Retos; natus in Dardania; civis Pannoniae; de provincia Dalmatia*) of origin' (Handley 2011: 81). About the Dalmatian soldiers see Danijel Dzino: Aspects of identity-construction and cultural mimicry among Dalmatian sailors in the Roman navy. *Antichthon* 44 (2010) 96-110.
[20] For the *nationes* and *numeri* in the Roman army, see Le Roux 1986; Haynes 2013.
[21] Speidel 1986.
[22] BGU VII 1689 = HGV 63754 = ChLA X 423. See also Speidel 2007.

in the Greek translations of these phrases. The *natio* obviously means ἔθνος, but—surprisingly—the Greek equivalent of *domo Roma* is γένι Ῥωμαῖα (CIL III 14184 = AE 1991, 1490) which is another ethnic term. According to our modern preconceptions the Greek γένος (Latin *gens*) has nothing to do with the city of Rome, if not only metaphorically, like in Vergil's famous verse on the *gens togata* (Aeneid 1.282).[23] This is why I am concerned that the *domo Roma* simply means 'originating from Rome'.[24] Just like the *domo Iudaeus* on the above mentioned inscription from Carnuntum means nothing else but 'Jewish in origin'. As to my mind, the ablatives *natione* and *domo* became epigraphic formulas by the 2nd–3rd century AD. Michael A. Speidel in his important article 'The soldiers' homes' argued that 'a Roman citizen, when living abroad, as a rule, indicated his home in the form of a town. A non-citizen, on the other hand, when indicating his home, as a rule referred to his province'. As we have seen from the above examples, this is a gratuitous overgeneralization. Most of Speidel's examples: 'Afer, Lusitanus, Britto, Raetus, Noricus, Pannonius, Dalmata, Thrax, Cappadox, or Syrus'—are not only names of provinces but can be interpreted as ethnic 'umbrella names', just like today the Portugese, British, Hungarian etc. which can equally refer to somebody's citizenship or ethnic origin.[25] If today someone say 'I am a Hungarian', we simply cannot decide if he is (1) a citizen of Hungary who is ethnically also Hungarian; (2) a citizen of Hungary who is ethnically non-Hungarian; (3) an ethnically Hungarian, who lives in another country. According to Speidel the term a *natione Gallus* refers to his native province, but he 'might come from Narbonensis, Lugdunensis, or Belgica'.[26] But a *natione Gallus* could also be referring to his ethnic origin with this phrase: 'by his origin Gaulish'.[27] Tatiana Ivleva (Newcastle University) published an interesting article about 'expression of identities by Britons on the continent

---

[23] Fraser 2009.
[24] This expression was thoroughly investigated by Ricci 2000.
[25] For the use of modern ethnic terms see Safran 2008.
[26] We are aware of the 'temple of three Gauls' in *Lugdunum*, but we know almost nothing about its purpose, see Fischwisk 1972. For the late antique 'Gaulish' identity see Kazanski 2008. We do not know if the Narbonensian, Lugdunensian and Aquitanian Gauls had a special identity, but the Belgians certainly did, see Colling 2013. Regarding the connection of Roman provinces and modern nation-states see Geary 2002; Le Roux 2013.
[27] Mark Handley has called our attention to an interesting phenomenon: 'Amongst the Gallic travelers within Gaul, the most common expression of identity was a reference to the *civitas* of origin. No one was identified by his or her province of origin, and certainly not as a 'Gaul'. What this shows is that the particular identity expressed at any one time is likely to have been chosen to reflect both the circumstances and milieu. It would appear that a person who might describe himself as Gallus while in Rome would never do so while in Gaul, where a *civitas* identity is more likely to be expressed—and there are no examples of such a label being used by non-travelers inside Gaul either' (Handley 2011: 67).

during the Roman Empire'.[28] She claims that originally there was no such thing as a British pan-tribal identity. Among the very few epitaphs published in the *Roman Inscriptions in Britain* we find mention of the tribes *Canti, Cornovi, Dobunni, Ctuvellauni, Dumnonii*—but not by any means *Britannici*. The pan-tribal names such as *Caledones* and *Brittones*, however, were classic ethnonyms primarily used by Romans to indicate the confederacies of tribes in northern and southern Britain respectively. In the case of 'Caledonian' and 'Briton', pan-tribal identity was used to stress the group identity of those who lived in the North and the South. These two broad groupings in a society brought some degree of uniformity in overall diversity, but it was not accepted by everyone. Outside the borders of the province the ethnonym *natione Britto* meant simply 'a man/woman from Britannia'. Ivleva has also suggested that in the 3rd century AD the trend might have shifted to naming the provincial origin rather than that of a tribe or a city.

References

Andrade, N. J. 2013. *Syrian Identity in the Greco-Roman World.* Cambridge, Cambridge University Press.

Bagnall, R. S. 1993. Egypt and the Lex Minicia. *Journal of Juristic Papyrology* 23: 25-28.

Beutler, F. and Kremer, G. 2013. Domo Iudaeus – Zwei neue Grabinschriften aus Carnuntum. *Tyche* 28: 5-20. < http://dx.doi.org/10.15661/tyche.2013.028.01>

Bonjour, M. 1975. *Terre natale: études sur une composante affective du patriotisme romain.* Paris, Les Belles Lettres.

Borhy, L. 2006. Vezető Komárom város római kori kőemlékeihez. *Acta Archaeologica Brigetionensia* I. 5. Komárom, Klapka György Múzeum.

Brein, F. 1973. Bücher auf Grabsteinen. *Römisches Österreich* 1: 1-5.

Carbonell i Manils, J, Gimeno Pascual, H. and and Stylow, A. U. 2007. 'Pons Traiani', Qantara es-saif, puente de Alcántara: Problemas de epigrafía, filología e historia. In *Provinciae Imperii Romani inscriptionibus descriptae: Barcelona, 3-8 septembris 2002.* Barcelona: Institut d'Estudis Catalans: 247-258.

Carroll, P. M. 2013. Ethnicity and Gender in Roman Funerary Commemoration: Case studies from the empire's frontiers. In Liv Nilsson Stutz and Sarah Tarlow (eds.), *The Oxford Handbook of the Archaeology of Death and Burial*: 559-579. Oxford, Oxford University Press.

Colling, D. 2013. Natio Belga. Latomus 72(3): 770-780.

Derks, T. 2009. Ethnic identity in the Roman frontier. The epigraphy of Batavi and other Lower Rhine tribes. In Ton Derks and Nico Roymans (eds.), *Ethnic Constructs in Antiquity: The Role of Power and Tradition*: 239-282. Amsterdam Archaeological Studies 13. Amsterdam, Amsterdam University Press, 2009.

---

[28] Ivleva 2014. See also Ivleva 2016.

Delia, D. 1991. *Alexandrian Citizenship during the Roman Principate*. (American Classical Studies, 23.) Atlanta, Scholars Press.

Dzino, D. 2010. Aspects of identity-construction and cultural mimicry among Dalmatian sailors in the Roman navy. *Antichthon* 44 : 96-110.

El-Abbadi, M. A. H. 1962: The Alexandrian Citizenship. *JEA* 48:106-123.

Fischwisk, D. 1972. The Temple of the Three Gauls. *JRS* 62 : 46-52.

Forni, G. 1997. L'indicazione della tribù tra i nomi del cittadino romano. Osservazioni morfologiche. *Athenaeum*. 65:1-21977: 136-140.

Forni, G. 2006. *Le tribù romane. Scripta minora*. vols. 1–4. Historica 6. Roma, Bretschneider.

Fraser, P. M. 2009. Greek Ethnic Terminology. Oxford, Oxford University Press for the British Academy.

Garnsey, P. 2008. Roman Citizenship and Roman Law in the Late Empire. In Simon Swain and Mark Edwards (eds.), *Approaching Late Antiquity: The Transformation from Early to Late Empire*. Oxford, Oxford University Press: 133-155.

Geary, P. J. 2002. *The myth of nations: the medieval origins of Europe*. Princeton, Princeton University Press.

Gregoratti, L. 2014. North Italic settlers along the 'Amber Route'. *Studia Antiqua et Archaeologica* 19, 1: 133-153.

Gonzalez Fernandez, R. and Molina Gomez, J. A. 2011. Precisiones a las menciones de origo con la formula domo + toponimo/gentilicio en la epigrafia romana de Hispania. *Emerita* 79(1): 1-29.

Gorostodi Pi, D. 2013. L'epigrafia paleocristiana de Tarraco. Característiques generals i estat de la qüestió. In Josep Maria Macia Solé and Andreu Muñoz Melgar (eds.), *Tarraco christiana ciuitas*: 43-68. (Documenta, 24.) Tarragona, Institut Català d'Arqueologia Clàssica.

Grüll, T. 2016. Jewish presence in the Danubian provinces of the Roman Empire. In Magdaléna Hrbácsek (ed.), *Židovský kultúrny fenomén v stredoeurópskom kontexte. / Zsidó kultúra közép-európai kontextusban*: 9-18. Nitra: Univerzita Konštantía Filozofa v Nitre.

Hainzmann, M. 2011. 'Provinz-Identität' und 'nationale' Identität. Das Beispiel Noricums. In Antonio Caballos Rufino and Sabine Lefebvre (eds.), *Roma generadora de identitades. La experiencia Hispana*: 321-336. (Coleccion de la Casa de Velázquez, 123.) Madrid, Casa de Velázquez, Universidad de Sevilla.

Handley, M. 2011. *Dying on Foreign Shores. Travel and Mobility in the Late-Antique West*. (JRA Suppl. 86.) Portsmouth, R.I., Journal of Roman Archaeology.

Haynes, I. 2013. *Blood of the Provinces: The Roman Auxilia and the Making of Provincial Society from Augustus to the Severans*. Oxford–New York, Oxford University Press.

Hoyos, D. B. 1978. In defense of CIL II 760. *Athenaeum* 56: 390-395.

Hope, V. 1998. Negotiating identity and status: the gladiators of Roman Nîmes. In Ray Laurence and Joanne Berry (eds.), *Cultural Identity in the Roman Empire*: 179-195. London–New York, Routledge.

Hope, V. 2000 (a). Essay Five: Status and identity in the Roman world. In Janet Huskinson (ed.), *Experiencing Rome: Culture, Identity and Power in the Roman Empire*. London–New York, Routledge: 125-152

Hope, V. 2000 (b). Fighting for identity: the funerary commemoration of Italian gladiators. *BICS* 44: 93-113.
Ivleva, T. 2014. Remembering Britannia: expressions of identities by Britons on the Continent during the Roman Empire. In Brita Alroth and Charlotte Scheffer (eds.), *Attitudes towards the Past in Antiquity. Creating Identities: Proceedings of an International Conference held at Stockholm University 15-17 May 2009*: 217-231. (Stockholm Studies in Classical Archaeology 14.) Stockholm, Acta Universitatis Stockholmiensis.
Ivleva, T. 2016. Britons on the Move. In Martin Millett, Alison Moore, and Louise Revell (eds.), *The Oxford Handbook of Roman Britain*. Oxford, Oxford University Press: 245-261.
Just, R. 1989. Triumph of the *ethnos*. In Elizabeth Tonkin, Maryon McDonald, and Malcolm Chapman (eds.), *History and Ethnicity*: 71-88. London, Routledge.
Kazanski, M. and Périn, P. 2008. Identité ethnique en Gaule à l'époque des Grandes Migrations et des Royaumes barbares. *Antiquités nationales* 39: 181-216.
Kiss. G., Tóth, E. and Balázs, Z. C. (eds.). 1998. *Savaria – Szombathely története a város alapításától 1526-ig*. Szombathely, Szombathely Megyei Jogú Város Önkormányzata.
Kovács, P. 2010. Notes on the 'Jewish' inscriptions in Pannonia. *JAJ* 1: 159-180.
Kovács, P.. 2015. Natione Boius, or what happened to the Boii? In László Borhy (ed.), *Studia archaeologica Nicolae Szabó LXXV annos nato dedicata*: 173-182. Budapest, L'Harmattan, ELTE.
Laurence, R. and Berry, J. 2001. *Cultural identity in the Roman Empire*. London–New York, Routledge.
Lefebvre, S. 2011. Onomastique et identité provinciale. In Antonio Caballos Rufino and Sabine Lefebvre (eds.), *Roma generadora de identitades. La experiencia Hispana*: 153-170. (Coleccion de la Casa de Velázquez 123.) Madrid, Casa de Velázquez, Universidad de Sevilla.
Mathisen, R. W. 2006. Peregrini, barbari, and cives Romani: Concepts of citizenship and the legal identity of barbarians in the later Roman Empire. *AHR* 111, 4: 1011-1040.
Van Minnen, P. 1995. Paul the Roman citizen. *JSNT* 17: 43-52.
Mrozewicz, L. 1989. Domo Dacia (zu AE 1957, 306). *ZPE* 78: 163-164.
Nicolet, C. 1976. *Le métier de citoyen dans la Rome républicaine*. Paris, Gallimard.
Oltean, I. 2009. Dacian ethnic identity and the Roman army. In William S. Hanson (ed.), *The Army and Frontiers of Rome. Papers Offered to David J. Breeze on the Occasion of his Sixty-Fifth Birthday and His Retirement from Historic Scotland*: 90-103. (JRA Suppl., 74.) Portsmouth, R.I., Journal of Roman Archaeology.
Ricci, C. 2000. Domo Roma. Il contributo della capitale all'esercito di confine e alle milizie urbane (età imperiale). In Géza Alföldy (ed.), *Kaiser, Heer und Gesellschaft in der römischen Kaiserzeit: Gedenkschrift für Eric Birley*: 193-206. (Heidelberger althistorische Beiträge und epigraphische Studien, 31.) Stuttgart, Franz Steiner.
Le Roux, P. 1986. Les diplômes militaires et l'évolution de l'armée romaine de Claude à Septime Sévère: auxilia, numeri et nations. In Werner Eck and

Hartmut Wolff (eds.), *Heer und Integrationspolitik. Die römische militärdiplome als historische Quelle*: 347-374. (Passauer historische Forschungen, 2.) Köln–Wien, Böhlau.

Le Roux, P. 2013. Provinces romaines d'Occident et nations modernes. *Historika: Studi di storia greca e romana* 2: 205-230.

Safran, W. 2008. Names, labels, and identities: sociopolitical contexts and the question of ethnic categorization. *Identities: Global Studies in Culture and Power* 15, 4: 437-461

Sherwin-White, A. N. 1973. *The Roman Citizenship*[2]. Oxford, Clarendon Press.

Speidel, Michael A. 1985. Domo Hispanus. *Gerión* 3: 347-349.

Speidel, Michael A. 1986. The soldiers' homes. In Werner Eck and Hartmut Wolff (eds.), *Heer und Integrationspolitik. Die römische militärdiplome als historische Quelle*: 467-481. (Passauer historische Forschungen, 2.) Köln–Wien, Böhlau.

Speidel, M. A. 2007. Rekruten für ferne Provinzen. Der Papyrus ChLA X 422 und die kaiserliche Rekrutierungszentrale. *ZPE* 163: 281-295.

Speidel, M. A. 2010. Pro patria mori... La doctrine du patriotisme romain dans l'armée impériale. *CCGG* 21: 139-154.

Stegemann, W. 1987. War der Apostel Paulus ein römischer Bürger?. *ZNW* 78, 3-4: 200-229.

Thomas, Y. 1996. *Origine et commune patrie: étude de droit public romain (89 av. JC-212 ap. JC)*. (Collection de l'École française de Rome, 221.) Rome, École française de Rome.

Tovar, A. 1989. *Iberische Landeskunde. Segunda parte. Las tribus y las ciudades de la antigua Hispania*. Tomo 3. Tarraconensis. Baden Baden, Heitz.

Walbank, F. W. 1972. Nationality as a factor in Roman history. *HSCPh* 76: 145-168.

Whitehorne. J. E. G. 2001. Becoming an Alexandrian citizen. *Communicazioni* (Universita degli Studi di Firenze, Istituto Papirologico 'Girolamo Vitelli') 4: 25-34.

Wiedemann, T. 1992. *Emperors and Gladiators*. London–New York, Routledge.

Williams, M. H. 1997. The meaning and function of Ioudaios in Graeco-Roman inscriptions. *ZPE* 116: 249-262.

Wilson, S. J. 2000, ΟΙ ΠΟΤΕ ΙΟΥΔΑΙΟΙ. Epigraphic evidence for Jewish defectors. In Stephen G. Wilson and Michael Desjardins (eds.), *Text and Artifact in the Religions of Mediterranean Antiquity. Essays in Honor of Peter Richardson*. ESCJ, 9. Waterloo, Wilfred Laurier University Press: 354-371.

Yébenes, S. P. 2007. Las patrias de soldado romano en el alto imperio. In Julio Mangas and Santiago Montero (eds.), *Ciudadanos y extranjeros en el mundo antiguo: segregación e integración*: 143-174. (Antigüedad 1.) Madrid, Edicones.

Centurions: military or social elite?

George Cupcea

Questions

The matter of military personnel and their involvement in civil life has long been a question of debate. The particular aspects which I would like to focus upon in this paper are related to one specific rank – the centurion. The questions I would like to answer in the following pages are basically, but not limited to: *Why centurions? Are centurions soldiers? What is their place in and relation to the civil society? Are they society members or political agents? Are they any kind of an elite?*

Why centurions?

Centurions are of special interest because of their particular manner of recruitment, promotion and social status. Academics have been debating the origin of centurions for more than a century, starting from two different positions. The creator of the first view, A. von Domaszewski, started from the idea that the Roman-Italian component of legionary centurions, in order to obtain tactical and loyal unity of the army, obtained until the 3rd century AD.[1] The other view was based on an analysis of epigraphic evidence and reached different conclusions. E. Birley, proposed a brand new direction in the study of this rank, and reached the conclusion that the simple centurion names, without the indication of *origo*,[2] especially if they were Roman, could not indicate clearly the origin of the officer.[3] When noticing the multitude of centurions who did not have Italian origin, Domaszewski's further opinion is not known.[4] The conclusions were stated in brief by B. Dobson: the gradual provincialization of legionary and implicitly centurion recruitment.[5]

---

[1] Domaszewski 1908: 83-90; Dessau 1910: 2-24.
[2] CIL VIII 18084.
[3] Birley 1941: 190.
[4] Birley 1941: 191-198. Another essential contribution is that of G. Forni who centralized the origins of legionaries from the Empire in two contributions twenty years apart and although he did not necessarily focus on the origins of centurions, sometimes even excluding them from his statistics, his study confirms what was already known: the theories regarding the increasing provincial character of the legions starting in the 1st century but especially from the 2nd century onwards. Forni 1953: especially 65-75 and Forni 1974: 380-390.
[5] Dobson, Mann 1973: 192-197: At the beginning of the Principate, the Italians dominated the legions, but rapidly their numbers begin to dwindle in favor of colonies already Romanized, from Narbonensis, Hispania and Africa. Starting with Hadrian the Italians no longer volunteer to serve

Access to the rank is another question of debate, but most opinions agree concerning the sources of the legionary centurionate, namely three categories: former legionary *principales*, former praetorian *principales* and directly-appointed centurions. A closer look might reveal several subcategories in these groups.[6] A conclusion that can be obtained from these statistics is that for the *ex caligati* in most cases the post of centurion was the culmination of a fine career that could include service in the auxiliary or praetorian troops.[7] Directly-appointed centurions belong to the provincial elite, they may or may not be knights or even sons of centurions; in any case, their possibilities depended on the quality of their origin and that of their father.

With regard to their social status during their service in the army, just as much ink has been spilled. The social role of the centurion varies a lot; he is probably the officer who best defines Roman imperial society. But what about his own social status? Is he associated with the knights, or this is false even in theory? What is certain is that the Roman military environment allowed for the greatest social mobility and the centurionate was the only way legally to advance up the steps of the social pyramid.[8] When in service, the advantages of centurions were limited to the military domain. The emperor was not opposed to relations of camaraderie,

---

in the legions, preferring praetorian cohorts and until the end of the 2nd century all legions received recruits from colonies of veterans of the provinces and also from the men living in the *canabae*. Once veterans settled down in the area where they served, military families are created, several specialized generations, which will offer the majority of recruits in the 2nd century, for the whole frontier army, as well as the majority of centurions and officers of equestrian ranks. P. Le Roux discusses the situation of centurions from Hispania. Le Roux, 1982: 294-299. Similar situations in Le Bohec 1989: 184; Christol 1994: 181-187, for the legion *III Augusta*, in Traverso 2000 for *II Augusta* and in Dabrowa 1993: 102-103 for *X Fretensis*. To all of this we must add the contributions for each legion published together in the papers of a conference on this subject by Y. Le Bohec, as well as more recent contributions. Le Bohec 2000; Mosser 2003; Malone 2006.

[6] Dobson, Breeze 1969: 100: A(1) – legionnaires, only towards legionary centurionate, until Severus, following 15-20 years of service; B(2a) – praetorian *principales*, towards legionary, but not praetorian, centurionate; B(2b) – *evocati*, towards legionary, but not praetorian, centurionate; B(3) – *evocati*, towards centurionate in Rome and then in the legions; B(4) – centurions from Rome, without serving in the legions, but who can become *primipili* directly (late cases); C(5) – directly appointed, only legionary centurions; C(6) – directly appointed, served as centurions in legions and in Rome.

[7] Richier 2004: 445.

[8] Stein 1927: 136-139, 208; Zwicky 1944: 89-91; Speidel 1993: *passim*. In the dissolution period from the end of the Republic we also encounter abuses but admittance into the equestrian order following a professional military career was restricted only to those soldiers who, after a long and arduous service had become superior officers; this was one of Augustus' inventions. The connection between soldiers and knights was created by the *primipilaris* who, as a soldier has passed through all ranks of *principales*, then through the centurionate to finally be *primus pilus*. Centurions are part of the third category of officers, next to soldiers, but the position is also open for knights and they do not have to give up membership in the equestrian order.

choosing to keep group unity even after discharge.[9] Thus centurions remain, even after discharge, officers, spokesmen and even venerable parental figures for the soldiers.[10] What happened to their status as knights while serving as centurions? It has been proven on several occasions that they did not have to give up being members in the *ordo equester*. From the time of Severus, moreover, the barrier between the *militia* and the *ordo equester* seemed to dissolve completely.[11]

Finally, to answer the main question, we are considering centurions because of their particular social status, their involvement in the most reliable machine for social mobility, their variation in the practice of the rank, their being the most socially-active group of the Roman army and most involved in provincial civil life.

Are centurions soldiers?

With regard to the payment grades in the Roman army, a centurion must have been paid 15 times the *stipendium* of a legionary, a *primus ordo* 30 times and a *primus pilus* 60 times that amount. At the beginning of the Principate a legionary centurion must have received 4,5 times the *stipendium* of a praetorian (1,5 that of an *evocatus*). Another principle is the constant increase in the centurion's *stipendium* in direct proportion to that of the soldier, during the first three centuries of the Empire, because the hierarchy of the army and the promotion systems did not change radically in this period.[12] Moreover, some centurions preferred to call their earnings *salaria*, instead of *stipendia*, like the praetorian *evocati* or other contracted specialists.[13] The *praemium* received at discharge only served to supplement the possible businesses centurions might have started while still enlisted.[14]

The literary competence of centurions is relevant for their individual level of culture and, although they came from different classes, as an indication of their general level.[15] It was unacceptable for a centurion to be illiterate. The army

---

[9] Tacitus, *Ann.* 14.27.3. The fact that hierarchical relations were still respected even after discharge can be also deduced from AE 1975, 570, AE 1923, 33. MacMullen 1984: 442.
[10] Caesar, *BG* 1.43, 7.17, *BC* 1.64. MacMullen 1984: 455.
[11] Richier 2004: 463.
[12] Speidel 1992: 101-102, and most recently Speidel 2014: esp. 56.
[13] Speidel 2014: 53 and n. 4.
[14] AE 1978, 635. Q. Atilius Primus, who goes from *interprex* to *centurio* and *negotiator*, sent in mission at the *Quadi* owned a considerable enterprise, which he leaves for his four freedmen to inherit. Centurions and soldiers are also involved in economic transactions and as witnesses at contracts, meaning they received a percentage. IDR I TabCerD VIII; Verboven 2007: 18-19.
[15] The difference between promoted centurions and those directly appointed resided in their education. For example, a legionary centurion, probably *ex equite Romano*, addresses Cerealis on a familiar tone. *Tab. Vind.* 2.255.

needed a number of educated men,[16] maybe even to the point of knowing several languages.[17] As far as the religious role of the centurion is concerned it seems this was rather monopolized by the *pimus pilus*. Most of the *ex-voto* monuments discovered to have been set up by centurions are set up in the name of the soldiers under their command. It falls to the centurion to commemorate the fulfillment of the vexillation's mission, but his religious role is strongly diminished in the legion, where he is overtaken by the *primus pilus*, the one whose honour it is to celebrate the *aquila* in the name of the whole legion.

Starting with Severus, from the rank of centurion and above, the military make up a rather coherent social group, with political influence, prestige and a safe economic position. This social elevation of the military can best be observed in the offering of the golden ring, the statutory symbol of the *equites*,[18] to centurions and *principales* as proof of their being considered as potential knights. This 'esprit de corps' can also be noticed from the banding of soldiers according to rank in those associations called *collegia*. Also they share the same cults and become proud of the political role of the army because it is the same Severus who grants them the right to legal marriage, thus they become active members of the urban society around the forts. Even more so, the inheritance of the military profession is another contribution to the solidification of this new social layer.[19]

In general, we cannot consider the centurions mere soldiers, simply because there is a fundamental hierarchical difference – that of command. Authority is generally assumed, as well as *iure gladii* over the soldiers under his command. The living quarters and mobility opportunities are substantially increased, plus, their variety of tasks involves them in all aspects of Roman life and society. Furthermore they never become veterans in the general sense of the word.

In relation to society, centurions can play a panoply of roles: political, juridical, economic, cultural/religious or simply an active role in the local civil society.

---

[16] The famous writer M. Valerius Probus tried for many years to become centurion and although he failed this example does not prove the exclusion of very educated men from the army. P. Alfenius Varus, a *trecenarius* makes a *chirographum*, indicating he knows how to write but not also his intellectual level. Vegetius, *Epit*. 2.19; Suetonius, *Gramm*. 24.1.

[17] Not all centurions who speak two languages know Greek and Latin. The future emperor Maximinus Thrax, whilst still a young soldier serving under Severus, did not speak Latin and addresses the emperor in 'an almost Thracian' language but, later on, he becomes a centurion and *primipilus* and thus must have learnt Latin at an acceptable level. *HA, Maxim*. 2.5. Another example of bilingualism is when a barbarian language is learnt as is the case of the centurion discovered in Slovakia, translator and *negotiator* with the Quadi. To conclude we can say that the education of the officers of the Roman army, particularly that of centurions, was just as heterogeneous as their social origin. Adams 1999: 132-133.

[18] *Digest* 3.8.5.

[19] Alföldy 1979: 151-152.

'Political' centurions

Most of the centurions involved in politics are in practical terms administrators. In this role, they are acting as managers of a particular administrative units – *regionarii* – in at least 26 examples in the entire Roman Empire: Britannia, Pannonia, Lower Moesia, Dacia, Asia, Syria, Egypt, Africa. These are military men, in charge of the administration and security of non-urban administrative units, sometimes temporarily, but very few are actually attested in close relation to the society they manage. Community administration is a task especially for those units which are of a lesser scale than a proper urban Roman establishment, with all its civil administrative features. Another function close to this registry is the public security of settlements, even urban, or areas of imperial property. The most relevant examples come from the eastern half of the Empire.

The matter of the involvement of the centurions in civil communities first came to attention at the beginning of the 20th century, alongside that of the *centuriones regionarii* in the East, when a particular inscription of Antioch in Pisidia was discussed.[20] Aurelius Dionysius, the centurion, transliterated into Greek as *regionarius* (ἑκατόνταρχος ῥεγεωνάριος), is honoured by the community of Antioch for his work in the service of the citizens and 'peace and justice keeping'; he is considered as the officer in charge of order and internal security in the city and its surroundings.[21] The term used specifically in this instance reveals that the authority of the *centurio regionarius* is extended over an entire *regio*, which must have had a specific significance in Roman administrative practice. In this particular case, *Mygnonia* most probably extended south of Phrygia and it had a police/internal security character, because of attestations of *stationarii*, *beneficiarii consularis*, probably under the command of the centurion in Antioch.[22] In fact, all of Asia Minor is an entirely particular area of the Empire in its administrative evolution, Phrygia is not acting as a province *per se*, but rather as a unit of imperial estates, *regiones* and *tractus*, gathered in a wider district, under a freedman imperial procurator, starting with Hadrian.[23] In this particular case, Aurelius Dionysius is honoured by the local community for his kindness, the peace he helped keep and the numerous lives he saved.[24]

---

[20] IGRR III 301.
[21] *Regio Phrygia*, according to Calder 1912, 80-4. The statue base has a couple of hexametric verses on the side, describing the dedication from the community of Mygdonia (poetic/Homeric name of Phrygia), Merkelbach, Stauber 2001: 403.
[22] Hirschfeld 1891: 863-864; Calder 1912: 82-83; Fuhrmann 2012: 224; Faure 2013: 130.
[23] Hirt 2010: 114.
[24] Brélaz 2005: 266. Full text: Αὐρ(ήλιον) Διονύσι/ον τὸν ἀξιο/λογότατον ἑ/κατόνταρχον/ ῥεγεωνάριον/ ἡ λαμπρὰ τῶν Ἀν/τιοχέων μητρό/πολις ἐπι(ι)εκίας/τε κ[α]ὶ τῆ(ς) εἰρή/νης ἕνεκα...

The monument, attesting a very special relationship between the dedicators and the honoured centurion is not relevant for any such situation present in the Eastern cities, where, at least in theory, the military would have preferred not to interfere with the civilian administration and public order institutions. There are, however, a few exceptions to this, out of which the case of Dionysius of Antioch in Pisidia is the most resounding. But he is not the only one in such a situation. Aulus Instuleius Tenax, centurion of *X Fretensis*, is highly honoured by the *boulé* and *demos* of the city of Ashkelon, in Palestine, on account of his goodwill towards the city.[25] The honorific inscription of Ashkelon is set on a statue base, precisely in the civil centre of the city (the basilica and *bouleuterion*), together with one other dedicated to another, important local citizen.[26] His role and relation to the community must have been highly important to the city, if they decided to honour him in such an official manner, practically identical to the case of Antioch.

In Syria and Mesopotamia, centurions and other soldiers, *beneficiarii*, *stationarii*, are mentioned in relation to police duties, public order and surveillance or sentence enforcement.[27] Here, the centurions of *III Gallica* and *XIV Flavia firma*,[28] are benefactors of the local communities, as they contributed to several infrastructure projects in the city, and to road security in Trachonitis,[29] a peripheral region, non-urbanized, crossed by important trade routes. In another case, a series of centurions of *IIII Scythica*, from Henu, a small Nabataean sanctuary on the road from Damascus to Bostra, are probably in charge of road surveillance and security for the entire region.[30] A certain status seems to be revealed in the title of a legionary of *VIII Augusta*, α κούστως Σεἰα, which can very well be the equivalent of an *agens regionis*...[31] To these we can add the numerous attestations of the involvement of centurions and other military in the police duties of Palestine, in the Gospels, recently argued in a very comprehensive publication.[32]

---

[25] AE 1923, 83, also known from CIL III 30, dated AD 65, when he became a *primus pilus* of the legion XII Fulminata. On his story see Eck 2015: 145–160.
[26] Boehm, Master, Le Blanc 2016, 271 324.
[27] *P.Euphr.* 2: κατὰ τόπους ἑκατοντάρχῳ; and *P.Euphr* 5: Ἰουλ(ίῳ) Μαρείνῳ (ἑκατοντάρχῳ) τῷ ἐπὶ τῆς εὐταξίας Σφωρακηνῆς...
[28] CIG III 4542=IGR III 1120 and CIG III 4543=IGR III 1121, 1122, Phaena.
[29] Pollard 2000: 96; Stoll 2001: 73.
[30] Speidel 1998: 185-186.
[31] Pollard 2000: 96-97.
[32] Kyrychenko 2014.

Centurions as judges

The general assumption is that centurions can be in charge of order/security maintenance and justice for entire regions, both rural and urban.[33] Ancient literary sources indicate such prerogatives: Juvenal, *Sat.* 16.13-4 (a centurion acting as judge for a case between a soldier and a civilian); Eusebius, *HE* 6.41.21; *Digest* 47.2.73; 5.1.61.1, attesting centurions as *iudices dati*. They are appointed by provincial governors, especially in regions where the proper civilian institutions were missing (two centurions of the XIth legion appointed judges by the governor in Dalmatia).[34] These were probably investigators of a certain kind who would consequently forward the results of their inquiries to the superior courts. Quantitatively, they are best attested in Egypt, where the role of centurions and other officers in the administration of justice is clearly visible, but whose competence apparently is limited to common felonies.[35]

In the West we have but a few such attestations in highly-Romanized regions of the Empire such as Spain, Dalmatia or Italy. More precisely, in Hispalis, Baetica, southern Spain, a community of sorts of sailors, operating small boats, on rivers or along the shoreline – *scapharii*[36] – dedicate a statue base to the *primus pilus* L. Castricius Q. f. Honoratus, a 'good man', due to his 'innocence and singular justice'.[37] Regarding the dedicators, these *scapharii* from Hispalis, apparently both marines and tradesmen, are very active official dedicators in this region, making themselves noticed also with a statue to emperor Hadrian.[38] The more interesting fact is their connection to official Roman power and its representative in the field, in this case a former centurion. His presence here is somewhat peculiar: the region was Roman since Republican times, highly assimilated and completely non-militarized. How then does a *primus pilus* come to act as a judge in such a substantial, Roman civilian environment? We can only assume that his role was to bring justice in a particular commercial dispute that these *scapharii* had at one time, by appointment from the emperor himself – acting thus as *iudex datus*. Another similar situation from the west, is the tombstone of C. Manlius Valerianus, of Aquileia, former cavalry officer (?), acting as a judge in the interest of the city.[39] Finally, the most eloquent such appointment of centurions dates from the time of Caligula, in Promona,

---

[33] MacMullen 1963: 55-56.
[34] CIL III 9832, according to Pollard 2000: 94.
[35] MacMullen 1964: 315; Campbell 1984: 433-434; Fuhrmann 2012: 223.
[36] Cf. Campbell 2012: 260.
[37] CIL II 1183, Hispalis, Baetica: *L. Castricio Q. f./Honorato p(rimo) p(ilo)/homini bono/scaphari(i)/Romul(ae) consist(entes)/ob innocentiam/et singularem/iustitiam eius/d(e) s(ua) p(ecunia) p(osuerunt)*. Other mentions of *scapharii* in Strabo, 5.3.5; *Digest* 14.2.4; CIL II 1168.
[38] CIL II 1168, Hispalis, Baetica.
[39] CIL V 923, Aquileia.

Dalmatia, where centurions of XIth legion are *iudices dati*, appointed directly by the governor.[40]

In the East, the evidence is of another kind. A significant number of *papyri* from both Egypt and Syria attest Roman officers, centurions, decurions and *beneficiarii*, acting as judges in rural, non-Romanized areas of the provinces. They are probably investigators of a certain kind, which would consequently forward the results of their inquiries to the superior courts. They are styled mostly as 'centurions/officers of this place', in some cases the settlement or region in their area of competence being named.

In a series of recent works on the matter,[41] all petitions to military men were collected, leading to very interesting statistics. In total,[42] 41 are sent to centurions (four for centurions ἐπὶ τῶν τόπων and one for a Ἀρσινοείτῃ ἑκατοντάρχῃ), 13 for *beneficiarii* (five for *beneficiarii* ἐπὶ τῶν τόπων, one for a βενεφικιαρίῳ ἐν τῳ Ὀξυρυγχίτῃ and another two for the same βενεφικιαρίῳ στατίζοντι ἐν Ἀρσινοείτῃ) and ten for decurions.[43] The situations do not seem to indicate any clear relation between the competences of the centurions and the administrative limits of the *nomes*. Therefore, the geographic extent of their authority was vague,[44] leading to the conclusion that the denomination ἐπὶ τῶν τόπων must have been a popular attribute of the military officer closest in the field (*of this place*).[45] With regard to the contents and significance of these petitions, evidence is mixed. On one hand, a part of them seem only to draw attention to the military in the victim's closest vicinity (thus the personalisation of state authority) and to demand an inquiry, but a large part of them actually demand the act of justice to be pursued by the officer amid reparations of all kinds.[46] Where there is a clearly-defined area of competence, they attend only to small matters and petty justice and their authority is semi-official and rather given by their military reputation. At the same time, we have at least three examples in which the officer is named along with the locality he is active in (Ἀρσινοείτῃ, Ὀξυρυγχίτῃ). However, in the northern part of Fayoum, where most of this

---

[40] CIL III 9832, Promona, Dalmatia: *Vib]ullius t[rib(unus?)]/[le]g(ionis) VII et L(ucius) Sa[l]/[vius] M(arcus) Sueto ce[n]/[t]uriones leg(ionis) X[I]/[iu]dices d[a]ti ex/[co]nventione a/[L(ucio) V]olusio Satur/[ni]no leg(ato) pro pr(aetore)/[C(ai) C]aesaris Aug(usti)/[Ger]manici inter/...*

[41] Alston 1995; Peachin 2007: 79-97; Gallazzi 2007: 90-100; Whitehorne 2004: 155-169.

[42] By now, at least 81, acc. to Whitehorne 2004: 161-169.

[43] Alston 1995: 88-90. Updated by Whitehorne 2004: 161-169.

[44] However, noticeable for some *beneficiarii* in CBFIR 647 (Montana), P.Cair.isid. 63 and 139 (Arsinoe), P.Mich.inv, 1960 (Oxyrichos) and a centurion in P.Mich 6.425 (Arsinoe).

[45] *Contra* Alston 1995: 93.

[46] Peachin 2007: 89-91. Peachin debates the particular case of P.Sijp 15, dated AD 50-51, an extensive petition for violence and theft, to a centurion that is in office since AD 46 (P.Thomas 5).

evidence comes from,⁴⁷ there is no other form of Roman authority present, and they may represent the only means by which Roman law gets to this rural and remote environment. Therefore, even with no formal legal training they are the only images of authority available to the simple peasants in any marginal, scarcely Romanized area.⁴⁸

Concluding, acting as judge (*sella pacis sedere*) was a crowning accomplishment for a centurion, worth mentioning along with the primipilate.⁴⁹

Centurions in culture and religion

The involvement of centurions and officers in civil, cultural and religious life is a fact. Their presence and contribution to provincial society is important, because they are seen, along with the veterans, as agents of Romanisation, practically as the integrators of new civil structures in the Roman way of life.

In this sense, centurions are involved actively in the religious and cultural life of the community, through the erection of monuments, restoration of temples and many other charity works, for the profit of the community. The more significant their work, considering that the majority do not originate in the communities they assist, the more developed social relation between the benefactor and the beneficiary is suggested. Reaching this conclusion, I only took into consideration dedications made outside the military milieu, these corresponding, somewhat logically, mostly to detached soldiers or officers.

To exemplify this, I have chosen a few cases, from both the western and eastern halves of the Empire. Britain has its share of architectural munificence deriving from soldiers, and present not exclusively in militarized zones.⁵⁰ A *centurio regionarius*, C. Severius Emeritus raises an altar mentioning the restoration of a holy spot, wrecked by insolent hands and cleansed afresh, to the virtue and numen of the Emperor, in Bath-Aquae Sulis.⁵¹ This gesture implies that the centurion was on some kind of official duty in the well-known spa centre of Bath, as *regionarius*, and was able, through his own means, which were not negligible, as was seen above, to restore a destroyed sanctuary. This is the only public work effected by a military person at Bath. There are other examples of

---

⁴⁷ There are only 10 examples coming from the Oxyrhynchite (urban), but more than 64 coming from the Arsinoite (predominantly rural). Whitehorne 2004: 158.
⁴⁸ Peachin 2007: 83-84, 95-96.
⁴⁹ AE 1928, 37 = IDRE II 456, Aquae Flavianae, Numidia.
⁵⁰ See Blagg 1990: esp. 20.
⁵¹ CIL VII 45 = RIB 152, Bath – Aquae Sulis: *Locum reli/giosum per in/solentiam e/rutum/virtuti et n(umini) /Aug(usti) repurga/tum reddidit /C(aius) Severius /Emeritus >/(centurio)/reg(ionarius)*.

centurions, *primi pili* and other, higher officers involved in public works, but most of them are in the close vicinity of forts.⁵² In fact, the only other public works effected by military men are those of soldiers or officers on detatchment duty, mostly *beneficiarii* or guards.⁵³

In Lower Moesia, especially in the *regio Montanensium*, a very particular region administered by military men,⁵⁴ I choose to deliver two examples, both referring to the restoration of the temple of Diana in Gromšin – Montana, apparently a very important holy place for the military serving in the region. The first is a common effort, by the entire squadron of *regionarii*, under the leadership of the centurion, in the form of a construction dedication, datable to Marcus Aurelius and Lucius Verus, mentioning the restoration of the temple affected by old age, by the governor M. Servilius Fabianus, through the military present on the spot - *per reg(ionarios) Mont(anenses)*.⁵⁵ The second is an altar to Diana and Apollo, for the health of the governor, put up by Ael. Artemidorus, a centurion of *I Italica, regionarius*.⁵⁶ Even though these gestures are made in a somewhat military context, they are actually public works, in the furtherance of a Roman society in this remote region of the Empire.

In Dacia, another so-called military province, soldiers and officers are deeply involved in civil life and society, as they are one of the main cohesive factors of the provincial structures, especially in the two 'capitals', Sarmizegetusa and Apulum. Here the situation is even more significant, as veterans alongside active soldiers are actual members of civil society, being awarded municipal honours, even in exception to the general rule, that excludes active military from this.⁵⁷

In particular, a centurion of *XXII Primigenia*, P. Tenacius P. f. Papiria Vindex, probably originating in Apulum, is a *bouleutes* of the *civitas Nicopolitanensis*, and honoured with a statue by his *augustalis* in his home town, on land offered by the decree of the decurions.⁵⁸ The decurions of Apulum seem to compensate the lack of municipal distinctions for Vindex with the grant of public land, probably in the city centre, for the erection of a statue, honouring the now

---

⁵² RIB 583, 587, 850, 886, 1272, 1334, 1396, 1988, cf. Blagg 1990: 20.
⁵³ RIB 88, 235, 725, cf. Blagg 1990: 20.
⁵⁴ See most recently Cupcea 2016: *in print*.
⁵⁵ CIL III 12385, Gromšin Montana, dated AD 162.
⁵⁶ CIL III 12371, Gromšin – Montana, dated AD 159-160.
⁵⁷ IDR III/2 113, Sarmizegetusa, where two officers on duty, a *b(ene)f(iciarius) co(n)s(ularis)* and a *scriniarius praef(ectorum) praet(orio)* are distinguished as *dec(uriones) col(oniae)* in absence, just because they are part of an important military family of the city. Also the *medicus* of the legion *VII Claudia*, from Drobeta (IDR II 42) is *ornat(us) ornament(is) decu[r(ionalibus)]*. Discussion in detail in Ardevan 1994; Cupcea 2014: 70-71, 110-112.
⁵⁸ CIL III 1481, 6265 = IDR III/5 582, 518, Apulum.

regional notable. The second case that I wish to exemplify is more than a regional celebrity, being the possessor of no less than five honorary statues in two different provinces, Italy and Dacia.[59] He is the famous P. Ael. P. f. Papiria Marcellus, again, probably originating in Apulum, centurion and Roman knight, bearing seven distinctive municipal honours, while in service:[60] *flamen Lucularis, sacerdos Laurentium Lavinatium, patronus et decurio coloniae Apulensis, patronus rerum publicarum Fulginiatium, Foro Flaminensium itemque Iguvinorum*. Again, we are dealing with an exceptionally well-established member of the provincial elite, who has a prodigious military career simultaneously with a civil, municipal and religious one.

On the other side of the Empire, evidence from Syria brings most of the contributions to the matter in discussion. For example, most of the inscriptions from Phaenae come from a monumental building, now destroyed, which may have been a temple.[61] The inscriptions attesting centurions seem to come in sequence, beginning with C. Egnatius Fuscus (AD 166-169), T. Aurelius Quirinalis (AD 169), Petusius Eudemus and finally C. Helvius Marianus. All are distinctive benefactors of this rural community, and are honoured, each, separately by the community. Among them, Marianus, centurion of *III Gallica* is mentioned precisely as 'donating a shrine and a statue on his own expense'.[62]

Conclusions

Are we able to answer the main question of this paper? Are centurions an elite? If so, what kind of an elite?

First, they are definitely a **military** elite. They have a superior, privileged status, huge salary, marvellous perspectives for their career. This is best noticed from the dedication in verse made by a centurion in Aquae Flavianae, Numidia: *[O]ptavi Dacos tenere caesos tenui/[opt]avi in sella pacis residere sedi/[o]ptavi claros sequi triumphos factum/optavi primi commoda plena pili hab[ui]/optavi nudas videre Nymphas vidi.*[63]

Second, **socially** they rather seem like an *imported/conjunctural* elite, in my opinion, because of the following reasons:

---

[59] CIL III 7795, 1181, 1182=IDR III/5 442, 441, 439 - Apulum; CIL XI 5215, 5216 – Fulginiae.
[60] His career was vast and prodigious: *centurio frumentarius, suprinceps peregrinorum, hastatus, princeps* and *primus pilus* of *VII Claudia* (all three centurionates in the first cohort!) and prefect of two legions – *VII Claudia* and *I Adiutrix*.
[61] IGRR III 1113-1118.
[62] IGRR III 1116, CIL III 162.
[63] AE 1928, 37 = IDRE II 456, El-Hamma – Aquae Flavianae, Numidia.

- They are active socially only where regular, civil elites are lacking;
- They perform acts of munificence only in strict relation to the community they oversee;
- Most of them are actually performing a political task or a military mission in a civilian environment;
- As political/military agents, the communities with which they are in contact seem to adopt them in their elite structure;
- This can merely be an act of political loyalty towards the central authority, symbolized by the governor and the emperor, which it actually is, in some instants;
- Nevertheless, most of the cases discussed are clear images of personal connection between the community and its overseer, only situations like this being able to generate acts of public gratitude as the ones presented.

The Roman military environment ensures the most effective plan of social mobility and, more precisely, the centurionate is the only way legally to climb the steps of the social pyramid. The mixture of military and civilian milieus produces this alternate form of local elite, the centurion in service, if not general practice, was surely widespread at least in the time of the Principate. However, in the end, ancient literate society would still look on military men, regardless whether they were soldiers, centurions or even *primi pili*, with reserve, mixed feelings and contempt – **men in boots!**

References

Adams, J. N. 1999. The Poets of Bu Njem: Language, Culture and the Centurionate. JRS 89: 109-134.

Alföldy, G. 1979. *Römische Sozialgeschichte²*. Wiesbaden: Franz Steiner.

Alston, R. 1995. *Soldier and Society in Roman Egypt. A Social History*, London: Routledge.

Alston, R. The Ties that bind: soldiers and societies. In: A. Goldsworthy and I. Haynes (eds.), *The Roman Army as a Community*, JRA Suppl. 34: 175-195.

Ardevan, R. 1994. Die Beneficiarier im Zivilleben der Provinz Dakien. In E. Schallmayer (ed.), *Der römsiche Weihebezirk von Osterburken II*, Stuttgart: Theiss. 199-204.

Birley, E. 1941. The Origins of Legionary Centurions, LAq 11: 47-62 (MAVORS IV, 189-205).

Blagg, T. F. C. 1990. Architectural Munificence in Britain: The Evidence of Inscriptions. Britannia 21: 13-31.

Le Bohec, Y. 1989. *La Troisième légion Auguste*, Paris: De Boccard.

Le Bohec, Y, Wolff, C. (eds.). 1998. *Les légions de Rome sous le Haut-Empire (Actes du Congrès de Lyon, 17-19 septembre 1998)*. Lyon-Paris: De Boccard.

Boehm, R., Master, D. M. and Le Blanc, R. 2016. The basilica, bouleuterion and civic center of Ashkelon. AJA 120, 2: 271-324.

Brélaz, C. 2005. La sécurité publique en Asie Mineure sous le Principat (Ier-IIIème s. ap. J.-C.). Institutions municipals et institutions impériales dans l'Orient romain, *SBA* 32.

Calder, W. M. 1912. Colonia Caesareia Antiocheia. *JRS* 2: 78-109.

Campbell, B. 1984. *The Emperor and the Roman Army*. Oxford University Press.

Campbell, B. 2012. *Rivers and the Power of Ancient Rome*. North Carolina University Press.

Christol, M. 1994. Sur quelques centurions de la légion III Augusta. *ZPE* 103: 101-107.

Cupcea, G. 2016. On Police and Administrative Duties of the Roman Military: *Regionarii*. *ActaMN* 53/I: in print.

Dabrowa, E. 1993. *Legio X Fretensis. A Prosopographical Study of its Officers (I-III c. AD)*. *Historia Einzelschriften* LXVI. Stuttgart: Franz Steiner.

Dessau, H. 1910. Die Herkunft der Offiziere und Beamten Römischen Kaiserreichs. Während der Ersten Zwei Jahrh. Seines Bestehens. Hermes 45/1: 1-26 & 45/4: 615-617.

Dobson, B., Breeze, D.J. 1969. The Rome Cohorts and the Legionary Centuionate. *EpSt* 8: 100-124.

Dobson, B., Mann, J.C. 1973. The Roman Army in Britain and Britons in the Roman Army. *Britannia* 4: 191-205.

von Domaszewski, A. 1908/1967. *Die Rangordnung des römischen Heeres* (and the 2nd edition, ed. B. Dobson), Bonn/Köln-Graz.

Eck, W. 2015. Statuenehrungen als Zeugnis für den Einfluss römischer Amtsträger im Leben einer Provinz. In: L. Bryce and D. Slootjes (eds.), *Aspects of Ancient Institutions and Geography: Studies in Honor of Richard A. Talbert*. Leiden: Brill, 145-160.

Faure, P. 2013. *L'aigle et le cep. Les centurions légionnaires dans l'Empire des Sévères*, Scripta Antiqua 54, Bordeaux : Ausonius.

Forni, G. 1953. *Il recrutamento delle legioni da Augusto a Diocleziano*, Milano-Roma: Fratelli Bocca.

Forni, G. Estrazione etnica e sociale dei soldati delle legioni nei primi tre secoli dell'impero. *ANRW* II.1: 339-391.

Fuhrmann, C. 2012. *Policing the Roman Empire*. Oxford University Press.

Gallazzi, C. 2007. Petizione a un beneficiaries. In: A. Sriks and K. A. Worp (eds.), *Papyri in memory of P. J. Sijpesteijn*, American Society of Papyrologists. Chippenham: University of Michigan Press, 98-100.

Hirschfeld, O. 1891. *Die Sichercheitspolizei im römischen Kaiserreich* (Sitzungsberichte der Königlich Preussischen Akademie der Wissenschaften zu Berlin), Berlin: 845-877.

Hirt, A. M. 2010. *Imperial Mines and Quarries in the Roman World (Organizational Aspects 27 BC - AD 235)*, Oxford.

Kyrychenko, A. 2014. *The Roman Army and the Expansion of the Gospel. The Role of the Centurion in Luke-Acts*. Berlin: De Gruyter.

MacMullen, R. 1963. *Soldier and Civilian in the Later Roman Empire*. Harvard University Press.

MacMullen, R. 1964. Imperial Bureaucrats in Roman Provinces. *HSPh* 68: 305-316.

MacMullen, R. 1992. *Enemies of the Roman Order². Treason, Unrest and Alienation in the Empire*. London: Routledge.

Malone, S.J. 2006. *Legio XX Valeria Victrix. Prosopography, archaeology and history*. BAR IntS. 1491. Oxford: Archaeopress.

Merkelbach, R., Stauber J. (eds.). 2001. *Steinepigramme aus dem griechischen Osten Band 3: Der 'Ferne Osten' und das Landesinnere bis zum Tauros*. Berlin: De Gruyter.

Mosser, M. 2003. *Die Steindenkmäler der legio XV Apollinaris*. Wiener Archäologische Studien 5.

Peachin, M. 2007. Petition to a centurion from the NYU papyrus collection and the questioof informal adjudication performed by soldiers (P.Sijp.15). In: A. Sriks and K. A. Worp (eds.), *Papyri in memory of P.J. Sijpesteijn*. American Society of Papyrologists. Chippenham: University of Michigan Press, 79-98.

Pollard, N. 2000. *Soldiers, Cities and Civilians in Roman Syria*. Ann Arbour: University of Michigan Press.

Richier, O. 2004. *Centuriones ad Rhenum. Les centurions légionnaires des armées Romaines du Rhin*. Paris: De Boccard.

Richmond, I. A. 1945. The Sarmatae, Bremetennacvm Veteranorvm and the Regio Bremetennacensis. *JRS* 35: 15-29.

Le Roux, P. 1982. *L'armée romaine et l'organisation des provinces Ibériques*. Paris: De Boccard.

Speidel, M. A. 1993. Miles ex cohorte. Zur Bedeutung der mit ex Eingeleiteten Truppenangaben auf Soldatenischriften. *ZPE* 95: 190-196.

Speidel, M. A. 1992. Roman Army Pay Scales. *JRS* 82: 87-106.

Speidel, M. A. 1998. Legio IIII Scythica, its movements and men. In: D. L. Kennedy (ed.), *The Twin Towns of Zeugma on the Euphrates. Rescue Work and Historical Studies*. JRA Suppl. 27: 163-204.

Speidel, M. A. 2014. Roman army pay scales revisited: responses and answers. In: M. Redde (ed.), *De l'or pour les braves! Soldes, armées et circulation monétaire dans le monde romain. Actes de la table ronde organisée par l'UMR 8210 (AnHiMa) a l'Institut national d'histoire de l'art (12-13 eptembre 2013)*, Bordeaux: Ausonius. 53-62.

Stein, A. 1927. *Der römische Ritterstand, München*.

Stoll, O. 2001. Garnizon und Stadt im römischen Syrien und der Arabia: Eine Symbiose im Spiegel städtischer Münzprägungen und der Epigraphik. In: O. Stoll (ed.), *Römisches Heer und Gesellschaft*. MAVORS 13: 59-78.

Traverso, M. 2000. Il centurionato nelle legioni romane: la legio II Augusta. *Athenaeum* 88: 219-252.

Verboven, K. 2007. Good for Business. The Roman Army and the Emergence of a Business Class in the Northwestern Provinces of the Roman Empire (1st Century BCE – 3rd Century CE), (L. De Blois, E. Lo Cascio eds.) Impact of Empire 6, Leiden: Brill, 295-314.

Whitehorne, J. 2004. Petitions to the Centurion: a Question of Locality?. *BASP* 41: 155-169.

Zwicky, H. 1944. *Zur Verwendung des Militärs in der Verwaltung der römischen Kaiserzeit*. Zürich: Winterthur.